D1164445

INTRODUCING CATHOLIC THEOLOGY

Interpreting Jesus

INTRODUCING CATHOLIC THEOLOGY

Interpreting Jesus

Gerald O'Collins

GEOFFREY CHAPMAN • PAULIST PRESS
LONDON RAMSEY

209950

232
0 17¿

A Geoffrey Chapman book
published by Cassell Ltd
1 Vincent Square, London SW1P 2PN

© Gerald O'Collins, SJ 1983
De licentia superiorum ordinis

All rights reserved. No part of this publication may be reproduced, stored in a retrieval system, or transmitted, in any form or by any means, electronic, mechanical, photocopying, recording or otherwise, without the prior permission in writing of the Publishers.

First published 1983

ISBN 0 225 66357 0

Nihil obstat: Anton Cowan, *Censor*
Imprimatur: Monsignor Ralph Brown, *V.G.*
Westminster, 20 December 1982

The *Nihil obstat* and *Imprimatur* are a declaration that a book or pamphlet is considered to be free from doctrinal or moral error. It is not implied that those who have granted the *Nihil obstat* and *Imprimatur* agree with the contents, opinions or statements expressed.

British Library Cataloguing in Publication Data
O' Collins, Gerald
Interpreting Jesus.—(Introducing Catholic
theology; 2)
1. Jesus Christ
I. Title   II. Series
232   BT268

Introducing Catholic Theology is a Geoffrey Chapman series.
Interpreting Jesus is published in the USA by Paulist Press, 545 Island Road, Ramsey, NJ 07446
ISBN 0-8091-2572-2

Phototypesetting by Georgia Origination, Liverpool.

Made and printed in USA

Contents

Foreword

Introducing Catholic Theology has been conceived and planned in the belief that the Second Vatican Council provided the Church with a fundamental revision of its way of life in the light of a thorough investigation of Scripture and of our history, and with fresh guidelines for studying and reflecting upon the Christian message itself. In common with every other form of human enquiry and practical activity, the Christian faith can be set out and explained in ways appropriate to human intelligence: it calls for scientific textbooks as well as for other forms of writing aimed at expressing and conveying its doctrines.

It is hoped that these volumes will be found useful by teachers and students in that they will supply both the information and the stimulus to reflection that should be taken for granted and counted upon by all concerned in any one course of study.

Conceived as expressions of the Catholic tradition, the books draw upon the contribution to the knowledge of God and the world made by other religions, and the standpoint of other patterns of Christian loyalty. They recognize the need for finding ways of reconciliation where differences of understanding lead to human divisions and even hostility. They also give an account of the insights of various philosophical and methodological approaches.

The series opens with an examination of the Christian understanding of the process of revelation itself, the special communication between God and humanity made available in the history of Israel and culminating in the person of Christ; its second volume is about the Catholic understanding of Christ, the Word of God and the source of the New Testament faith. The volumes immediately following will deal with the human person as understood in the light of that faith and with the work of the Holy Spirit through whom the Word is continually made present and comprehensible to humanity.

Michael Richards

Preface

Christians have had no problem accepting Christ as holy, as God. But they always have problems accepting him also as a human being at the same time. I want to dust off all the sand that has encrusted the character of Christ after too many story-book interpretations and parochial films.

FRANCO ZEFFIRELLI

Since the Second Vatican Council closed in 1965, Church teachers, theologians, biblical scholars, historians and others have continued to produce a steady flow of books, articles and further works on the person who makes Christianity distinct and different – Jesus Christ. Much of this material is only available in French, German and other foreign languages. Some of it is also highly technical. Yet a great deal of it can contribute to this project, an attempt to provide a textbook in Christology for a wide range of English-speaking students in departments of religious studies, theological faculties and seminaries. I hope that my work may also appeal to some professional colleagues, clergy, religious, laity, interested non-Christians and other readers whose questions and bewilderments can fuel their desire to know more about the Founder of Christianity.

Long ago the Book of Acts summarized the Christian faith in the statement 'God has made both Lord and Christ, this Jesus whom you crucified' (2:36). This can be put more briefly: 'The crucified Jesus is the risen Christ' or 'Jesus is the Christ'. Christology is nothing more or less than the careful clarification of that basic proposition. On the one hand, there is that unique, historical individual, Jesus of Nazareth, who acted in particular ways and ended his earthly existence by crucifixion under Pontius Pilate. On the other hand, he is identical with the risen Christ, the Messiah and divine Saviour sent by the Father and filled with the Holy Spirit to bring history to its completion and save the world. This particular individual (Jesus) has absolute and universal significance (as the Christ).

In detail, this book aims

(a) to provide basic factual information about Christian (and, specifically,

Roman Catholic) beliefs concerning the person and saving function of Jesus Christ (as truly human and truly divine);
(b) to analyse, reflect on and organize this material systematically; and
(c) to suggest some further lines of enquiry and discussion.

As regards (a), the mainline teaching coming from Anglican, Orthodox and most Protestant Churches has hardly differed from received Catholic teaching on Christ's person and saving 'work'. Documents of the Reformation like the Augsburg Confession (Lutheran; from 1530), the Thirty-Nine Articles (Anglican; from 1563) and the Westminster Confession (Presbyterian; from 1648) illustrated that general agreement. Nowadays debates in Christology tend to take place between individual theologians or schools of theology rather than between Churches, and to an extent these differences concern methodology and interpretation rather than doctrinal content. It is instructive that recent 'bilateral' conversations between the Catholic Church and other Christian Churches have taken up themes like authority, Eucharist and ministry. In general, it seems to have been agreed that the Churches share in common the essential faith in Jesus Christ as Son of God and Saviour of the world.

However, disputed questions will not be passed over in silence, whether they involve the positions of particular theologians or those of some Church groups. In such cases I will attempt to show where and why such positions arose and how they differ from what seems a proper Catholic stance in the matter. Possible ways towards reconciliation may also be indicated.

For the sake of convenience this book will speak of 'the Catholic Church' rather than 'the Roman Catholic Church'. No theological judgement as such is thereby implied.

Besides noting the teaching of other Christian Churches and of representative non-Catholic theologians, I will also take some account of other religions, Marxism, other ideologies and contributions from modern science.

The scriptural quotations in this book are taken from the Revised Standard Version of the Bible, copyrighted 1946 and 1952 by the Division of Christian Education of the National Council of the Churches of Christ in the United States of America and used with permission.

Two years ago a student painted for me an artistic and prayerful icon, the face of the crucified Christ. When I contemplated that icon, I could see the face of the artist as well. Whether we do it through painting, words or some other medium, to identify and portray Christ is to identify and portray ourselves.

It is an awesome thought. If all theology comes across as a species of auto-biography, this is especially true of Christology. Writing about Jesus Christ betrays what we have experienced and done as human beings and where we stand as his disciples.

It is not difficult to state the ideal. Theologians should have deeply experienced Christ in faith and been led by his Spirit before attempting a Christology. Only such a lived commitment will rightly support and guide their scholarly reflections. Their theology demands constant conversion as much as critical analysis. Christology above all should be born of prayerful discipleship and feed back into it.

At this point I always find it tempting to make two moves: to criticize others and to take refuge in technical scholarship. First, years of living in Europe have encouraged me to ask some questions about the generation of theologians just ahead of me: Where and how did they spend the Second World War? What prior commitments and experiences at the political, economic and social levels have helped to shape their theology and, specifically, their Christology? Of course, one might correctly observe that to dismiss their theologies as *nothing but* the expression of other interests and experiences would be to repeat the reductionist errors of interpreters like Karl Marx and Sigmund Freud. It is much more relevant to ask myself in all honesty: What personal interests and experiences lie behind my own theological reflections?

Second, nowadays progress in biblical studies and other disciplines has made available for Christology greater resources of scholarship. But can my generation say in all honesty 'We *know* more about Jesus Christ than Athanasius, Anselm, Thomas Aquinas and other such great Christian writers of the past'? Progress in biblical scholarship and other academic disciplines has not automatically brought progress in sanctity. In Christology holiness is a decisive factor – that deep 'knowing' or experience of Jesus which St Paul insisted on (Phil 3:8, 10). I can only pray for a renewed conversion and discipleship which might form and fashion my Christology.

Many friends and other persons have made this book possible or contributed in some way to its making. In particular, I would like to recall and express my warm thanks to the following people: Raymond Brown, Peter Carnley, William Dalton, Robert Faricy, John Fuellenbach, Tim Galligan, Kathy Halvey, Peter Kenny, Margaret Hebblethwaite, Adrian Lyons, Chris McElroy, Kevin McGeever, Martin Molyneux, Emilio Rasco, William Reiser, Cosima Resta, Alfred Singer, David Stanley, Elizabeth Mary Strub, Frank Sullivan, George Sullivan, Ruth Swalenberg, Miles Walsh, Leslie Wearne, Archbishop Sir Guilford Young, Brian Zimmer, colleagues at the Gregorian University, members of a special study circle in Rome, and those who have taken my courses, seminars or workshops on Christology in Rome, Australia, England, India, Japan, New Zealand and the United States of America. Finally, I am most grateful to Michael Richards for asking me to contribute this volume to his series and for his encouraging help in seeing the work through to completion. This book realizes my long-standing dream of writing a coherent and substantial

Christology in the light of what I have already published on Jesus Christ in various periodicals (especially the *Gregorianum*, *Heythrop Journal* and *The Way*) and in the following works: *The Calvary Christ* (London and Philadelphia, 1977), *The Cross Today* (Sydney and Dublin, 1977), *The Easter Jesus* (London, 1973; new ed. 1980; published in Valley Forge [U.S.A.] as *The Resurrection of Jesus Christ*), *What are they saying about Jesus?* (New York, 1977) and *What are they saying about the Resurrection?* (New York, 1978).

Originally I had intended to dedicate this book simply to the memory of Steve Biko (1947–77) and that of an alumnus of the Gregorian University, Archbishop Oscar Romero (1917–80). In different ways they shared the Lord's passion and expressed it for us. Then I started to add the names of other noble victims of human violence: Maura Clarke, Jean Donovan, Ita Ford and Dorothy Kazel (December 1980), Godofredo Alingal (April 1981), Jay Jackson (May 1981) and Rosa Judith Cisneros (August 1981). But there is no end. 'Jesus will be in agony to the end of the world. We must not sleep during that time' (Blaise Pascal).

Rome, Easter Sunday 1982   *Gerald O'Collins, S.J.*

Abbreviations

CD	K. Barth, *Church Dogmatics* (ET: Edinburgh, 1936–69).
Christology	J. Sobrino, *Christology at the Crossroads* (ET: New York and London, 1978).
DBT	*Dictionary of Biblical Theology*, ed. X. Léon-Dufour (2nd ed.: ET, London, 1973).
DNTT	*Dictionary of New Testament Theology*, ed. C. Brown (Exeter, 1975–78).
DS	*Enchiridion Symbolorum, definitionum et declarationum de rebus fidei et morum*, ed. H. Denzinger, rev. A. Schönmetzer (25th ed.: Freiburg, 1973).
DV	*Dei Verbum*, the Dogmatic Constitution on Divine Revelation from Vatican II.
EJ	G. O'Collins, *The Easter Jesus* (new ed.: London, 1980).
EncBrit	*The New Encyclopædia Britannica* (Chicago, 1974–77).
EncTh	*Encyclopedia of Theology. A Concise Sacramentum Mundi*, ed. K. Rahner (ET: London, 1975).
ET	English translation.
Foundations	K. Rahner, *Foundations of Christian Faith* (ET: New York, 1978).
Fundamental	G. O'Collins, *Fundamental Theology* (New York and London, 1981).
GS	*Gaudium et Spes*, the Pastoral Constitution on the Church from Vatican II.
HJKC	*The Historical Jesus and the Kerygmatic Christ*, ed. C. E. Braaten and R. A. Harrisville (New York and Nashville, 1964).
IDB	*The Interpreter's Dictionary of the Bible*, ed. G. A. Buttrick (New York and Nashville, 1962); supplementary vol., ed. K. Crim (Nashville, 1976).

JBC	*The Jerome Biblical Commentary*, ed. R. E. Brown and others (Englewood Cliffs, 1968).
Jesus	E. Schillebeeckx, *Jesus. An Experiment in Christology* (ET: London and New York, 1979).
JGM	W. Pannenberg, *Jesus – God and Man* (ET: London and Philadelphia, 1968).
NCE	*New Catholic Encyclopedia* (New York, 1967); supplementary vol. (1974).
OBC	H. Küng, *On Being a Christian* (ET: London and New York, 1977).
ODCC	*The Oxford Dictionary of the Christian Church*, ed. F. L. Cross (rev. ed., London, 1974).
par(r).	and parallel(s) in other Gospel(s).
RH	Pope John Paul II, *Redemptor Hominis*.
SM	*Sacramentum Mundi* (ET: London and New York, 1968–70).
TDNT	*Theological Dictionary of the New Testament*, ed. G. Kittel (ET: London and Grand Rapids, 1964–76).
ThInv	K. Rahner, *Theological Investigations* (ET: London and New York, 1961–).

Note: In this book the translation of documents from the Second Vatican Council is taken from *Vatican Council II: The Conciliar and Post-Conciliar Documents*, ed. A. Flannery (Dublin, 1975).

Glossary

Apocalyptic: A term used for biblical and non-biblical books (from the period *c.* 200 B.C. to A.D. 100) which reveal hidden mysteries, especially those concerned with the future end of all things.

Apologetics: The defence of Christian belief through rational arguments.

Arianism: The heresy which held that the Son of God was only a perfect creature.

Atonement: Literally 'setting at one'; reconciliation between God and human beings through the expiation of sins.

Beatific Vision, the: The face-to-face vision of God enjoyed by the blessed in heaven.

Christology: The theological interpretation of Jesus Christ, clarifying systematically who and what he is in himself.

Christology from above: The kind of Christology developed from the theme of the pre-existent Son of God who descended into the world.

Christology from below: The kind of Christology developed from an examination of Christ's human life.

Communicatio idiomatum: Literally the interchange of properties. The union of divinity and humanity in the one person of Jesus Christ means that the attributes of one nature may be predicated of the person even when the person is being named with reference to the other nature: for example, 'the Son of God died', or 'the Son of Mary created the world'.

Docetism: From *dokein*, to seem; the heresy which held that the Son of God only appeared to be a human being.

Enhypostatic: Derived from 'in' and 'hypostasis' or person; refers to the fully human existence of Christ, inasmuch as it was personalized through being assumed by the divine person of the Logos.

Eschatology: Literally the doctrine of the last things; refers to the final destiny of individuals and the world in general.

Expiation: The making amends for sin; the reparation for offences against the moral order.

Functional Christology: A Christology which does not focus on who and what Christ was/is in himself (= ontological or 'substantial'

Christology), but on the saving activity of Christ and can thus largely coincide with Soteriology (see below).

High Christology: As opposed to 'low Christology', a Christology which highlights Christ's divinity. This distinction should *not* be confused with the distinction, explicit/implicit Christology (= a clearly stated versus a merely implied Christology).

Homoousios: Literally 'of one substance'; a term referring to the one divine substance shared in common by the Father and the Son.

Hypostasis: Earlier meant 'substance', but by the fifth century A.D. had come to designate a distinct *personal* existence.

Hypostatic Union: That union between divinity and humanity in the one (divine) person of Jesus Christ.

Incarnation: Taking or being made flesh; the assumption of a full human nature by the pre-existent Son of God.

Kenosis: The self-emptying or limiting involved in the incarnation; see Phil 2:7.

Logos: The Word of God or second person of the Trinity.

Messiah: The promised (kingly) deliverer of the Jewish people.

Monophysitism: The heresy which maintained that in the person of Christ the humanity was merged into the divinity and hence there was only *one* (divine) nature.

Monothelitism: The heresy which maintained that Christ lacked a human will and possessed only one (divine) will.

Nestorianism: The heresy which maintained that in Christ there were two separate persons, the divine Logos and the man Jesus.

Parousia: Christ's coming in glory at the end of the world and its history.

Passover: Jewish spring festival celebrating the exodus from Egypt.

Propitiation: An explanation of redemption in terms of God's anger being appeased through Christ's sacrificial death.

Redemption: Deliverance from sin and evil through Christ's incarnation, life, death and resurrection.

Satisfaction: The restoration of God's honour after the moral order had been damaged by sin.

Soteriology: Literally the doctrine of salvation; the systematic interpretation of Christ's saving work for human beings and the world.

Synoptic Gospels: The Gospels of Matthew, Mark and Luke which very frequently parallel each other in content and phraseology.

1
Preliminaries

Right from the outset any book about Jesus Christ risks becoming confused and confusing, unless it explains how it envisages its task. Such a preliminary statement, I believe, should respond at least to the following questions: What are some major reasons for undertaking such a study? Which sources should be drawn on? Can one map the main lines of Christology's past history? What are the most significant issues in current Christology? Lastly, what are my own methodological presuppositions and aims in writing this work?

REASONS FOR STUDYING CHRISTOLOGY

If Christology involves the believer in carefully thinking about and systematically interpreting Jesus Christ, one can very well ask: Why take the trouble to engage in this exercise? After all, for those who have faith in him, no systematic reflection should be necessary. For those who do not have faith in him, no such reflection will be possible or, for that matter, interesting.

Oppressed by the burden of all the books on Christology, believers could well feel the temptation to make a liberating leap from the ambiguities of debate to the moral purity of a sincere self-commitment to Jesus and his cause. But it should be clear that fundamental questions will not be solved that way. Reason will re-assert itself to ask: What can we coherently say about Jesus Christ and his cause? A kind of mindless fideism that embraces certainty and refuses to seek understanding may be tediously familiar but is no real option. Intelligent reflection has its role to play *in* and *for* Christian faith and, above all, when that faith is focused on Jesus himself. Critical thought clarifies and supports one's commitment to him.

In general the First Vatican Council's Constitution on Catholic Faith, *Dei Filius*, endorsed the place of reason in establishing God's existence, presenting the case for the Church, and seeking some clarification of the various revealed mysteries. Of course, both before and after that Council (1869–70) academic theology and, specifically, Christology often lost itself in abstract concepts and hair-splitting analysis. Ideally, however, clear and precise thinking should serve the faith of believers and never divorce itself from, let alone threaten, the practice of their faith. Christians know *that* they believe in Jesus Christ. An intelligent Christology can help them clarify and express just *what* it is they believe about him.

For those who do not share this faith a systematic account of what Christians believe about Jesus can supply information about the person who makes Christianity distinctive. The Christian religion stands or falls by what its adherents believe Jesus of Nazareth to be and to have done 'for us'. And if non-Christians seriously wish to face the truth or falsity of that religion, they should first ascertain what Christians mean by their beliefs about Jesus. Here, as elsewhere, questions of meaning enjoy a priority over questions of truth.

Thus far I have been justifying the study of Christology on general grounds. Rational, systematic reflection enjoys its proper place in Christianity and other religions. Can I indicate more particular motives for such a study?

(1)   Understanding, accepting and interpreting Jesus of Nazareth as Son of God and the world's Saviour immediately touches upon our personal identity, deepest needs and final destiny.

First, *our personal identity*. St Augustine's prayer 'Lord, that I might know myself! That I might know thee!' classically indicated how the search for oneself coincides with the search for God. The question of one's own identity is ultimately the question of God and vice versa. The Second Vatican Council's Declaration on Non-Christian Religions, *Nostra Aetate*, nicely summed up the basic issues which human life spontaneously raises. The list moves naturally from self-questioning ('What is man?') to our search for God ('What is the ultimate mystery... which embraces our entire existence?'):

> The problems that weigh heavily on the hearts of men are the same today as in the ages past. What is man? What is the meaning and purpose of life? What is upright behavior, and what is sinful? Where does suffering originate, and what end does it serve? How can genuine happiness be found? What happens at death? What is judgment? What reward follows death? And finally, what is the ultimate mystery, beyond human explanation, which embraces our entire existence from which we take our origin and towards which we tend? (n. 1; cf. *GS*, n. 10).

In these terms the mystery of our own identity merges with the mystery of God.

Hence to answer Jesus' question 'Who do you say that I am?' (Mark 8:29) by confessing him as Son of God is in effect to state *who we think we are*. To acknowledge in Jesus of Nazareth the mystery of the divine presence among us entails committing ourselves about our own personal identity

('Who do I say that I am?'). Here no confession of faith is possible without accepting 'the innermost truth' about ourselves, the meaning of our own existence and the nature of our ultimate goal. In sum, when we identify Jesus as Son of God, we take an ultimate stand on 'the mystery of man' (*GS*, nn. 22, 41).

There is no chance of speaking about Jesus Christ *in himself* without at least implying what the same Jesus says *about us*, and – as we shall now see – acknowledging what he did/does *for us in our needs*.

Right from the choice of its title, Pope John Paul II's encyclical *Redemptor Hominis* (1979) highlights what we receive from Christ our Redeemer. One glimpses here a certain shift of emphasis from, let us say, the spirit of the First Vatican Council which called the first of its two dogmatic constitutions *Dei Filius* (Son of God). So far from being simply preoccupied with the correct description of Jesus' personal identity, our age makes much of what he promises to do for us through his saving work. On 3 November 1976, Pope Paul VI told an audience in Rome: 'There are two simple yet formidable questions which we ought always to put to ourselves: "Who is Christ in himself? Who is Christ for me?" '

The Christ 'for me' or 'for us' (*pro nobis*) also establishes the importance of some systematic reflection which goes beyond Christology (understood as a clarification of Jesus' personal identity in himself) to take up Soteriology or the doctrine of his saving 'work' for us.

The questions here are obviously urgent ones. What does Jesus promise to redeem us 'from' and redeem us 'for'? We might agree that the evil and sin from which we yearn to break loose largely concern three things: (a) annihilation or death in its many forms, (b) absurdity and meaninglessness, and (c) isolation and hatred. How does Christ set us free from these threats to our existence and bring us life, meaning and love? If the need to ponder carefully the issue of personal identity (Christ in himself as Son of God) fails to grip us, at least the issue of redemption should appear inescapably significant (Christ for us as the world's Saviour).

The questions with which Immanuel Kant (1724–1804) ended his *Critique of Pure Reason* ('What can I know? What ought I to do? What may I hope for?') can be slightly rearranged to suggest the basic motives for studying Christology (and Soteriology): What can I know about Jesus' personal identity? What salvation can I hope for from him? What ought I to do if I submit my entire existence to him who is Son of God and Saviour of the world?

(2) Christian believers worship and act together within *the community of the Church*. This fact recalls a further motive for the systematic study of Christ's person and work. The Second Vatican Council produced sixteen documents, all of which dealt with the updating of the Catholic Church

both within herself and in her relationship with other religious bodies and the contemporary world. In 1963 Paul VI became Pope during the Council and naturally devoted his first encyclical to the theme of the Church, *Ecclesiam Suam* (1964). But then the years since the Council closed have shown how all reform remains theologically shallow and pastorally ineffective unless it clearly bases itself on the Founder of Christianity himself and our faith in him as Son of God and Saviour. What we believe and practise vis-à-vis the Church depends essentially on what we believe about Christ himself. Karl Rahner expresses this point succinctly: 'The mystery of the Church is only the extension of the mystery of Christ' (*Foundations*, p. 213).

Hence, to admit that our theory and practice of Church life is and should be shaped by our belief in Christ is to accept the more basic task. We should use all the resources of faith and reason to express and interpret faithfully who Jesus is and what he does for us.

(3)   If this brief list of motives for studying Christology is not to remain patently inadequate, it should also move beyond the inner life of the Church to recall the motivation provided by the multi-faceted *Christian dialogue with various world religions and ideologies*.

How should Christological reflection be renewed, once we recognize contemporary Jews as in some sense our partners rather than dismiss them as precursors who have survived beyond their time? In the dialogue with Islam a proper understanding of the prophetic role of Jesus obviously plays a crucial role. How should an articulate Christian belief interpret and present the death and resurrection of Jesus to Hindus who find difficulty at that point but can readily understand the incarnation of the Logos? What new possibilities arise for expounding the salvation brought by Jesus when Christians encounter the different branches of Buddhism – in Burma, Japan, Sri Lanka, Thailand and elsewhere?

Christians may then pursue a dialogue with the other monotheistic faiths of West Asia (Judaism and Islam), with the world religions that arose in India (Buddhism and Hinduism), with the traditional religions of Africa, Asia, Melanesia and elsewhere, with Marxism in its various forms, with Confucianism, or with other religions and ideologies. In every case the meeting with these other systems of belief can be expected to sharpen our perception of what accepting Jesus of Nazareth as Son of God and Saviour essentially entails. Over and over again Christians have experienced this happy result from such a dialogue with 'others'. Practically nothing else promises to be so effective for *distinguishing* between primary elements and secondary accretions in the faith we profess in Jesus Christ. This can only bring an increase in our knowledge of him. A medieval axiom applies here: *Cognoscere est distinguere* (making distinctions is knowing).

SOURCES

What sources provide the appropriate material for our systematic account of Jesus Christ's identity and function? Where can we learn about Jesus Christ and find what Christians have believed about him and done because of their faith in him? Here a comprehensive answer is required. We need to respect the full range of Christian and Catholic experiences, expectations, teachings, reflections and activities which span *the present, the future* and *the past*. Certainly there are some privileged sources like the New Testament and the Christological confessions from the early centuries of the Church's history. Nevertheless, it would be an unwarranted diminishment of our source material if we ignored the many other ways in which believers have experienced and then narrated, symbolized and interpreted that experience of Christ, who is 'the First and the Last' (Rev 1:17) and 'the same yesterday, today and forever' (Heb 13:8).

To be sure, one can rightly maintain that for Christology, no less than for other sectors of theology, there is only *one* source, the self-revelation of the Triune God which reached its ultimate expression in the life, death and resurrection of Jesus of Nazareth, was then transmitted (and interpreted) through the apostolic traditions, and finally received its fixed record in the written scriptures. Nevertheless, the composition of those inspired scriptures and the end of the apostolic age did not abolish the principle of tradition. The many-faceted traditions of the Christian Church, while they must be scrutinized in the light of the scriptures, rightly contribute to any systematic account of who Jesus is and what he did/does. For a fuller account of the complex interplay between revelation, tradition (both past and present) and scripture, let me refer readers to my *Fundamental Theology* (practically everywhere).

As revelation, tradition and scripture operate in a profoundly social way, that book reminds me of an essential methodological point for this Christology. Truth and faith take place and are known in an intersubjective way. Both as human persons and believers, Christians are social beings through and through. Hence we can expect to find the truth about Jesus Christ within the Church. Faith in him began in the context of that community, has been expressed in countless ways by members of that same community, and will be properly articulated only within that same con-text.

(1) *The Christ of the present.* The Christ of present Christian experience extends beyond the sectors of liturgy and teaching to the entire life of Christians. This is the Christ of the Church's 'doctrine, life and worship' (*DV*, n. 8). Let me take up these three sectors in this order: first worship, then doctrine, and lastly life and experience.

In a now classic passage the Second Vatican Council spelled out the various *liturgical* presences of Christ:

> Christ is always present in his Church, especially in her liturgical celebrations. He is present in the Sacrifice of the Mass not only in the person of his minister . . . but especially in the eucharistic species. By his power he is present in the sacraments so that when anybody baptizes it is really Christ himself who baptizes. He is present in his word since it is he himself who speaks when the holy scriptures are read in the Church. Lastly, he is present when the Church prays and sings, for he has promised 'where two or three are gathered together in my name there am I in the midst of them' (*Sacrosanctum Concilium*, n. 7).

Here the Constitution on the Sacred Liturgy spoke affirmatively of Christ's presence in worship and did not intend to deny or discard his 'extra-liturgical' presences. In fashioning our Christology we would not do justice to the 'whole Christ' of present experience if we passed over those other presences.

Moreover, the Church's worship contains many texts which aim to articulate what believers experience and know of Christ's person and work. Thus any Christology must reckon among its (written) sources the creeds which remain in liturgical use (the Apostles' Creed and the Nicene Creed), the various Eucharistic Prayers, a full range of Prefaces, the *Gloria*, and other texts which here and now continue to embody and express the community's faith in Christ.

Over and beyond the official liturgy of the Church, devotional practices often vividly interpret what Christians believe about Christ. Stations of the Cross, Christmas cribs and pictures of the Sacred Heart – both the objects themselves and the hymns and other texts which comment on them – fill out in various ways what it means for people to accept Jesus as Son of God and Saviour.

Lastly, the music and visual art which accompany worship also feed into Christological reflection. Byzantine art, for instance, enjoys an integral role in the liturgy of Eastern Christians. In general their art has been steadfastly theological and a graphic witness to their faith in Christ as the incarnate Son of God and 'Cosmocrator' or ever-present ruler of the universe.

At various times in the Church's history iconoclasts or opponents of images rejected the possibility of creating images of Christ. They maintained that the union of *divinity* and humanity put him beyond such visual description. Over and against such a position, the Second Council of Nicaea (787) indicated that an image or icon of Christ properly witnesses to Christian belief in the incarnation. Since the Logos assumed all the essential characteristics of a human being, he can and should be described.

Contemporary Church *teaching* also provides material for the study of Christ. Many documents from the Second Vatican Council, even if none of them was explicitly dedicated to Christ, still had significant things to say about his saving function and personal identity.[1] The same point holds true of papal documents like 'On Evangelization in the Modern World' (*Evangelii Nuntiandi*), which followed from the work of the 1974 bishops' synod in Rome and was published by Paul VI in 1975 to mark ten years since the closing of the Council. This 'apostolic exhortation' devoted sections to Christ (nn. 6–12; 26–27) and to human liberation (nn. 30–39). It described salvation, for example, in the following terms:

> As the kernel and center of his Good News, Christ proclaims salvation, this great gift of God which is liberation from everything that oppresses man but which is above all liberation from sin and the Evil One, in the joy of knowing God and being known by him, of seeing him, and of being given over to him (n. 9).

Any listing of current teaching on Christ should include Pope John Paul II's *Redemptor Hominis* and his 'apostolic exhortation' on catechetics, *Catechesi Tradendae* (1979), which draws from the bishops' synod of 1977. That exhortation takes a thoroughly Christo-centric stand: 'At the heart of catechesis we find . . . the person of Jesus of Nazareth'. Hence 'the primary and essential object of catechesis' can only be 'the mystery of Christ' (n. 5). *Catechesi Tradendae* dedicates a lengthy section to Christ the 'one Teacher' (nn. 5–9). In doing so, it promotes 'Jesus the Teacher' as a title for Christ.

The Church's doctrine on Jesus Christ also gets expressed through the writings of current theologians. Here we need to admit a broad and representative range of writers and not remain contented simply with European figures of the 'centre' – be they Catholics like Walter Kasper and Karl Rahner or Protestants like Wolfhart Pannenberg. No matter what one-sided, irrelevant or even false elements one may find in the work of a given author, I know no modern Christology which does not contain important elements of truth. In fact, as so often happens in the history of Christianity, misguided and even partly erroneous presentations may succeed better than others in highlighting certain truths. Thus Albert Schweitzer's *The Quest of the Historical Jesus* (which first appeared in German in 1906) has been relentlessly and rightly criticized for its final thesis. It developed a one-sided picture of Jesus as an uncompromising apocalyptic preacher who announced the last hour, attempted to bring it about, and fell in the attempt. Despite its shortcomings, the last lines of Schweitzer's book capture hauntingly the mystery of Jesus' person and the fact that real knowledge of him comes only through the pain and practice of discipleship:

> He comes to us as One unknown, without a name, as of old, by the lake-side, He came to those men who knew Him not. He speaks to us the same word: 'Follow thou me!' and sets us to the tasks which he has to fulfil for our time. He commands. And to those who obey Him, whether they be wise or simple, He will reveal Himself in the toils, the conflicts, the sufferings which they shall pass through in His

fellowship, and, as an ineffable mystery, they shall learn in their own experience Who He is.

Contemporary teaching on Christology includes catechisms, sermons, joint statements from various groups, and other such sources which in our times witness to and articulate Christian faith in Jesus of Nazareth. Here I think, for example, of the report from the First Assembly of the World Council of Churches (Amsterdam, 1948). It confessed 'our Lord Jesus Christ' as 'our God and Saviour', 'the Son of God incarnate' who 'gave the Holy Ghost to dwell in His Body the Church' (nn. 1 and 4). That First Assembly began by defining the World Council of Churches as being 'composed of Churches which acknowledge Jesus Christ as God and Saviour'. Similar confessions of Jesus Christ (as Son of God, Lord and Saviour) have turned up repeatedly in other documents of the World Council of Churches and, specifically, in texts prepared by its Faith and Order Commission.

We can also learn a great deal about actual belief in Jesus from the artistic images developed in films, literature and popular music. Such depictions may at times exploit the story of Jesus, misrepresent his identity and function, and largely mirror the religious spirit of the period and place in which they were made. Nevertheless, the images of Jesus in fiction and popular music and on the screen belong among the most widely influential ways in which faith (or partial faith) in him is expressed and formed.

In sum, we should avoid any narrow view of current Christian belief and teaching when we list sources for Christology. The Constitution on Divine Revelation from the Second Vatican Council encourages such a 'total' approach:

> What was handed on by the apostles comprises *everything* that serves to make the people of God live their lives in holiness and increase their faith. In this way the Church, in her doctrine, life and worship, perpetuates and transmits to every generation *all* that she herself is, *all* that she believes (n. 8; italics mine; ET corrected).

Thirdly, all the experiences and activities which make up *Christian life* today can directly or indirectly provide source material for Christology. To begin with, we should reckon with the living presence of Christ brought to us through all the men and women around us. In *Redemptor Hominis* John Paul II emphasizes the mystery of Jesus Christ, 'in which each one of the four thousand million human beings living on our planet has become a sharer from the moment he is conceived beneath the heart of his mother' (n. 13). The Lord comes to us behind four thousand million faces; they are all signs and sacraments of his presence. What does the mystery of his union with them say to us now as we seek to clarify systematically his person and saving work?

In particular, we can expect *those who suffer* to be privileged carriers of his presence. Left to ourselves, we would not turn to sectors of human suffering for help in understanding and interpreting Christ as Son of God and Saviour. But the point comes through clearly from the Gospels, St Paul's letters and other parts of the New Testament. Jesus points to hungry, imprisoned, sick and displaced persons as identified with him in a special way (Matt 25:31–46). Then he dies in seeming failure and atrocious pain, crucified between two criminals. That is precisely the moment when the Roman centurion breaks through to the deepest secret of Jesus' identity and declares: 'Truly this man was the Son of God' (Mark 15:39). This episode of powerless suffering (which together with the resurrection forms the climax of Christ's revealing and saving work) remains paradigmatic. Paul discerns and interprets the passion of his own missionary experiences as *the* means through which Christ remains particularly present and active in the apostle's life (2 Cor 4:8ff.; 6:4ff.; 11:23ff.; 12:7ff.).

Events of contemporary history also manifest something of Christ's lordship and the working out of the salvation which he has brought. St Paul sees all humanity and creation 'groaning' in a history of suffering as they move together towards the fullness of Christ's liberating redemption (Rom 8:18ff.). Through Christ the story of the world unfolds as a story of cosmic and human reconciliation (2 Cor 5:18ff.; Col 1:20ff.). By means of its vivid scenarios and apocalyptic language the Book of Revelation invites the reader to contemplate the triumph of Christ in human history. Now it would be unaccountably odd to agree in theory that Christ's reconciling power is presently shaping the world's history towards the day of full and final salvation, and at the same time refuse to acknowledge any visible signs of his presence among the sources of Christology. In 'the signs of the times' Christians recognize and seek to read off current indications of Christ's person and work.[2]

Lastly, an increasing dialogue with non-Christian religions and ideologies – partly interpreted through a return to the thought of Justin, Clement of Alexandria, Irenaeus and other Fathers of the Church – has alerted Catholics and other Christians to further areas of present experience which might enrich their Christological reflections. The Second Vatican Council initiated a theme which was taken up by Paul VI, by the closing statement from the bishops' synod of 1977 (n. 15), and by John Paul II in *Redemptor Hominis* (n. 11): the *'semina Verbi'* (seeds of the Word) which disclose a kind of 'inchoate' presence of Christ before and beyond Christianity. In *Evangelii Nuntiandi* Paul VI described non-Christian religions as 'all impregnated with innumerable "seeds of the Word" ' (n. 53).

This attitude encourages Christians to acknowledge and reverence Christ already actively present in other religions even before any contact takes place with the gospel. These other faiths and their cultures have proved a matrix in which his revelation and salvation have been in some way effectively expressed. For Christology this raises the question: What can Christians learn about Christ as *the* Revealer and *the* Saviour from discerning and pondering the 'seeds of the Word' which they find outside Christianity?[3] I will return to this matter, above all in Chapter 7.

(2) *The Christ of the future.* In seeking material for its reflections Christology needs to look also to the future. Here it may learn from that warning with which Ernst Bloch begins his *Das Prinzip Hoffnung* (*The Principle Hope*): 'Philosophy will have a conscience for tomorrow, a bias for the future, a knowledge of hope, or it will no longer have any knowledge at all'. Christology, we might add, will have a conscience for tomorrow, a bias for the future, a knowledge of hope, or it will no longer be a worthwhile Christology at all. To a degree we do our Christology more out of our hopes for the future than out of our Christian memories (of the past) and experiences (of the present).

This is because Christ is not only the one whom we remember and experience but also the one whom we expect. Our Eucharist means 'proclaiming the death of the Lord until he comes' (1 Cor 11:26). We live with the bridegroom still absent (Mark 2:18 ff.) and the master of the household still away (Mark 13:33–37). His profoundly real presence in the Eucharist reminds us, paradoxically, that he is not yet fully with us.

Of course, the future coming of Christ will be much more than the return of one who seemed to be absent. It will be the full realization of his position and power as God's Son. He will then complete the process inaugurated by his resurrection, which was and is the beginning of the end. To be sure, his risen existence has let something of that future already appear in anticipation. Elements of the future are with us now and give life its present meaning. Nevertheless, Christ will be truly and fully Christ for us only when the final stage comes:

> Then comes the end, when he delivers up the kingdom to God the Father, after abolishing every kind of domination, authority and power. For he is destined to reign until God has put all enemies under his feet; and the last enemy to be abolished is death . . . When all things are thus subject to him, then the Son himself will also be made subordinate to God who made all things subject to him, and thus God will be all in all (1 Cor 15:24–28).

We will never rightly express and interpret Christ if we leave aside that future end of all things.

On this point the Book of Revelation is strikingly instructive. The work opens with an ecstatic vision experienced one Sunday by 'John, your brother' on the island of Patmos. He sees the radiant, risen Christ who reassures him: 'Fear not, I am the first and the last, and the living one; I died, and behold I am alive for evermore' (1:9–18). Revelation begins with this encounter between John and the risen Lord who recalls his death and resurrection before delivering messages to seven churches of Asia Minor (2:1 – 3:22). But then the whole perspective of the book widens so as to include all heaven and earth, a series of cosmic struggles between good and evil, and finally the vision of the new heaven, the new earth and the new Jerusalem. With this promise of a divine future when all present conflicts will be resolved, Revelation ends by praying 'Come, Lord Jesus' (22:20). In sum, the writer of this work recognizes the 'whole Christ' to be much more than the one who in the past died and rose to 'sit enthroned with his Father' (3:21). He is also not simply the one who now sends his words of prophecy through his servant John and stands at the door and knocks (3:20). The 'whole Christ' is also – or rather we should say, pre-eminently – the Lord Jesus who is coming soon (22:20). The Christ of that final end shapes and determines everything, including our Christological reflections.

All in all, the Book of Revelation vigorously reminds us that the risen Jesus, who now forms the object of our faith and reflection, does so as the light of the future (20:23; 22:16) and the Lord of the coming world. In these terms he is the 'Ad-vent' Christ, who comes to us out of the future. If you like, it is rather a matter of our now experiencing and systematically reflecting on *the presence of the coming Christ* than of our acknowledging (in a theoretical way) the future of the present Christ.

(3) *The Christ of the Christian tradition.* Among its main sources Christology also exploits what it can learn from the *total* Christian tradition of the past. Under the guidance of the Holy Spirit the *lex orandi* and *lex vivendi* of Christians have fed into their *lex credendi*, while the *lex credendi* has in its turn affected and shaped the former. It is at its peril that Christology neglects the accumulated traditions of worship (*lex orandi*) and lived experience (*lex vivendi*) from the past to concentrate simply on the official teaching and classic theology which in a special way articulated the *lex credendi*.

Specifically this means that Christology should respect but go beyond the teaching about Christ developed by early Church Councils and classical theological treatises. It should recognize as well and draw on the rich range of ways in which his followers have stated and transmitted their faith in him. To begin with, they have left us hymns, poems, sermons, liturgical texts, scripture commentaries and other writings that centre on him. The broad Christian tradition speaks of its faith through items like that very personal and deeply felt prayer to the Eucharistic Lord, *Adoro te devote*, attributed to St Thomas Aquinas and translated by Gerard Manley Hopkins as 'Godhead here in hiding, whom I do adore'. In his *Imitation of Christ* Thomas à Kempis records just what 'familiar friendship with Jesus' brings in terms of spiritual experience (II, 8). Edmund Spenser's 'Easter', in witnessing to the poet's faith in Christ as Saviour of the world, incorporates those three major models for describing redemption which this book will discuss in Chapter 6.

Almost from the foundation of Christianity believers have expressed through *art* their experience of and faith in Jesus Christ: from the simple tender frescoes in Roman catacombs to the vast bronze statue of the risen Christ in the main audience hall at the Vatican, from the carvings on Chartres Cathedral to the paintings of Tadao Tanaka in Japan, from the old Coptic paintings in Ethiopia to the Latin American representations of the crucified Liberator. Christian art has consistently mirrored with a peculiar intensity the essence of faith in the Word made flesh. It has attempted to present the whole person of Jesus Christ, his character and universal significance as Son of God and Saviour. Of course, this art has varied and continues to vary from sublime masterpieces to dull mass-productions. Yet either way it has attempted to tell the truth about Jesus and deserves to be numbered high among the witnesses from Christian tradition.

To sum up. In assessing the material which Christology can use from Christian history, we dare not take a reduced view and sell short the *total* tradition. We should draw not only from the teaching Church but also from the praying and living Church of the past. At every level of the Church's past (and present) existence we can expect to uncover at least some hints of the Holy Spirit's presence guiding believers to (and back to) the full truth about Christ.

(4) *The Christ of Christian origins.* All Christology looks back through the history and traditions of the Church to find the figure of Jesus there at the origins of Christianity. Through the Old Testament preparation for his coming, the incarnation, his ministry, the crucifixion, the resurrection and the sending of the Holy Spirit, he did not so much communicate to the founding fathers and founding mothers of the Church some organized body of revealed truths, but he left them wrestling with the mystery of his person and saving function.

A number of them had known Jesus during his ministry. Some of these, St Paul and perhaps others also (who like Paul had not known Jesus in his lifetime), encountered him risen from the dead. All of them knew themselves to be incorporated permanently into him through baptism and to have received his Holy Spirit. They celebrated his presence at the Eucharist and other gatherings for worship. They looked forward to his coming in glory. All these memories, experiences and expectations led the first Christians to richly varied ways of naming, describing and proclaiming Jesus of Nazareth. For example, when they thought of his being uniquely related to the Father for the salvation of the world, they called him 'Son of God'

(Rom 1:3f.; Gal 4:4–7). When they spoke of him as they experienced him in the worshipping community, they named him 'Lord' (1 Cor 12:3).

Either directly or indirectly, the whole New Testament does nothing more or less than record and witness to what the first Christians had known and experienced of Jesus. These inspired writings, which portray the Christ of Christian origins, supply the essential data for any Christology. We later Christians depend upon that record whenever we seek to clarify systematically what Jesus has done for us and who he is in himself.

Such then are the 'places' or sources which provide data for a systematic reflection on Jesus Christ's personal identity and saving function. Here we need to take a broad attitude towards our sources. A restricted view of what counts as material and evidence for Christology will devalue the 'whole' Christ and produce partial results, if not worse. To attend only to 'the Christ of the present' will overvalue contemporary experience and tamper with the historical nature of Christianity. A preoccupation with 'the Christ of the future' could support a revolutionary hope, but will have little to do with the many ways in which Christ's saving presence is *already* experienced. A certain kind of preoccupation with 'the Christ of Christian tradition', especially when it concentrates only on the written documents from early Church Councils and ignores the full range of traditions coming from Christian life and worship, may produce a hyper-orthodox 'clarity' which may refuse to pay the cost of true discipleship. Lastly, an over-emphasis on 'the Christ of Christian origins' will need to be reminded of the further fact that through the centuries the Holy Spirit truly guided the Church in her essential interpretation of Jesus' identity and saving work. The evidence coming from the historical origins of Christianity is essential but not exclusive. In summary, to reduce our 'intake' and concentrate absolutely on one source means selling short the 'total Christ' of Christian faith.

THE HISTORY OF CHRISTOLOGY

In any Christology the material will overlap and criss-cross in various ways. It is always possible to see how a different order might have been followed or a different selection of material made. In fact, listing the sources of Christology necessarily indicates something about the history of systematic reflection on Jesus Christ's identity and function. Yet it seems useful to sketch briefly the way that history unfolded.

(1) *The New Testament period.* The inspired books of the New Testament record the first epoch of reflection on the personal identity and saving function of Jesus. As the following chapters will deal at length with the New Testament data, there is no need here to linger long over this first stage

of Christology (and Soteriology). But let me prime the reader a little for what will be developed later.

Christology properly began with what we can call the 'post-existent' Jesus. After his death he was experienced and worshipped by his disciples as risen to new life, exalted in glory, and existing in power and dignity on the divine level. What had been hinted at, implied and even partially claimed about his relationship with his Father now became revealed. Embedded in Paul's letters we find various formulas and titles for Jesus which Christians had fashioned during the thirties and forties A.D. in the light of the resurrection of the crucified Jesus. Two of these titles (*Kyrios* or 'Lord' and 'Son of God') with their attendant credal formulas show clearly how Christological reflections started with the 'post-existence'. Both these titles (with their formulas) *have a resurrection setting* and exhibit a close relationship in content.[4]

Here the *origin* of the title 'Lord' proves less significant than its *meaning*. Some scholars have argued that Christians took over 'Lord' from the Greek mystery religions of that time or from the Roman cult of the emperor as a divine being. But today probably more scholars recognize that the title had a Jewish (Palestinian) background and passed from Aramaic-speaking Christian communities to Greek-speaking ones. But what *meaning* attaches to *Kyrios* in Paul's letters?

In Rom 10:9 the apostle quotes a traditional formula (derived apparently from a baptismal liturgy): 'If you confess with your lips that Jesus is *Lord* and believe in your heart that God raised him from the dead, you will be saved'. In Philippians he cites a Christian hymn which gratefully rejoices that Jesus' exaltation after death now means that 'every tongue' should confess that he 'is *Lord*, to the glory of God the Father' (2:9–11). This hymn, while it is no careful, philosophical statement about Jesus' personal identity and status, shows Christians offering *worship* to him as one who enjoys a 'post-existence' *on the divine level*.

In 1 Corinthians Paul includes an expression from the worship of Aramaic-speaking Christians: '*Maranatha*' (16:22). This could be a credal statement: 'Our Lord is come, he is here and present with us'. Or it could be a prayer to the (present) Lord asking for the *parousia* to occur soon: 'Our Lord, come, come quickly'. Taken either way, '*Maranatha*' refers to *the risen and divine Lord*, who is both with his Father and through his Spirit present in the Church, especially when communities gather for worship.

To open his Letter to the Romans, St Paul inserted an early Christian confession of Jesus 'who was descended from David according to the flesh and designated *Son of God* in power according to the Spirit of holiness by his resurrection from the dead' (1:3f.). Here 'designated' did not mean that Jesus was 'adopted' and became Son of God only as a result of his resurrection. Rather the sense was that believers began to experience his powerful, heavenly existence in the aftermath of his resurrection from the dead – as opposed to the way people experienced Jesus in his earthly existence when he was born from the house of King David. For Paul to confess the 'post-existent' *Son of God* was to describe the content of the good news (Rom 1:3, 9). The title was associated both with the saving self-revelation of God which made Paul the apostle to the Gentiles (Gal 1:15f.) and with the full working out of the divine rule in the coming resurrection (1 Cor 15:28). Perhaps no other section in Paul's letters shows more clearly than the climax of Romans how – for the apostle himself and for the early Christians – the title 'Son of God' pointed to that intimate link between Jesus and his Father which was manifested when the events of Good Friday and Easter Sunday communicated the divine salvation to human beings. The God 'who did not spare his *Son* but gave him up for us all' will 'also give us all things with him' (Rom 8:32). That same Father has 'also predestined those whom he foreknew to be conformed to the image of his *Son*', so that Christ's resurrection might not be just an isolated privilege but might make him 'the first born among many brethren' (Rom 8:29).

To sum this up. Those early titles 'Son of God' and 'Lord' both refer to the risen, exalted Christ, who now enjoys life, power and authority after death (a 'post-existence') on the divine level. There are differing nuances. The first title points to his unique relationship to God his Father in the work of bringing salvation to human beings. 'Lord', however, expresses more the link between the risen and exalted Christ and his worshipping community or the individual believers (1 Cor 12:3). But both titles illustrate how the 'post-existence' of the risen Christ provided the starting-point for Christology. The confessional statements which the earliest believers and Paul made in the light of the resurrection initiated that never-ending process of evaluating the personal identity and saving function of Jesus Christ.

In the development of the New Testament that process of evaluation soon showed a desire to clarify and express Christ's origins. When he composed his Gospel around 65, Mark took matters back to Jesus' baptism and left us with a work which has often been described as a Passion story with a long introduction. In a thoroughly Pauline way Good Friday and Easter Sunday continued to loom over this Gospel's view of Jesus. It included no nativity narrative, but recognized Jesus' oneness with God only as far back as the baptism (1:11). When they wrote later with Mark's Gospel in front of them, Matthew and Luke decided to start with accounts of Jesus' birth and childhood. Finally, John towards the close of the first century began his Gospel with the announcement: 'In the beginning was the Word, and the Word was with God, and the Word was God . . . . And the Word became flesh and dwelt amongst us.' If we follow the development of thought from Paul and the early Christological confessions which he quoted, through the Gospels of Mark, Matthew and Luke, to the Fourth Gospel, we find an increasing concern to interpret and express Christ's origins and his divine 'pre-existence'. As we will see, that movement continued beyond the New Testament period to culminate in Chalcedon's teaching about Christ's one person in two natures.

In general, the later books of the New Testament moved from statements about the function and identity of Christ in his 'post-existence' to statements about his 'pre-existence'. However, something of that process began early and here and there got reflected even in Paul's letters. Galatians and Romans seem to acknowledge the pre-existent Son of God sent into the world to save the human race. Despite his oneness with God, Christ appeared as the divine envoy sent to live among us, become a sacrifice for sin and make human beings the adopted children of God (Gal 4:4; Rom 8:3). In both these texts, however, Paul is clearly thinking less of Christ's pre-existence than of his function to redeem those who have suffered under the bondage of law and sin. If the hymn incorporated into Philippians emphasized Christ's exaltation after his death, it began by confessing that, although divine by nature, he 'emptied himself' (2:6f.). In 1 Corinthians Paul even recognized the 'Lord, Jesus Christ' as mediator of creation itself (8:6). In such ways hints about Christ's functions and identity in a state of *divine pre-existence* surfaced early in the writings of the New Testament.[5]

(2) *The Patristic period.*   After the New Testament the next great stage in Christological development spans the period of the first Councils and the Church Fathers. This period, roughly speaking, runs down to the end of the seventh century. *False interpretations* of Christ, struggles for *the right terminology* to use about him, and *differing methodologies* all slip in and out of the story.[6]

Oddly enough, the first heretical tendency in Christology, Docetism (from *dokein*, to seem), which emerged in the late first century, took the form of affirming that Christ the Son of God only appeared to be a human being. He left the man Jesus before death and thus it was only the man Jesus who was crucified. Before his martyrdom (*c.* 107) St Ignatius of Antioch warned against such Docetic tendencies. Then Paul of Samosata (third century) and others maintained various forms of *adoptionism*: the one God adopted Jesus as his Son and gave him the Spirit. Sabellius (third century) held that, as God was only a single person, the Son and the Holy Spirit could be no more than *modes* in which God had appeared.

The immediate occasion of the first Ecumenical Council, Nicaea (325), came with the teachings of Arius (*c.* 250–*c.* 336). He had maintained that the Son was a perfect creature, at best a kind of demigod subordinated to the Father. Hence Arius' slogan about the Son: 'There was a time when he was not'. To counter Arius and assert Christ's genuine divinity, the Council excluded this way of talking and adopted a term which had been used by

Origen (*c.* 185–*c.* 254) to indicate Christ's unity of being with the Father: *Homoousios* (of one substance). What kind of oneness or identity was being affirmed here? Seemingly the Council meant a numerically identical substance – one common divine being in which both the Father and the Son shared.[7]

In the event Nicaea's teaching did not meet with universal agreement. For decades St Athanasius (*c.* 296–373) and his followers battled to uphold the Council's term for expressing Christ's divinity. Nicaea had also left certain questions to be answered. In the light of its teaching how could one sustain Christ's true humanity? And how were the divine and human elements in Christ related?

Apollinaris of Laodicaea (*c.* 310–*c.* 390), himself a defender of Nicaea and a supporter of Athanasius, went ahead with language that threatened Christ's genuine humanity: 'The flesh-bearing God' and 'the one incarnate nature [*physis*] of the divine Word'. He seems to have used this terminology to deny that Jesus had a human soul. In the incarnation the divine Logos assumed only a body and itself took the place of the human spirit. Against Apollinaris the First Council of Constantinople (381) taught that Christ had a true human soul. It also reaffirmed Nicaea's teaching.

Thus the two Church Councils from the fourth century had insisted, respectively, that Christ was divine (Nicaea) and human (Constantinople). But how then were the being divine and the being human related? An Archbishop of Constantinople, Nestorius (d. *c.* 451), was pressed to take a position on the Marian title *Theotokos* (Mother of God). To affirm it would have been to hold a personal unity of divinity and humanity in Jesus right from his conception and birth. The child born from Mary of Nazareth was truly the Son of God. As he wanted to defend the full humanity of Jesus and had difficulty in finding the right categories, Nestorius refused to endorse that Marian title. He seemingly held a moral rather than a true personal unity between Christ's divinity and humanity. A divine being (the Logos) co-existed side by side with a human being (the man Jesus).

St Cyril of Alexandria (d. 444) and others saw to it that the Council of Ephesus (431) condemned Nestorius, deposed him and upheld the title of *Theotokos* for Mary. Cyril's commitment to the *unity* of Christ, however, led him to take over (unwittingly) the language of Apollinaris in his formula about the 'the one nature of the divine Logos, which [nature] became flesh'. Unlike Apollinaris, Cyril understood 'flesh' in the sense of a *full* human nature, but he wanted to insist that right from conception the human nature of Christ belonged entirely to the Logos.

Almost inevitably Cyril's teaching caused others to move beyond orthodox bounds in defending the *unity* of Christ's divinity and humanity. Eutyches of Constantinople (*c.* 378–454) held (really or only verbally?) that Christ's divinity absorbed his humanity – the so-called 'Monophysite' heresy for which the one divine nature (*physis*) swallows up Christ's humanity. The orthodox reaction to Eutyches came with the 'Tome' of Pope Leo I (449) and the Council of Chalcedon (451), which recognized in Christ 'two natures in one person'. This personal unity left the divine and human natures quite intact and in no way confused or intermingled them with each other.

We can go ahead and describe the sequence of teaching through the first Councils as follows: Christ is divine (Nicaea); Christ is human (Constantinople I); the human and divine elements are personally united (Ephesus); yet this personal unity does not destroy or reduce the integral individuality of either the human or the divine nature (Chalcedon). Against four successive errors these Councils moved to affirm *both* the full divinity and full humanity of Christ *and* the union which preserves the proper distinction between his two natures.

Two subsequent Councils added footnotes to Chalcedon. Constantinople II (553) introduced the term 'hypostatic union' to interpret the unity of Christ which Chalcedon had upheld. A century later Constantinople III (680) added one detail to the teaching about the integrity of his two natures. Christ possessed a divine *and* a human will, and these two wills (the doctrine of *Dyothelitism*) were not confused with each other.

Issues of *terminology* played a crucial role in all those early Christological controversies. Popular Greek philosophy offered Christians various options for expressing Christ's nature and person. Earlier on, many used *ousia* (as in *homoousios*) and *hypostasis* somewhat indiscriminately to refer to the common (divine) substance shared by Christ and his Father. (Cicero had translated the Greek *hypostasis* as *substantia*. Hence our English word 'substance'.) But then the two terms were differentiated, *ousia* being understood as the common substance and *hypostasis* as the individual essence, distinct personal existence or acting subject. In the controversies *physis* was frequently used synonymously with *hypostasis*, but eventually Chalcedon adopted the term in the sense of nature. St Cyril had preferred *hypostasis* over the rival term *prosōpon* (*persona* in Latin) which some theologians of Antioch favoured. *Prosōpon* appeared to be somewhat vague and even to preserve something of its original meaning of 'mask'. Nevertheless, Chalcedon incorporated both *hypostasis* and *prosōpon* into its final text. The Council spoke of the two natures (*physeis*) of Christ coming together to form one person (*prosōpon*) or subsistence (*hypostasis*). In its aim to regulate Christian language about Christ, Chalcedon had a lasting success. Its language of 'one person in two natures' became the normative terminology down to the twentieth century.

Before leaving the period of the Church Fathers, I should like to recall briefly how two different *methodologies* organized many of the answers to the central Christological question: How are the divine and human elements in Christ related? The school of *Alexandria*, which included leading figures like Origen and St Cyril, pursued a descending Christology 'from above'. This 'Logos–sarx' (Word–flesh) approach centred on the pre-existent Logos who descends into our world and then returns to the place from which he came. Its high concern for Christ's divinity entailed a strong stress on faith. This Alexandrian Christology, as it began with the unity of Christ as subject, normally did well in maintaining that unity but had trouble in showing his real humanity. Its most difficult challenge was the question: How could the eternal Logos take on a genuinely and fully human way of acting?

The school of *Antioch*, which included figures like Theodore of Mopsuestia (*c*. 350–428) and Nestorius, pursued an ascending Christology 'from below'. This 'Logos–anthropos' (Word–man) approach safeguarded the full human nature of Jesus Christ. As part of its concern for the human side of things it stressed history and reason. As the Antiochenes began with the duality of natures (the full human nature of Christ and his divine nature), their gravest problem was the question: How are Christ's divinity and humanity united in one acting subject? This Christology could go astray in abandoning the real unity of Christ, and ending up with two subjects: the assuming Word and the man Jesus who is assumed.

The Council of Chalcedon effected a brilliant synthesis between the two schools. It took from Alexandria an insistence on Christ's unity and from Antioch a clear regard for the duality of distinct natures.

A final word on these two schools. An Alexandrian Christology finds its New Testament support above all in John's Gospel with its majestic scheme of the Word become flesh. An Antiochene Christology looks more to the Synoptic Gospels. St Thomas Aquinas (*c*. 1225–74) and Karl Barth are classic examples of the first school. Pannenberg and Edward Schillebeeckx have produced Christologies which exemplify, albeit differently, an Antiochene approach.

(3) *The Middle Ages.*   The third period of Christological development saw Aquinas and others employ stricter philosophical categories (frequently derived from Aristotle) to explore further the hypostatic union, and the types of knowledge, grace and freedom possessed by Christ. Christology became more and more centred on the incarnation – even if Aquinas, for instance, continued to discuss Christ's ministry, death and resurrection. Later the resurrection and themes from Christ's ministry would largely disappear from Christological treatises. As we shall see in Chapter 6, the Council of Chalcedon itself had unwittingly prepared the way for this shift from a Pauline Christology (which focuses on the crucifixion and resurrection) to a Christology which draws its identity from the incarnation.

It is not unfair to note a certain monophysite tendency in medieval theology. For instance, in his human consciousness Christ was credited with enjoying the beatific vision. Like the blessed in heaven he saw God directly and hence could not be a believer. He lived his earthly life by vision, not by faith. In this way his human life was understood to be more 'divine' and more distant from that of normal men and women. I return to this point, especially in Chapters 3 and 6.

When theology tended to present Christ largely in terms of his divinity, popular devotions arose to defend his genuinely human existence and experience. Thus the devotion to the Christmas crib, the Stations of the Cross and (later) the devotion to the Sacred Heart witnessed to the ordinary faithful's instinctive attachment to the authentic humanity of Jesus.

The most lasting medieval contributions to our understanding of Christ's person and work came in the field of *Soteriology* – from St Anselm (*c.* 1033–1109) and Abelard (1079–1142). Of course, right from New Testament times Christians had attempted to interpret the redemption which they knew Christ to have brought them. Let me fill in briefly something of that background to Anselm and Abelard.

Often the Christological controversies (over Christ's person and natures) were only a thin veil covering concerns about his saving 'work'. Sometimes the Soteriological motive bolstered the belief in Christ's *divine identity*. Thus Cyril of Alexandria insisted that unless it was God who endured the crucifixion, that event could not truly have saved us. Earlier, St Gregory of Nazianzus (329–389) had expressed a similar conviction: 'We needed a God made flesh and put to death in order that we could live again'. At other times, the Church Fathers called on the Soteriological motive to support a genuine incarnation. As the Word of God truly took on a *human nature*, he could heal human beings and 'divinize' them through his grace. It was feared, for example, that Apollinaris' error simply undercut the divinization of human beings effected by the Logos being united with a full human nature in the person of Jesus Christ. Thus Gregory of Nazianzus wrote: 'What has not been assumed has not been restored; it is what is united with God which is saved'. Here Gregory was endorsing a principle that had become common currency in the East since the time of Origen and Athanasius: unless the incarnate Son of God had assumed an integral human nature, his redemptive grace could not have healed and divinized human life in all its dimensions. To quote Athanasius: 'He assumed humanity, that we might become God'.

We can draw together as follows much of what the Patristic period had to say about Soteriology. (a) *As such*, the key controversies were not directly concerned with Christ's saving function (Did his redemption save, heal and divinize human beings?) but rather his ontological state (How were and are the human and divine elements related in him?). (b) We saw above how the *incarnation* (the assumption of human nature by the Logos) shaped the Soteriological convictions of Church writers like Origen, Athanasius,

Gregory of Nazianzus and Cyril of Alexandria. (c) At times the Fathers interpreted Christ's death as a ransom paid to the devil to set human beings free from bondage. (d) Finally, the Latin hymns of Venantius Fortunatus from the sixth century (*Vexilla Regis* and *Pange, lingua, gloriosi*), an Anglo-Saxon religious poem (*The Dream of the Rood*) and an eleventh-century Easter Sequence (*Victimae Paschali*) remind us that images of conflict and battle also organized Christian interpretations of the redemption. Despite the apparent defeat of the crucifixion, Christ gained the victory and won the day over sin and death.

But it was not till Anselm's book *Cur Deus Homo* that we find a Christian writer devoting a work explicitly to the redemptive activity of Christ. Here Anselm maintained that as human disobedience offends the divine honour, either 'satisfaction or punishment must follow every sin' (I, 15). By making satisfaction, Christ restored God's honour and punishment was *not* imposed. Anselm has been criticized for including punitive elements in his version of redemption. Such elements did turn up in those who drew on him: from Thomas Aquinas, through John Calvin (1509–64), down to Karl Barth. But Anselm himself clearly rejected the alternative of punishment. What critics of Anselm have sometimes missed is the fact that more than anyone else he helped to move Soteriology away from Christology.

This separation later flowered in some Protestant theology, which frequently showed itself preoccupied with what Christ did and does '*pro nobis*' (for us) or '*pro me*' (for me), and could eventually produce positions like that of Rudolf Bultmann. In his writings Soteriology edges out Christology. At the time of the Reformation itself the trend to reduce Christology to Soteriology had already become more pronounced with Philipp Melanchthon (1497–1560) than with Martin Luther (1483–1546).

On the Catholic side Anselm's move helped to bring about almost the opposite situation. Christology took pride of place and Soteriology got treated subsequently – sometimes very briefly. One thing, however, did keep alive the link between Christology and Soteriology. When Catholic theologians discussed *the motive* for the incarnation (Why did God become man?), they were admittedly raising a Christological question, but they could not do so without entering the field of Soteriology. In one way or another, the incarnation – whether associated closely with creation (the Scotist view) or not (the Thomist view) – was understood to be an intrinsic element, if not the major factor, in human redemption.

In Chapter 5 I will come back to Anselm's interpretation of redemption and also discuss an Abelardian approach which turns on the theme of love.

(4) *Modern times.* From the end of the eighteenth century Christology began to be deeply affected by the rise of scientific history and, in particular, by critical methods in biblical research. One could say that the debates about

the historical Jesus have tended to become *the* Christological issue.

(a)   The modern quest of the historical Jesus began in 1778 with the posthumous publication of extracts from Hermann Reimarus. He portrayed Jesus as a would-be political insurgent who died as a self-confessed failure. The disciples of Jesus, however, stole his corpse, fabricated the story of the resurrection, and set up the Christian Church. Inevitably and rightly the theory of Reimarus raised a storm of protest and was widely rejected. Yet he made an assured contribution at least in one point: the real Jesus of history (or the earthly Jesus) and the Christ preached by the Church would need to be shown to coincide. The quest of the historical Jesus was on the way.

The classical period for this historical study of Jesus' life ran from the end of the eighteenth century to the early years of the twentieth century. Writers like Ernest Renan, D. F. Strauss and Adolf von Harnack attempted to penetrate beneath the later dogmatic overlay and discover the authentic picture of the real Jesus. They held that the early Christians had made a 'Christ' out of Jesus. 'Free from Paul' (*Los von Paulus*) was their slogan as in various ways they tried to get behind the Christological doctrines of the early Church back to the rabbi from Galilee. By precise, unprejudiced use of the earliest sources, in particular Mark's Gospel, they expected to uncover Jesus of Nazareth as he really was. Frequently this search for the 'true Jesus' was carried on by the unorthodox – by rationalists (who removed the miraculous elements of Jesus' life), by humanitarians (who concentrated on his ethical teaching), and by liberal Christians (for whom Church membership and practice were often of no great moment).

What common picture resulted from all this intensive work on the life of Jesus? Notoriously the enterprise led to no agreed consensus. Doubts arose, but they were suppressed. Eventually, however, the truth had to be faced. The disparity between the portraits of Jesus by no means derived simply from differences in critical judgements about the New Testament evidence. The writers were affected by their differing attitudes towards God, human life and the world. In some measure their portrayals of Jesus were the products of highly subjective interpretation. A number showed themselves unbelievably confident about their power to penetrate the mind of Jesus and offer sound reflections on his psychology.

The story of this nineteenth-century search for 'the real Jesus' was told in classic form by Albert Schweitzer in *The Quest of the Historical Jesus*. He summed up his findings as follows:

> Each successive epoch of theology found its own thoughts in Jesus . . . . But it was not only each epoch that found its reflection in Jesus; each individual created Him in accordance with his own character. There is no historical task which so reveals a man's true self as the writing of a Life of Jesus (p. 4).

Nineteenth-century research had fatally 'modernized' Jesus.

Schweitzer himself voiced the conviction that Jesus' preaching did not turn on ethics, but on eschatology – on the proclamation of God's coming kingdom. We have already seen how Schweitzer went on to develop that theme in a distorted fashion. Nevertheless, he made a twofold contribution. He successfully challenged the conventional wisdom of nineteenth-century research into the life of Jesus. Henceforth his account of his predecessors would exercise an inhibiting influence, at least in Protestant academic circles. Faced with this perceptive critique of a long line of writers from Reimarus to Schweitzer's own day, others were dissuaded from attempting to write a biography of Jesus. Second, Schweitzer broke decisively with the attempts to turn Jesus into a contemporary. The earthly Jesus is to be seen within the historical framework of the first century. In particular, the eschatological nature of his message must be respected.

If Schweitzer's critique proved inhibiting to Protestant scholars, Catholic writers continued to compose what purported to be more or less exact historical lives of Jesus. The stream of biographies by Daniel-Rops, Fouard, Prat, Ricciotti and others continued at a steady rate. However, in general *Catholic Christology as such* for decades took little notice of any discoveries and debates about the history of Jesus (and the origins of the Church) which came from the historians and biblical scholars.

The Second Vatican Council brought a decisive shift, which had already been prepared by the 1943 encyclical by Pope Pius XII on scriptural studies, *Divino Afflante Spiritu*. It was not merely that the Constitution on Divine Revelation encouraged theologians (and hence those specializing in Christology) to regard the Bible as 'the very soul' of their work (n. 24), and gave pride of place to the notion of salvation history. The Council exemplified the need to reflect on the history of Jesus himself by incorporating data from his ministry in its Declaration on Religious Liberty, *Dignitatis Humanae* (n. 11).

From the early 1970s Kasper, Hans Küng, Schillebeeckx, Jon Sobrino and other Catholics have taken up into their Christologies the findings of biblical scholarship and included lengthy accounts of Jesus' ministry. In a sense this represents a return to a theme which Aquinas and some later theologians like Francesco de Suarez (1548–1617) handled and which largely disappeared in post-Reformation Catholic textbooks of Christology: such 'mysteries' of Christ's life as his baptism, preaching, miracles, transfiguration and so forth. But the contemporary theologians, of course, make use of historical and exegetical techniques and findings which were simply not available in earlier centuries.

To pull matters together. Both for Catholics and other Christian theologians *the emergence of scientific history* has decisively affected what modern theology says about Christ's life, death and resurrection. I will come back to the role of history in Christology later in this chapter and in subsequent chapters.

We can rightly summarize the characteristic differences between the four periods of Christology as follows. The contemporary Jewish, largely *pre-philosophical*, thought-forms heavily shaped the New Testament's Christologies. That was a period in which Jesus Christ was proclaimed and interpreted through the gospel stories, the metaphors of Paul and the symbolic language of John's Gospel and the book of Revelation. *Popular philosophical* notions (often coming from some form of Platonism) proved important in the Patristic period. *Aristotelian categories* helped to form the academic Christology of the Middle Ages. Finally, *scientific history* has been Christology's special dialogue partner in modern times.

(b)   At the same time *other modern influences* on Christology should be recalled. A whole range of academic and cultural changes have brought new challenges and offered fresh help to those who would systematically interpret Jesus Christ.

Sigmund Freud (1856–1939) discovered the unconscious, and that discovery remains enduringly significant for our understanding and interpretation of the New Testament data. What can the depth psychology of Freud and, even more importantly, that of his successors contribute to our appreciation of Jesus? And what light can modern psychology throw on the work and conclusions of historians, exegetes and theologians who seek to interpret and express Christ?

Charles Darwin (1809–82) brought the theory of evolution into popular consciousness. In this century Teilhard de Chardin developed insights into Christ's person and function within an evolutionary framework. Somewhat more cautiously, Rahner has argued that the incarnation, while it was not a necessary consequence of evolution, nevertheless can be interpreted within an evolutionary scheme (*Foundations*, pp. 178–203; *ThInv* 5, pp. 157–192).

Marxist social analysis, when adopted and modified by liberation theologians, has helped to organize their Christologies. The existentialist philosophy of Martin Heidegger affected the way Bultmann and others presented Christ.

I have been selecting examples almost at random. But I hope the point is clear. Besides history, other non-theological disciplines have significantly affected modern theological reflections on Jesus' person and saving function.

(c)   *Within Christology itself* we can spot *several other important shifts*. First, Kasper and most other Catholic theologians now attempt to heal the split between Christology and Soteriology, between what Jesus is in himself (*in se*) and what he is for us (*pro nobis*). They realize that his person and work are distinguishable but not separable. On the one hand, these Catholic writers will rebuke some of their predecessors for forgetting that everything about Christ concerns our salvation. On the other hand, they will not adopt the almost totally functional (if very different) approaches of Bultmann and Oscar Cullmann.

Second, many theologians (for example, Kasper, Moltmann and Pannenberg) construct their Christologies around Christ's death and resurrection. They accept the Easter mystery not only as the starting-point but also as the organizing centre for Christology.

Third, there has been a general tendency to recognize the close link between creation and redemption. This means a vindication of the view which reaches back through the Anglican theologian Charles Gore (1853–1932) to Duns Scotus (c. 1265–1308) and St Irenaeus (c. 130–c. 200). The Son of God came to bring the created world to its appropriate fulfilment, a fulfilment that as a matter of fact entailed repairing the harm done by human sin. The incarnation and redemption did *not* occur *only* because human beings were lost in and through sin and no solution could be found other than the coming of a divine Saviour. Rahner typifies the present unwillingness to let the incarnation (and redemption) appear as anything like a 'subsequent' rescue operation mounted because the initial divine scheme had failed. He describes the creation and incarnation as 'two moments and two phases in the *one* process of God's self-giving and self-expression, although it is an intrinsically differentiated process' (*Foundations*, p. 197).

Lastly, Christology has altered its nature wherever there has been a return to the radical centring of all *Christian theology* on the person and functions of Jesus Christ. Barth practised just such a thorough-going Christocentrism in his monumental *Church Dogmatics* (1932–67). In documents like *Dei Verbum*, *Lumen Gentium* (n. 8), *Gaudium et Spes* (n. 22) and *Sacrosanctum Concilium* we can spot the same phenomenon in the work of the Second Vatican Council. Christological convictions focused the Council's reflections in such 'particular' areas as fundamental theology, grace, eschatology, ecclesiology, liturgy and sacramental theology. John Paul II followed suit in emphasizing Christ's saving work in presenting the Eucharist and the sacrament of reconciliation (*RH*, n. 20). Further, it is widely agreed today that Christology provides the way into the doctrine of the Trinity. I will take up that point again in Chapter 5.

So much for the four periods in the story of Christology. Modern questions and developments will show up everywhere in the chapters that follow. But a brief account of what I believe to be the major contemporary concerns can also help to clarify the present situation.

PRESENT ISSUES

I will not attempt to list here all the issues about Christ's person and work which are being currently discussed. I have already touched on some of them. But any account of serious contemporary questions should include the following matters.

(1)   The Synoptic Gospels permit and even encourage us to raise a number of *historical questions*. How did Jesus understand his own identity? Did his knowledge and consciousness leave room for or even demand an attitude of faith? How did he interpret his mission? What were his intentions when death loomed up? The story of Jesus' ministry, passion and death leaves us to face these and associated questions.

(2)   When we move beyond Jesus' life and death, we need to enquire about the origin and nature of *Easter faith*. What did Paul, the Gospel-writers and other New Testament authors mean by their claim that Jesus was risen from the dead? How did they come to make this and related claims about the resurrection? What should we include in a detailed exposition of what faith in the risen Christ entails?

(3)   The nature of the *redemption* effected by Christ's incarnation, life, death, resurrection and sending of the Spirit continues to call for attention, not least because evil and sin assume new forms. Certainly there are 'constants' from which human beings need to be saved: for instance, death, the fear of death and that basic self-assertion which is sin. At the same time, scientific progress (while it has dramatically extended human power over nature and increased life-expectancy) has also brought menacing new forms of slavery and evil, as noted by recent Church documents like *Gaudium et Spes* (nn. 4ff.) and *Redemptor Hominis* (nn. 15, 16). In a world which experiences the reckless exploitation of natural resources, environmental pollution, the greed of the consumer society, international problems of terrorism and drugs, the North–South tension, the East–West conflict and the threat of nuclear annihilation – in such a changed context the salvation brought by Christ must find expression in some fresh ways. What models interpret best his redeeming work for contemporary men and women? Can we, for example, still describe this redemption in terms of expiation and reparation? Or should we decide that only models of victory (or liberation) and love can carry conviction when we proclaim Christ as Saviour of the world?

(4)   *The* perennial question for Christology is relating *the divine and human elements* in Jesus Christ – his being true God and true man. How can we most helpfully articulate today his divinity, his humanity and their union in his divine person?

(5)   Lastly, a shrinking and ever more interconnected world has given

even greater urgency to the interpretation of Christ's person and saving work for *non-Christians*. How might we understand his redemptive role beyond (and before) Christianity? And how can we clarify and justify theologically what faith suggests about Christ's powerful presence in the general history of the human race and, indeed, in the story of the whole cosmos?

THEOLOGY, HISTORY AND PHILOSOPHY

If this chapter on preliminaries is not to remain patently incomplete, I should briefly clarify three further points. How do I envisage the role of the theologian? How do history and philosophy function in Christology (and for that matter in theology at large)?

(1) *Theology*. The preface of this book and some sections of this chapter have already indicated something about the work of the professional theologian. Chapter I of my *Fundamental Theology* fills out that picture. Here it seems enough to note two features of theological practice that affect Christology.

First, theologians bear their own responsibility for analysing, clarifying, interpreting and systematically articulating the common faith in Jesus Christ. In doing that they draw on the New Testament, official Church teaching and the other data I listed above under 'Sources'. This work always involves ever so much more than merely quoting certain scriptural passages and repeating traditional formulations of faith. Faced with classical expressions of Christology (Christ is 'of one substance with the Father') and Soteriology ('Christ expiated our sins'), theologians must move from asking 'What did this language mean then?', to asking 'What can it mean today?', and to fashioning new ways of presenting to the contemporary world Jesus Christ as Son of God and Saviour.

Second, such Christological reflection by theologians should take place in 'close collaboration' with the bishops who together with the Pope make up the *magisterium* or body of official teachers in the Church (*RH*, n. 19). Here, as elsewhere, the members of the *magisterium* and the theologians share the same goal – that of serving the community by expressing clearly and fruitfully the good news which is the divine salvation and self-communication in Christ. This service takes place in a reciprocal relationship. On the one hand, official formulations of Christian faith coming from Councils, bishops and Popes should guide subsequent theological reflections. Thus the teaching of Chalcedon has rightly directed Christology for over fifteen hundred years. On the other hand, the fruits of theology have been fed into the teaching of the *magisterium*. Thus the Second Vatican Council drew on theologians in many ways – for instance, in its use of 'salvation history' and other terms. If and when the Third Vatican Council meets and produces some document(s) on Jesus Christ, the approach, theses and terminology of theologians currently working in Christology will be seen to affect and contribute to that Council's texts.

(2) *History*. Christianity, while it is more than simply a historical and reasonable religion, does possess both those characteristics. Hence it necessarily entails historical knowledge and rational (philosophical) reflection. To apply this to the present work: Like all theology, Christology is an exercise of Christian faith seeking understanding. In particular, philosophical reason and (as we saw above, especially in modern times) historical research have taken a conspicuous part in that search for understanding about Jesus Christ's person and functions. Hence it seems reasonable to insert here some preliminary remarks about the place of those two disciplines in the Christological reflection which follows.

Several 'slices' of history are obviously crucial for the development of this book: the life and death of Jesus, the emergence of the early Church in the aftermath of his resurrection, and the centuries of Christological controversy which found their classical solution in the teaching of Chalcedon. In each case we should distinguish that history which was actually lived and experienced from the historical reconstruction and inter-pretation which historians can offer us. Thus we can rightly contrast (a) the historical Jesus (= the earthly Jesus as he actually existed in space and time) and the historical early church with (b) the Jesus of history and the early Church of history. In the case of the latter, we deal with the picture of Jesus' life and death or the picture of the early decades of Christianity which historical research produces. (In this book the context should make it clear which of the two senses is intended.)

Here, as elsewhere, historians deal with 'the remembered and interpreted past'. In the nineteenth century when the natural sciences began to dominate the academic scene, Leopold von Ranke and other historians fondly imagined that they could describe with 'scientific', objective neutrality what had actually happened. Since then, however, not only in history but also in the social and even in the natural sciences, the proper role of subjective appropriation and interpretation has been widely recognized. If he had been living in the twentieth century, von Ranke might have been tempted to consider the movie camera the ideal method for recording events as they really happened. But this would have been to overlook the way in which 'documentary' films rightly (and sometimes notoriously) interpret what they record. Modern historical accounts of Jesus and the early Church (and even more the Gospels and the Book of Acts) interpret what they remember. Likewise historical scholars and writers create as well as discover the truth. They produce their pictures in the work of recovering data from the past.

What hangs upon this recognition of the place of interpretation? Just this. Over and over again interpretative and evaluative statements – for example, about the life of Jesus – will appear in the chapters which follow. But the *mere* presence of interpretation in these statements does not *as such* remove them from the realm of history to some separate, theological arena of faith.

In practice the historical methods and research which concern Christology are mainly identical with the work of *biblical scholars*. The results coming from historians of the Patristic period are more convergent and provoke fewer debates. The key problem is this. Which biblical scholars deserve a hearing and should provide the historical material for a Christology? In my opinion, the theologian should not rely so much on marginal scholars who promote possible, sometimes barely possible, theories. One is better advised to follow widely accepted results coming from mainline exegetes. Hence I will draw from biblical scholars *like* C. K. Barrett, Günther Bornkamm, Raymond Brown, Hans Conzelmann, J. D. G. Dunn, Joseph Fitzmyer, R. H. Fuller, Martin Hengel, Joachim Jeremias, Xavier Léon-Dufour, C. F. D. Moule, Rudolf Schnackenburg and Heinz Schürmann. The list is *not* at all complete and I am taking names almost at random. But it seems better at the outset to indicate with some specificity the kind of biblical scholars I intend to rely on.

Lastly, historical research investigates *particular* persons and *contingent* events. In our case it deals, for instance, with the concrete details of Jesus' life or with the specific schemes which the first Christians as a matter of fact used to interpret his death. Philosophy, however, commonly takes up *general* truths, *universal* norms and *necessary* principles. One might put the difference this way. In the pair of names 'Jesus Christ', history looks to 'Jesus' and philosophy to 'Christ'. To call Jesus 'the Christ' or by the name 'Christ' is to state that he belongs to the present and does so everywhere and for everyone. It is to state that he enjoys an absolute and universal value which lifts him beyond the relative and particular aspects of his history. What then can philosophy contribute to our study which after all is a 'Christology' and not a 'Jesuology'?

(3) *Philosophy.* Philosophy should begin its work here by accepting a situation. Christological reflection precisely as a theological activity presupposes in general that Christian faith is true and, specifically, that the crucified and risen Jesus is the Saviour of the world and the Son of God. Hence Christology does *not* appeal to philosophy for help in *proving* these truths about Christ's resurrection, saving function and divinity. Rather, philosophical reason plays its part in clarifying the meaning and presuppositions of such truths.

Thus philosophy will raise such questions as the following: How could an innocent man's atrocious death do anything to expiate and lift the burden of human guilt? What universal elements in human life does Christ's resurrection respond to? What basic experiences and hopes make it possible to believe in and interpret more fully his resurrection? In the common situation shared by human beings what makes them candidates for salvation? When we confess Jesus Christ to be true God and true man, what ultimately enters into our account of divinity and humanity? Can we think of God in such a way that we can understand, even very slightly, how God can 'become' something and, specifically, become matter as John's gospel affirms ('The Word became flesh')?

On all these issues philosophical reason has its points to make, but will also run up against limits. Thus, for example, philosophical reason can shed light on two elements which explain somewhat the human need for salvation: on the one hand, the pressure from evil of all kinds, and, on the other hand, the human drive towards life, meaning and love. Yet it takes theological faith to illustrate more fully how the sinful situation of human beings calls for redemption through Christ.

Philosophy's contribution comes in two ways. First, it offers specific insights, concepts and terms which, when adjusted and modified in the appropriate fashion, can prove useful in Christology. Later chapters will provide examples in the philosophical analyses of expiation, personhood and the Thomist understanding of consciousness as being returning to itself and being present to itself. Second, philosophical reason is the force which can organize Christology into a systematic and coherent whole. A comparison could help here – at least for those who know the work of Bultmann, Cullmann and Rahner. Their philosophical resources gave shape and strength to Bultmann's and Rahner's reflections on Jesus Christ. Cullmann's philosophical limitations, despite his very considerable biblical scholarship, meant that his Christology finally never enjoyed the impact it might otherwise have had. My own Christology, especially in Chapter 5, will be structured around Graf Dürckheim's insights into human existence as a radical quest for and experience of life, meaning and love.

THE AIM OF THIS BOOK

At the heart of the theory and practice of Christianity we find the person of Jesus Christ. If this book gives a little more intelligibility to the belief, worship and way of life which centre on him, I will be grateful.

At the same time, however, I am only too aware of what might be called the 'geography' of Christology. Like anyone else, I am conditioned by my present environment (Rome and the Gregorian University) and past experiences (in Australia, West Germany, England, North America, India and – through brief contacts – West Africa, Japan and Papua New Guinea).

It would be an impossible dream to write a Christology that might be equally valid for all human experiences, world cultures and geographical regions. I have never, for instance, lived in a country when ground fighting was taking place. I do not belong to a Third World nation which had to struggle for its independence from some colonial government. The limits of my lived experience inevitably condition my vision of Christ's identity and functions.

The New Testament itself indicates a certain 'geography' of Christology. For all their 'one faith' in the 'one Lord' Jesus Christ (Eph 4:5), the inspired authors and their sources produced many titles for Christ and different modes of reflecting on his person and work. This variety ran all the way from Phil 2:6ff. (the pre-existent Christ 'emptied himself') to the almost adoptionist language of Acts 2:36 ('God has made him both Lord and Christ, this Jesus whom you crucified'). This pluralism of Christological approaches was not only brought about by various religious and cultural causes, but was also undoubtedly motivated by the desire to proclaim Christ more effectively to different communities. Likewise today we should expect distinct Christologies to emerge *from* and *for* the various cultural, political and economic areas of the world. One region will respond to Christ as the Wisdom of God, another will be drawn to him as the suffering Son of Man, and so forth.

One way to establish this point is to look at the different experiences (and interpretations) of *evil* and the *man/woman* relationship. When I read contemporary Christologies from various parts of the world, read the lines, and then read between the lines, I ask myself constantly: How has this author experienced evil and what view of evil has he reached through his experiences? One author will imply that unorthodox belief (or expressions of belief) in Christ is *the* evil to be combated. Another will be deeply concerned with people drifting into unbelief as the consumer society deadens their religious feelings with its array of satisfactions and false beatitudes. ('Blessed are they who produce more, for they shall consume more.') Yet another theologian will focus on large-scale injustice, deadly hunger and senseless murder to ask: What does Jesus Christ say to such an environment?

The other question I keep raising for myself when I read current works in Christology is this: How do these authors understand what it is to be a man and what it is to be a woman? Differing cultural versions of male and female identity and the relationship between the sexes are rarely discussed explicitly by authors of Christological works. Yet what various cultures and individuals take for granted in this area deeply affects what will be said, for example, about the human characteristics of Jesus.

If then we enjoy 'one Lord, one faith and one baptism' but *not* one culture, what should I aim at? I plan to do at least this – to remain steadily aware of my own cultural experience (and its limitations), and every now and then to suggest how other cultural experiences might be linked with the point under discussion.

Lastly, in this book I intend to maintain Christ's death and resurrection as *the central mystery* around which everything takes shape. Earlier in this chapter I pointed to the fact that New Testament Christology properly began with the 'post-existent' Jesus. It took Good Friday and Easter Sunday (a) to disclose properly Christ's divine relationship to the Father in the Spirit, and (b) to communicate that life, meaning and love which make us children of God. Hence the end is where we start – with that climax of divine salvation and self-revelation which Christ's death and resurrection brought. From that midpoint Christology looks *backwards* (through Christ's life, the incarnation, the history of the Israelites and back to the creation), and *forwards* (through the coming of the Holy Spirit, the story of the Church, and on to the *eschaton*, the future consummation of all things).

The liturgy strongly supports the centrality of the Easter mystery. Right from the birth of Christianity believers have maintained liturgically the sense that Christ's crucifixion and resurrection (and not his incarnation, ministry or any other mystery) is the heart of the matter. Through baptism believers knew themselves to be drawn into the crucifixion and given the promise of resurrection (Rom 6:3–5). They were not baptized 'into the incarnation'. Their Eucharist proclaimed the death of the risen Lord until he comes in glory (1 Cor 11:26). They did not, and we do not, celebrate the Eucharist to proclaim the birth of Christ until he grows to manhood.

But before examining Christ's death and resurrection, I take up the story of his life. Who was it that was crucified and raised from the dead? How had he acted?

NOTES

1   See, for example, Decree on Ecumenism (*Unitatis Redintegratio*), nn. 1, 20; *GS*, nn. 10, 22, 45; Decree on the Church's Missionary Activity (*Ad Gentes*), nn. 3, 8; *Sacrosanctum Concilium*, n. 83.

2   On 'the signs of the times' see my *Fundamental*, pp. 102–107.

3   See *ibid.*, pp. 114–129.

4   See J. Fitzmyer, 'Pauline Theology', *JBC* II, pp. 810–812; W. Foerster, '*Kyrios*', *TDNT* 3, pp. 1039–1098; M. Hengel, *The Son of God* (ET: London and Philadelphia, 1976); S. E. Johnson, 'Lord (Christ)', *IDB* 3, p. 151; *idem*, 'Son of God', *IDB* 4, pp. 408–413; C. F. D. Moule, *The Origin of Christology* (Cambridge, 1977); H. Renard and P. Grelot, 'Son of God', *DBT*, pp. 561–563; E. Schweizer, '*Huios*', *TDNT* 8, pp. 334–399; P Ternant, 'Lord', *DBT*, pp. 321–322.

5   For helpful warnings against finding too much about pre-existence in these Pauline passages see J. D. G. Dunn, *Christology in the Making* (London, 1980), pp. 38–45, 111f., 114–121, 179–183.

6   See A. Grillmeier, *Christ in Christian Tradition* (ET: rev. ed., London, 1975); B. Lohse,

A Short History of Christian Doctrine (ET: Philadelphia, 1966), pp. 37–99; F. X. Murphy, 'Christological Controversy, Early', *NCE* 3, pp. 660–662; J. Pelikan, *The Christian Tradition* 1: *The Emergence of the Catholic Tradition* (Chicago, 1971), pp. 172–277. See also various articles in *ODCC*: 'Alexandrian Theology', 'Antiochene Theology', 'Apollinaris', 'Arius', 'Chalcedon, The Definition of', 'Christology', 'Docetism', 'Eutyches', 'Homoousion', 'Hypostasis', 'Monophysitism', etc.

7   It is not altogether clear that at Nicaea *homoousios* meant numerical identity of substance. See C. Stead, *Divine Substance* (Oxford, 1977), pp. 242–266.

QUESTIONS FOR DISCUSSION

(1)   In your situation, what are the most urgent reasons for studying Christology?

(2)   In *The Legacy of the Middle Ages* F. M. Powicke wrote: 'Only those who accept the dogma of the divinity of Christ as the central fact in a long process of divine revelation can escape bewilderment in the contemplation of the spread of Christianity, which has been so unlike other religions in its claim to penetrate and control the whole of life'. Do you agree that *unlike other religions* Christianity has claimed to penetrate and control the whole of life and that this has been due to the Christian belief in Christ's divinity?

(3)   What has been the history of Christology (both at the level of theory and practice) in your part of the world? What do teachings of the local Church, theological works, devotional practices, popular movements, artistic works or events of history in your country and culture indicate about the Son of God and Saviour of the human race?

(4)   What do you consider the most important Christological issues either for Christians in general or for Christians in your country and continent?

(5)   If you have already read some works in Christology, where do you think the authors stand on the questions of evil and the man/woman relationship?

ADDITIONAL READING

Besides the works indicated in notes 4 and 6, the following items could be helpful:

F. J. van Beeck, 'Christology', *NCE* 16, pp. 84–85.

R. E. Brown, ' "Who Do Men Say that I Am?" ' – a Survey of Modern Scholarship on Gospel Christology', *Crises Facing the Church* (New York and London, 1975), pp. 20–37.

S. E. Johnson, 'Christ', *IDB* 1, pp. 563–571.

W. Kasper, *Jesus the Christ* (ET: London and New York, 1976), pp. 15–61. This classic study stresses the need to interpret Jesus' person and work within the Christian tradition. Its use of German philosophy can make it hard reading.

H. Küng, *OBC*, pp. 119–144. Splendidly organized and very readable, this book offers – among other things – a good account of Jesus' ministry.

J. P. Mackey, *Jesus the Man and the Myth* (London, 1979), pp. 1–51. Perhaps the best written among recent Christologies.

I. Maisch and others, 'Jesus Christ', *SM* 3, pp. 174–209 (= *EncTh*, pp. 730–772).

W. Marxsen, 'Christology in the NT', *IDB* supplementary vol., pp. 146–156.

G. O'Collins, *What are they saying about Jesus?* (New York, 1977). This slim book concentrates on the work of Kasper, Küng and Schillebeeckx. A projected second edition will also discuss the Christologies of Mackey and Sobrino.

R. Orlett and others, 'Jesus Christ', *NCE* 7, pp. 909–955.

W. Pannenberg, *JGM*, pp. 19–49. A classic contemporary Christology which centres on Jesus' resurrection.

E. Schillebeeckx, *Jesus*, pp. 17–40. This book approaches Christology on the basis of the Synoptic Gospels.

J. Sobrino, *Christology*, pp. xv–xxvi, 1–40. A Latin American study which stresses the history of Jesus and the call to practical discipleship.

J. J. Walsh, 'Christology', *NCE* 3, pp. 662f.

2
The Ministry of Jesus

No sane person can doubt that Jesus stands as the founder behind the historical movement whose first distinct stage is represented by the oldest Palestinian community.

RUDOLF BULTMANN

The Christ that Harnack sees, looking back through nineteen centuries of Catholic darkness, is only the reflection of a Liberal Protestant face, seen at the bottom of a deep well.

GEORGE TYRRELL

Jesus is certainly more beautiful than anything in the world or even the world itself. When He appeared, then, like the sun, He dimmed the stars.

VASILY VASILYEVICH ROZANOV

When we investigate the data and try to settle some facts about the history of the earthly Jesus, questions of *fact* and questions of *principle* can mingle intriguingly.

First, how much can we say with any degree of historical probability or even certainty about the words, deeds, attitudes and fate of Jesus? Non-Christian sources provide some slight details. For instance, the Roman historian Tacitus mentions the historical existence of Jesus and his execution under Pontius Pilate (*Annals* XV, 44). What can we glean from those earliest Christian documents, the letters of St Paul? Jesus was born a Jew (Gal 3:16; Rom 9:5), from the house of David (Rom 1:3). He exercised a ministry for the people of Israel (Rom 15:8). He opposed divorce (1 Cor 7:10f.). Before his betrayal and death by crucifixion, he celebrated the Last Supper (1 Cor 11:23ff.). Paul's use and adaptation of the hymn to the exalted Lord in Philippians 2:6–11 shows that the apostle considers the obedient self-abasement 'even to death on a cross' as *the* great decision of Jesus' historical existence.

The Gospels make it clear that the prayer 'Abba! Father!' (Rom 8:15; Gal

4:6) came from Jesus, and that Paul echoed some sayings of Jesus about the right attitude towards enemies and persecutors (Rom 12:14; 1 Cor 4:12f.; 1 Thess 5:15). But if we only had Paul's letters, we would not know that that prayer and these sayings went back to Jesus himself. In the second lecture of his *What Is Christianity?* Adolf von Harnack remarked: 'Everything that we know, independently of these Gospels [= the first three Gospels], about Jesus' history and his teaching, may be easily put on a small sheet of paper, so little does it come to'. Here Harnack pointed to the challenge facing those who investigate the story of Jesus.

It would obscure the real nature of the Gospels to draw on them as if they were written to be biographies or history-books in some 'ordinary' or even 'modern' sense. These narratives constituted relatively brief testimonials of faith. For the Gospel-writers Jesus had become the central object of religious devotion. They offered an amalgam of believing witness and historical reminiscence with the aim of eliciting or at least developing the faith of those who read and heard their works. Certainly the Gospels may not be dismissed as nothing more than the devotional literature of the early Church. But neither may they be interpreted as if they were ordinary, disinterested historical sources from ancient times. I shall return in detail to the problems involved in using the Gospels to settle some facts about what the earthly Jesus said, did, intended and suffered. For the moment I wish only to note the challenge.

This challenge about the facts brings up an obvious set of questions. Then and there, how did Jesus of Nazareth understand his mission? Did he know himself to be Messiah and Son of God? As regards the immediate future, did he foresee his own early (and violent) death and speedy resurrection? And did he intend to redeem others through that coming death and resurrection? Looking to the less immediate future, did he envisage salvation being extended beyond the Jewish people to the Gentiles? Did he intend to found a community which would endure for centuries?

Second, how relevant *in principle* are such questions (and all else that we might establish about the history of Jesus) for the study of Christology and indeed for the whole life of Christian faith which supports our Christological reflections? Should it really make any difference theologically whether or not our historical investigation can establish very much? Does or should our Christian faith in Jesus depend upon some historical knowledge of his life? Do Christians accept him as Messiah and Son of God precisely because they know (historically) that he understood and revealed himself as such? Do we regard his death and resurrection as redemptive because in advance he intended them to have that effect?

It seems best to tackle *the issue of principle* before investigating various factual details of Jesus' ministry and life. As we shall see, certain convictions about matters of principle and presuppositions (at the level of theology and philosophy) can affect very deeply the factual work of methodically using the Gospels to reach conclusions about the history of Jesus.

THE SIGNIFICANCE OF JESUS' HISTORY

(1) *Faith and history.* Christian faith is tied to history in that it confesses God's self-communication to have occurred in a special way through a series of specific historical events and a specific set of persons – prophets, apostles and, above all, the person of Jesus along with the events in which he was involved. Christians see their own religious history and experience as based upon the history of Jesus. Preachers deliver sermons on the basis of Gospel stories. At baptism the faithful recite a creed and align themselves with certain historical events – confessing, for example, that 'For our sake he was crucified under Pontius Pilate'. Their Eucharist recalls and celebrates what 'the Lord Jesus' did 'on the night when he was betrayed' (1 Cor 11:23).

Their concern with historical roots has meant that Christians at large never make their peace with attempts to reduce their link with what happened back 'there' and 'then' in the life of Jesus (*c.* 6–7 B.C.–A.D. 30) under the Roman Emperors Augustus (23 B.C.–A.D. 14) and Tiberius (A.D. 14–37). The Danish philosopher Søren Kierkegaard (1813–55) in his *Philosophical Fragments* classically formulated the attempt to trivialize the historical existence of Jesus:

> If the contemporary generation [of Jesus] had left nothing behind them but these words: 'We have believed that in such and such a year . . . God appeared among us in the humble figure of a servant, that he lived and taught in our community, and finally died,' it would be more than enough.

In our own century Bultmann escalated this position to the point of first separating the historical Jesus from the Christ preached by the Church and then decreeing: 'It is the Christ of the kerygma and not the person of the historical Jesus who is the object of faith'.[1] Beyond doubt, Bultmann proved himself to be the arch-minimalizer of the relevance of Jesus' human history for Christian faith. It could be helpful to recall briefly his position and the main objections to it.

From data provided by the Synoptic Gospels Bultmann was ready to reconstruct the historical Jesus, but then he argued that details from the history of Jesus remain *neutral* for faith and theology. In his *Jesus and the Word* (1926) and later in the opening chapter of his *Theology of the New Testament* (1953) Bultmann outlined what he regarded as the known facts about the historical Jesus. It can be astonishing to note how far this account went. Jesus' demand for decision, Bultmann pointed out, indicated how he interpreted his call as God's last word to human beings. Conscious of his own authority, Jesus understood himself as a final, eschatological sign in relation to which human destiny would be decided. Bultmann was confident that we know this and other facts about the history of Jesus. It is good to remind ourselves of the extent of Bultmann's conclusions, in view of the charge of straight historical scepticism which has often been levelled against him.

Why then did Bultmann settle for a theologically neutral Jesus and thus the irrelevance of his ministry for Christian faith? To begin with, Bultmann insisted uncompromisingly that Christianity began *after* the crucifixion. The earthly Jesus remained within the framework of Judaism as a rabbinical teacher who drastically reinterpreted the Law and preached a more radicalized form of Old Testament faith in God. In brief, for Bultmann the history of Jesus formed the last stage of a superseded Judaism (*Theology of the New Testament*, I, ch. I). The real vitality of Bultmann's position, however, arose ultimately from his preoccupation with one question: How is God's word of salvation made present? Jesus' authoritative claim did not extend beyond his lifetime, but was confined to the past where it can no longer be effective for my salvation. It is only *the proclamation* here and now which constitutes the word which encounters me and can precipitate my faith.

For this kerygma no more than the sheer existence of the historical Jesus must be presupposed. Over and over again Bultmann insisted on this point: 'All that is necessary is to proclaim *that he has come*'. As crown-witness for this position Bultmann claimed the chief theologians of the New Testament: 'Paul and John, each in his own way, indicate that we do not need to go beyond the "that" ' (*HJKC*, p. 20). The content of Jesus' historical life and preaching should not be taken to inform faith. Christian faith remains dependent solely on the present kerygma. Here and here alone in the proclaimed word which elicits our decision to believe, Christ meets us. In short, for Bultmann the Christ of the kerygma and not the person of the historical Jesus constitutes the object of faith.

There is an attractive simplicity about Bultmann's minimalizing view. But a moment's reflection suggests serious flaws in the case he argued. As a matter of fact, the individual personality of the historical Jesus and the events of his ministry have proved (and remain) highly significant for the faith of very many Christians. One might parody a statement by Bultmann (to which we shall come later) and say: 'It is impossible to watch Zeffirelli's *Jesus of Nazareth* and notice the effect of this film on the Christian and non-Christian public, and at the same time accept Bultmann's veto on the relevance of the historical Jesus for faith'.

Further, to inform Christians that they need only to hear it announced 'that he has come' is to encourage serious doubts about the genuine historical existence of Jesus. Many theologians and other believers have felt uneasy over Bultmann's Docetic tendency which seems to trivialize a real incarnation out of a preoccupation with the present proclamation. This discomfort has sometimes been expressed by stating that in Bultmann's interpretation the Word does not become flesh, but the flesh becomes word. Many critics have rightly wondered whether Bultmann's view can be reconciled with the Johannine insistence that Jesus has 'come in the flesh' (1 John 4:2f.). There are certainly issues to be faced about the place of history and the amount of historical information in the Fourth Gospel. Yet John does offer his account of the divine Word in the form of a Gospel, and that means as a history of the Incarnate One.

What of Bultmann's other crown-witness, St Paul? We have already seen how the apostle included at least some data from the history of Jesus. Paul's letters (c. 50–c. 65) were largely 'occasional' writings composed to meet specific needs and problems of early Christian communities. It seems reasonable to suppose that he knew and took for granted material from the ministry and passion of Jesus which was circulating in oral and written form and which would be used by Mark (c. 65) and then by Matthew and Luke (c. 75). 2 Corinthians 5:16 should not be mistranslated to make Paul repudiate 'knowing Christ according to the flesh', as if the apostle were rebuking those whose weak faith led them to desire some knowledge of the historical Jesus: 'Though we once knew Christ according to the flesh, we regard him thus no longer'. The phrase 'according to the flesh' belongs rather with the verb, not with 'Christ': 'Even though we once regarded Christ from a human point of view, we regard him thus no longer'. Paul had believed the crucified Jesus to be someone accursed, but his conversion obviously led the apostle to disown that earlier attitude. As far as known traditions coming from the earthly life of Jesus were concerned, Paul did not repudiate them and occasionally showed that he recognized them as decisive. What Jesus was remembered to have said against divorce remained unquestionably valid for the apostle (1 Cor 7:10f.).

Nowadays there is probably little need to go on arguing against Bultmann's attempt to reduce the importance of Jesus' earthly life to an utter minimum. Bultmann's severest critics were stationed to his left – among those who found that he offered no convincing justification for the need to retain at least the sheer existence of the historical Jesus among the conditions for faith. Why should the 'that' of Jesus' having come enjoy such importance if everything else about him was to be quietly dropped? Why must one's authentic decision of faith remain tied to that historical point in the past?

In retrospect, it is a little baffling that many Protestant theologians could have solemnly accepted Bultmann's view during the 1930s and 1940s. The crash came in 1953 with a lecture by one of Bultmann's greatest students, Ernst Käsemann. He insisted that what we know about Jesus' life remains relevant for faith. The upshot among exegetes and theologians who had followed Bultmann's lead was to initiate a new interest in the history of

Jesus and the study of the Synoptic Gospels. Those who had never accepted Bultmann's veto naturally expressed satisfaction at this turn of events.

At the end of this chapter I want to pick up again the issue of the significance which the recoverable history of Jesus bears for Christian faith and theology. Here let me add just this. The understanding which the earthly Jesus had of his own *identity* and *mission laid some basis for what followed* – the subsequent Christian belief in him as Son of God and Saviour of the world. In experiencing and confessing him to be such in the aftermath of his resurrection, Christians were proclaiming things which had been at least prepared for and implied during his ministry.

(2) *Jesus and outsiders.* So far I have touched on the significance of Jesus' history for committed Christian believers. But here it would be outrageously wrong to forget *non-believers* and *half-believers*. Many people who hesitate to accept the Christ of full-blown Christian doctrines or even the heavenly Lord of St Paul's letters are still powerfully drawn to the earthly Jesus of the Synoptic Gospels which make claims about his function and identity in a subtler and less direct way.

It is one thing to accept the risen Lord of Christian faith and join in worshipping him with a community of believers. But it is another, less 'demanding', thing to yield to the fascination and attraction of Jesus of Nazareth. Many people who find themselves distressed at institutional Christianity or so far unwilling to confess Jesus as Son of God and Saviour are ready to reflect on what we know of Jesus' life and teaching.

Believers and non-believers have shared in common the growth of modern historical consciousness and witnessed together the emergence of professional historical methods. Together they can ask: What can historical enquiry establish about the earthly Jesus? Holding as far as is possible our belief or unbelief in abeyance and using the available historical methods, how much can we say about his life and death taken on their own terms and 'freed' as it were from the post-Easter conceptions of all New Testament sources?

In short, the historical Jesus offers common ground for Christians and non-Christians. At times the latter find that their experience will follow Augustine's principle 'Through the man Christ you move to the God Christ' (Sermon 261, 7). After all, Peter, Mary Magdalene and other early disciples enacted a similar movement, as they passed from contact with the earthly Jesus to their post-Easter belief in him as Son of God and Saviour of the world.

INTERPRETING THE GOSPELS

(1) *Presuppositions and procedures.* Some statements about presuppositions

and procedures should be made before examining the data and drawing various conclusions about the history of Jesus. To begin with, I accept the common view that Mark's Gospel was written first and was used in the composition of Matthew and Luke. Those two later Gospels, among other sources, also drew on Q, a collection of Jesus' sayings or *logia* which is no longer extant. In other words, I assume as a plausible and useful working hypothesis the Two-Source Theory (Mark + Q) and that the Gospels as we have them were finally written in the following order: Mark (*c.* 65), Matthew and Luke (*c.* 75), and John (*c.* 90). The traditional names 'Mark, Matthew, Luke and John' are used here for convenience and not to indicate precise claims about the specific authors of the four Gospels (see *Dei Verbum*, n. 18).

Here I should at once ward off a possible misconception arising from the order of the Gospels: Mark, Matthew, Luke and John. A later Gospel and, especially, particular traditions recorded by a later Gospel might be historically more accurate than earlier ones. Or, to put matters the other way, what was written down earlier need not necessarily prove a more faithful guide to the 'facts' than what was written down later. Further, as regards the interpretation of the events in question, an earlier writer might obviously grasp less of their significance than a later writer. *As such*, the chronological order of the Gospels does not automatically imply any conclusions about differences in the quality either of the historical content or the theological evaluation.

(2) *Form criticism and redaction criticism.* Next this book presupposes *the three-stage development* recognized by the Second Vatican Council in *Dei Verbum* (nn. 7, 18f.): the events of Jesus' life, then the period of apostolic preaching from the thirties into the sixties, and lastly the composition of the Gospels by the evangelists. At the end of the First World War the work of form criticism opened up stage two. After the Second World War redaction criticism brought new insights into stage three.

FORM CRITICISM. In the period of apostolic preaching the story or stories of Jesus' passion may have settled down fairly soon as pieces of narrative. But other traditions about his words, deeds and experiences seem to have been mainly passed on orally as separate units or small groups of units. The original geographical contexts and chronological order of these units could be lost, while the traditions themselves were preserved and shaped to meet the life and needs of the Christian communities. By noting the role of the early Church in selecting, transmitting, and adapting to its purposes the sayings and deeds of Jesus, form criticism brings out the difficulty of establishing the historical facts at the origin of these traditions. In that sense the Gospels are primary sources for the history of the early Church and only secondary sources for the history of Jesus himself. Faced

with a particular passage, our first question should be: What function did
this unit serve in the life of early Christians? How does it mirror their
situation?

Beyond question, New Testament scholarship is permanently indebted to
the form-critics for illuminating the development of the materials behind
and before the Gospels, Yet the value of their contribution should not lead us
to extremes. Specifically, form criticism seeks to classify materials on purely
formal grounds. These classifications are not always certain. Often
difficulties arise in correlating forms with a setting in the life of the early
Church. In fact, it is impossible to sustain the thesis that no traditions from
Jesus and about Jesus survived except insofar as they served some function in
the life and worship of the primitive Church. Further, the mere fact that
certain pronouncements or some story can be shown to have met certain
needs of early Christian communities does not necessarily demand the
conclusion that such words or events do not (or even, cannot) derive from
the history of Jesus himself. Community requirements could have dictated
not invention but selection out of the many (authentic) traditions which
were available.

REDACTION CRITICISM.   Those who launched redaction criticism after
the Second World War successfully corrected the impression communicated
by the form-critics that the Gospel-writers – and, specifically, Mark,
Matthew and Luke – were 'mere' collectors of community traditions rather
than active editors or even authors who selected and adapted materials for
their own purposes. They combined words and deeds of Jesus and set them
in new contexts, so as to present and interpret his story according to their
own theological insights and the needs of the specific communities they
were writing for.

In *Dei Verbum* the Second Vatican Council described the editorial work of
the evangelists as follows:

> The sacred authors, in writing the four Gospels, selected certain of the many
> elements which had been handed on, either orally or already in written form, others
> they synthesized or explained with an eye to the situation of the churches, the while
> sustaining the form of preaching, but always in such a fashion that they have told us
> the honest truth about Jesus (n. 19).

But how do we know that the Gospels give us 'the honest truth about
Jesus'? What arguments substantiate a similar claim made earlier in that
same chapter of *Dei Verbum*?

> Holy Mother Church has firmly and with absolute constancy maintained and
> continues to maintain that the four Gospels..., whose historicity she
> unhesitatingly affirms, faithfully hand on what Jesus, the Son of God, while he
> lived among men, really did and taught for their eternal salvation (n. 19).

(Here 'historicity', incidentally, should be understood in the context of the document and the discussion which produced it. It does *not* refer to sheer data or 'mere' facts – if indeed such could ever exist simply by themselves. Rather this 'historicity' and 'honest truth' are a matter of faithful reliability in the work of reporting and interpreting the past story of Jesus.)

(3) *Substantial reliability.* A number of considerations converge to encourage us to take the Gospels, or at least Mark, Matthew and Luke, as reliable guides to the last stage of Jesus' earthly existence – his ministry, passion and death. Like the communities which handed on the material about Jesus during the thirty or forty years before these Gospels were written, the evangelists themselves were selective rather than highly inventive. Just as they recast the Jewish scriptures for particular purposes, so too they transposed and added material when they set down in writing the community's memory of Jesus. But they remained substantially reliable in supplying data on Jesus, just as we know that they were substantially accurate in citing the Jewish scriptures. The Dead Sea Scrolls, which can be dated between 20 B.C. and A.D. 70 and which – along with other writings – include fragments and sometimes lengthy sections of nearly all the books of the Old Testament, startlingly confirm the substantial reliability of the Gospels in their quotations from these sacred scriptures.

Further, what we can learn about first-century Judaism and Palestine from Josephus (*c.* 37–*c.* 100), Philo (*c.* 20 B.C.–*c.* A.D. 50) and other non-Christian sources generally tallies well with what the Synoptic Gospels have to say about the Herod family, the Pharisees, Pontius Pilate (Roman procurator of Judaea A.D. 26–36), the Sadducees and so forth. A check with these outside sources creates a favourable impression.

Then in the case of Luke we can verify many details of his Acts of the Apostles through Roman records and other non-Christian sources. In such matters as the complex system of titles for the kings, governors, magistrates and petty officials he mentions, he shows a reasonable standard of historical accuracy in this second work. We can rightly conclude that this level of accuracy holds also for his Gospel and that he does carry out his promise to give an accurate account of Jesus' story (Luke 1:1–4). Of course, in writing history Luke took his standards at least partly from the conventions of his time. Yet the practice of Greek, Jewish and Roman historians, even if freer than that of modern historians, nevertheless maintained some fidelity to sources and facts.

Another argument derives from the chronology of the New Testament books. Galatians, Romans and other highly theological letters of St Paul appeared *before any of the Gospels were composed.* Yet Mark, Matthew and Luke remained relatively untheological. Although they wrote *after St Paul* and presumably had some contact with the apostle's thought, they did not read his theology back onto the lips of Jesus or in other ways impose Paul's theology on the story of the ministry and passion. Instead they recorded the sayings and doings of Jesus more or less as they were transmitted to them. Three examples. Repeatedly Paul interprets Jesus' death as having occurred 'for us' and 'for our sins'. But this theme of atonement rarely surfaces in Mark (10:45; 14:24), even though this Gospel shows such a strong orientation towards the crucifixion that, like the other Gospels, it has rightly been described as 'a passion story with a long introduction'. Mark draws on traditions about Jesus to give us in narrative form a theology of the cross. But he does not retroject into Jesus' ministry that explicit atonement theology which grew up between Jesus and Mark and which got lodged (and developed) in the Pauline letters.

Second, Mark obviously believes that Jesus was and is Son of God in a way that tallies with Pauline texts like Galatians 4:4. But Mark does not feel free to put in the mouth of Jesus a clear statement to that effect.

My third example comes from the Christian controversy over the possible obligation of Gentile converts to maintain the practice of circumcision and other items in the Jewish law. Chapters 10, 11 and 15 of Acts, the Letter to the Galatians and other Pauline writings document the way early Christians struggled with this issue. It would obviously have been tempting to have credited the earthly Jesus with some precise instructions in this area. But in Mark, for example, we find some pronouncements concerning Jewish traditions about washing and food laws (7:1-23) but nothing to indicate, let us say, that the obligation of circumcision was to lapse with Jesus' death and resurrection. Despite pressing Church interests in the matter, neither Mark himself nor the traditions on which he drew felt free to invent and retroject into the ministry of Jesus some clear statement that circumcision was no longer to be considered obligatory for salvation. In 1 Corinthians 7:10, 12 and 25 we see Paul carefully distinguishing between his own instructions and those which went back to Jesus and had been transmitted to the apostle by the Church tradition. It seems that like Palestinian Judaism (from which the first disciples of Jesus came), the early Christian communities were set to differentiate faithfully between the words of 'the teacher' (in their case Jesus) and subsequent additions and interpretations derived from his followers. And they maintained this distinction, even though some urgent questions in the emerging Church put them under pressure to look for traditions about Jesus which could directly meet these needs.

Let me add one final consideration in support of the substantial accuracy of the Synoptic Gospels in reporting Jesus' ministry and death – their tone. They come across as sober, unexaggerated documents when compared with the Apocryphal Gospels which were not accepted as genuine by the early Church. These latter books with their sensational fantasies, magic and legends highlight the quiet objectivity of our Gospels.

With these and other arguments it is relatively easy to mount a persuasive case for the basic trustworthiness of the account that Mark, Matthew and Luke offer of Jesus' earthly activity. We might wish that these evangelists had given us more facts about dates, names, places and numbers. But, by and large, their story from Jesus' baptism to his death appears substantially reliable. The interests of the communities (the period studied in form criticism) and of the evangelists (the object of redaction criticism) certainly shaped the Gospels. Yet, far from freely composing sayings and doings of Jesus, the early Church and its writers passed on with substantial fidelity what was remembered from Jesus' ministry.

What of *John's Gospel* as a source of information on Jesus? In this Gospel decades of interpretative and prayerful reflection have deeply modified the historical record. Theological and spiritual concerns are strongly to the fore. The picturesque language of the earthly Jesus has dropped away. He speaks repeatedly of 'light', 'life', 'truth', 'darkness', 'the world', 'testimony', 'glory', and the rest – not to call people to repentance and announce God's rule, as he did historically, but quite directly *to proclaim himself as divine*. In Mark, Jesus comes preaching 'the gospel of God, and saying, "The time is fulfilled, and the kingdom of God is at hand; repent, and believe in the gospel" ' (1:14f.). In John, long contemplation of Jesus' identity allows the evangelist to represent him in terms that recall Yahweh's self-revelation to Moses (Exod 3:14): 'Jesus said to them, "Truly, truly, I say to you, before Abraham was, I am" ' (8:58). If we are trying to retrieve the sayings and doings of the earthly Jesus, we should generally allow the Synoptic Gospels to guide us.

Nevertheless, an earlier scepticism which denied all historical value to John's Gospel would not be justified and in fact has largely given way to a more nuanced attitude. For example, John may be historically correct in presenting Galilee *and Jerusalem* as the setting for Jesus' activity. Where the Synoptic Gospels apparently present the ministry as lasting only for about a year and including only one (final) journey to Jerusalem, John reports Jesus as attending three Passover feasts in Jerusalem (2:13; 6:4; 11:55) and making four journeys there (2:13; 5:1; 7:10; 12:12). The more prolonged exposure to the Jerusalem public reported by John would explain more plausibly the hostility towards Jesus of the authorities in the capital. I shall return to this point in the next chapter.

(4) *Criteria of authenticity*.   Before completing these preliminary matters, I must answer one final question. What kind of criteria can guide our judgement that a particular saying or action reported by the Gospels does in fact have its basis in the actual history of Jesus' ministry? Let me indicate three among a number of criteria which can satisfactorily help in making such a judgement.

(a) MULTIPLE ATTESTATION.   Where something is recorded about

Jesus in different forms and layers of the early Christian tradition, we can be more confident of its historical authenticity than if it were reported in an isolated way by only one evangelist. We have such multiple attestation, for instance, for the fact that at some point during his ministry Jesus chose a core-group of twelve from the wider ranks of his disciples. The Marcan *narrative* includes a story of such a call (3:13–19 parr.) and a subsequent mission of the twelve (6:7–13 parr.). The logia or Q *tradition* on which Matthew and Luke draw also attests the existence of this core-group: 'Jesus said to them, ''Truly I say to you, in the new world, when the Son of man shall sit on his glorious throne, you who have followed me will also sit on twelve thrones, judging the twelve tribes of Israel'' ' (Matt 19:28 par.). Finally, *a faith formula* quoted by St Paul confirms that such a group existed before Jesus' death and hence could receive an appearance of the risen Lord: 'He appeared to Cephas [= Peter], then to the twelve' (1 Cor 15:5).

Perhaps I should point out that this criterion of multiple attestation does not simply as such apply to situations where Matthew and Luke have taken over a story or saying from Mark. In such a case the attestation is not strictly multiple. The criterion does, however, come into play where both Mark (followed by Matthew and Luke) and John (with his somewhat different traditions) jointly attest to some saying or an episode like the feeding of the five thousand (Mark 6:32–44 parr.; John 6:1–15).

(b) DISSIMILARITY AND DISCONTINUITY. Where the Gospels report Jesus as saying or doing things that have no background in Judaism and/or are not characteristic of the life of the emerging Church, we can conclude that such traditions stem from Jesus himself. For example, Jesus' use of 'Abba' (Father dear) and 'Amen' does not come from his Jewish background and is hardly taken up in early Christianity.[2] In such cases we rightly get the impression of finding language which was original to Jesus himself. It is the same with his language about the reign of God. The formulations are Semitic, but the language itself was characteristic neither of contemporary Judaism nor of the emerging Church. Again the reasonable conclusion is that this language derives from the person of Jesus himself.

This second criterion comes into play where the Gospels record traditions which conflict with the sentiments and interests of the early Church. A case in point would be an episode reported by all four evangelists: Jesus submitted to baptism at the hands of John. Despite its positive aspects, this act of Jesus clashed with the Church's tendency to keep John subordinated to Jesus and could only have embarrassed early Christians in any debates with those who remained disciples of John and did not move quickly to faith in Jesus himself (Acts 19:2f.). Moreover, as we will see in Chapter 6, different traditions and authors in the New Testament all witness to the conviction that Jesus was utterly sinless. How then could he have accepted 'a baptism of repentance for the forgiveness of sins' (Mark 1:4)? His baptism by John was a doubly embarrassing matter. We shall see other examples of traditions about Jesus which are not in line with the understanding and interests of the early Church. It is plausible to argue that such traditions (which it must have been tempting to suppress) enshrine authentic memories of Jesus' words and deeds.

Things would go astray here, however, if I failed to note how this second criterion is *inclusive and not exclusive*. It allows us to say '*At least this tradition goes back to Jesus*'. It encourages us to spot what was original and unique to Jesus. But it does not allow us to exclude other traditions as doubtful simply because we find a background for them in Judaism and/or a follow-up for them in the life of the early Church. It would be nonsense to expect Jesus to be either totally discontinuous with his Jewish past or radically dissimilar from emerging Christianity. As René Latourelle remarks in his *Finding Jesus through the Gospels*,

> To reason thus, would be to make of Christ a being outside of time, cut off from his environment and his era. This would be to place Christ in a *vacuum*, without influence received from Judaism, and without influence exercised on the Church (p. 226).

On the contrary, we shall note things he said and did which either derive from his Jewish heritage or lay the basis for subsequent Christian teaching and practice.

(c) COHERENCE. A third criterion for assessing historically authentic material is that of coherence. Early traditions which correspond to items already established as authentic on other grounds can also be accepted as authentic. For example, the parable of the prodigal son is found only in one Gospel (Luke 15:11–32), but it corresponds extremely well with Jesus' special concern for sinners which is attested in many ways by the Gospel traditions. Hence we may confidently accept the parable as genuinely coming from Jesus.

So much for these three criteria of authenticity. In what follows I want to appeal only to those Gospel traditions which, on the basis of these or other criteria, can be reasonably held to derive from the earthly Jesus himself.

THE STORY OF JESUS

(1) *The limits of reconstruction.* When we seek to reconstruct the ministry and message of Jesus, we should recall the limits imposed by the Gospels. We certainly cannot repeat the classical attempt to write a life of Jesus. For the writing of any real biography, four requirements seem indispensable:

(a) that we have access in some degree to the whole of our subject's life and development;

(b) that some chronological framework can be established;

(c) that we have some access to his motivation and psychology;

(d) that in our portrayal we can make use of biographical 'types'; by this I mean that, while paying proper attention to our subject's individual traits, we have some way of generalizing about him as, for instance, a dedicated social reformer, an antisocial recluse or a violent revolutionary.

In the case of Jesus the four requirements cannot be met. (a) Our knowledge of him is restricted to the last year or two of his life. (b) Even for those months not much chronology can be established. (See above what was said about the transmission of the traditions and the activity of the evangelists under the headings 'Form criticism' and 'Redaction criticism'.) (c) The Gospels rarely mention Jesus' motives or deal with his states of mind. These sources make it difficult to penetrate his inner life. (d) Finally, Jesus transcends ordinary biographical types. It remains quite unsatisfactory in any portrayals of him to make use of such typical figures as the religious revivalist, the wandering miracle-worker, or the high priest of a new cult.

Hence we would be unjustified in renewing the nineteenth-century attempts to write a life of Jesus. Nevertheless, our disagreement with that classical enterprise should not lead us to underrate what our sources do permit us to reconstruct about Jesus' ministry.

To start with, some basic structure and items are historically recoverable. Jesus came from Nazareth, was baptized by John, and began a wandering ministry in which he proclaimed that 'the Kingdom of God is at hand', associated with sinners and outcasts, called disciples to follow him, worked miracles and taught some memorable parables. His violation of some Sabbath laws, cleansing of the Temple and other 'offences' aroused the antagonism of some influential Jewish leaders. In Jerusalem (where he had come for the Passover celebration) he was arrested, interrogated by members of the Sanhedrin (the supreme Jewish council and highest court of justice), tried by the Roman authorities, and then executed as a messianic pretender on a cross which bore an inscription giving the charge against Jesus as 'King of the Jews'.

The test of multiple attestation and other criteria validate these conclusions. For example, all four evangelists attest that the charge of being a messianic pretender was attached to Jesus' cross.

What of Jesus' teaching? Can scholarly enquiry retrieve something of what he said – at least the substance of some sayings, if not the precise wording? Here the evidence points to the following passages in the Gospels: the repeated proclamation that 'the Kingdom of God is at hand', the shorter (Lukan) version of the Our Father (11:2–4), certain parables (minus the interpretations like Mark 4:10–20, which appears not to go back to Jesus himself), some 'aphorisms of reversal' such as Mark's 'many that are first will be last, and the last first' (10:31), and Jesus' familiar Aramaic word 'Abba' (Father dear) to which I will return shortly. This is not offered as a complete list but I want to indicate the kind of sayings that appear to provide, if not necessarily the actual words (*ipsissima verba*) of Jesus, at least the drift of what at times he said (*ipsissima vox*).

In short, the Gospels do allow us to reconstruct something of the message, activity, claim and impact of Jesus at least during the last year or so of his life.

(2) *The message and the claim*. We pull together many of the threads from Jesus' ministry by saying this: *To his own Jewish people he proclaimed God's reign with divine authority and compassion*. Several of these themes call for some closer attention.

(a) THE REIGN OF GOD. Hardly anything is more certain about the ministry of Jesus than that he proclaimed God's kingdom or reign – that final saving act of God which was coming not as a reward achieved through human merits but as sheer gift from the divine goodness. Jesus announced this climactic intervention of God as being 'at hand', 'coming' and 'appearing' in a way which was beyond human control. Men and women were 'invited' to enter this 'kingdom of heaven' or to accept it as a child does a gift. If Jesus gave himself totally in the service of the present (Matt 12:28 par.) and future (Matt 8:11 par.) rule of God, his proclamation and activity were actually initiating this final saving intervention of God (Matt 12:28). The divine reign was already operative through Jesus' preaching, teaching and healing (Matt 4:23; 9:35). In the deepest sense for Jesus to proclaim that 'the reign of God is near' was to say 'God is near'. We will generally catch the sense of what Jesus intended, if for that reverent circumlocution 'the kingdom of heaven' or 'the kingdom of God' we simply substitute 'God' or perhaps 'divine salvation'.

(b) DIVINE AUTHORITY. One particularly striking feature of Jesus' proclamation of the divine reign was the authority with which it was done. If at times elusive, his sense of personal authority remains thoroughly well attested. At least once, when faced with some critics, Jesus refused to trace the source of his authority: 'Neither will I tell you by what authority I do these things' (Mark 11:33). Yet his conviction of authority was unmistakably there. The classical prophets passed on God's word as something which came to them from the outside. They were often more vociferous about the divine origin of the message, insisting with their hearers, 'Thus says the Lord'. Jesus, however, lived in God's presence as one who belonged there. Through what he did and said he simply expressed in his own right the will of God. He directly acted in that way, without it ever being said about him what was stated of the last of the Jewish prophets: 'The word of God came to John the son of Zechariah in the wilderness'

(Luke 3:2). The way Jesus spoke and acted revealed a sense of his personal authority which sets him apart from the prophets. Let me give some examples.

Jesus showed a personal authority that did not flinch at going beyond *the Mosaic law*. In his day the principle of divorce was universally accepted among the Jews. But in that matter Jesus simply swept aside the law of Moses (Deut 24:1ff.) as irrelevant and judged matters on the basis of the original purposes in the creation of man and woman: 'What therefore God has joined together, let not man put asunder' (Mark 10:9). Over and over again Jesus exemplified the truth of Mark's summary observation: 'And they were astonished at his teaching, for he taught them as one who had authority, and not as the scribes' (1:22). No other Jewish teacher at that time could have uttered those antitheses, 'You have heard that it was said to the men of old.... But I say to you' (Matt 5:21–48). Here Jesus authoritatively *and in his own name* transformed the divine law, by honouring the real force and carrying to the ultimate the inmost spirit of the great commandment: 'You shall love the Lord your God with all your heart, and with all your soul, and with all your might' (Deut 6:5).

Another example. It would have been unthinkable for any other teacher of Jesus' time to have gone beyond the belief that the Mosaic law included all that God demanded of human beings. Yet that is what Jesus did with the man who asked 'Good Teacher, what must I do to inherit eternal life?' (Mark 10:17). Even though that man had proved loyal to the law in every detail, he still fell short of perfection: 'You lack one thing; go, sell what you have, and give to the poor, and you will have treasure in heaven; and come, follow me' (Mark 10:21). Here Jesus authoritatively indicated that the law was insufficient. Jesus' invitation showed how the divine demands cannot be circumscribed by some written formulae, even of the most sacred kind. On this and other occasions he invited people to follow him even at total cost to themselves (Mark 10:29 parr.).

Finally, Jesus offended religious sensibilities by overriding regulations about purity and other traditions (Mark 7:1–23). But the really startling claim to authority came when he set aside various interpretations of what constituted the Sabbath rest (Mark 3:1–5) and claimed the right to decide what should be done or not done on that sacred day (Mark 2:28).

In what appears to be an authentic saying Jesus stated the ultimate secret and basis of the high authority he claimed and employed: 'All things have been delivered to me by my Father; and no one knows the Son except the Father, and no one knows the Father except the Son and anyone to whom the Son chooses to reveal him' (Matt 11:27 par.). This uniquely intimate and reciprocal relationship with the One he called Father meant that Jesus knew himself to be absolutely reliable in revealing the divine will to others. As Ben Meyer puts it, 'Jesus understood himself to be the unique revealer of the full, final measure of God's will' (*The Aims of Jesus*, p. 151). I will come back to this Son–Father relationship later.

(c) DIVINE COMPASSION. Jesus exercised his extraordinary authority in a deeply compassionate fashion. Over and over again the Gospels report him as having behaved and spoken in a way that forces us to this conclusion: Jesus identified himself with the divine concern to forgive and save sinful human beings. Just as he understood his word and God's word to be identical, so he understood his presence and God's salvation to be identical. Jesus knew that in his own person the divine mercy had drawn near sinful men and women. Let us see some details of this.

In a special way Jesus proclaimed the divine compassion to those who were marginalized by the respectable society of their day: 'I come not to call the righteous, but sinners' (Mark 2:17 parr.). The 'little' people, those who felt afflicted by the requirements of the law with its 248 commands and 365 prohibitions, and those who had been made outcasts by the 'good' people now found themselves named and treated by Jesus as special beneficiaries of God's merciful reign, the ones to be singled out as 'blest'. 'Blessed are you poor, for yours is the kingdom of God' (Luke 6:20 par.). Tax-collectors and other close collaborators with the occupying Roman army, women of bad reputation, tanners and all those whose occupations made them religiously unclean, lepers and others whom religion and society had confined to some condition of misery found Jesus promising them happiness. God had decided to save the miserable. Unlike the righteous, such people could recognize divine salvation as pure gift. They knew that their repentance did not prompt God's forgiveness but was only a response to the loving offer of divine mercy extended to them through Jesus' call for conversion. Stories like that of Zacchaeus (Luke 19:1–10) witness to the joy Jesus aroused when he liberated those who had felt themselves lost in sin and misery.

The Gospels recall particular occasions when Jesus said to some sinner 'Your sins are forgiven' (Mark 2:5; Luke 7:48). His critics saw the implication of this: 'It is blasphemy! Who can forgive sins but God alone?' (Mark 2:7). Such people were scandalized also when Jesus showed the divine compassion by his practice of dining with sinners and so taking them into God's company. These critics derided him as 'a glutton and a drunkard, a friend of tax collectors and sinners' (Matt 11:19). Through the parable of the prodigal son (Luke 15:11–32) Jesus defended his own conduct. As God did, Jesus received and forgave returning sinners, expressing this through his table-fellowship with them.

The parables themselves, while at times forcefully proclaiming the divine mercy, aimed above all to provoke a response to the loving and demanding presence of God. They called on people to open themselves and submit with repentance and joy to the divine rule which was coming among them with power in the person of Jesus.

(d) THE PERSON OF JESUS. On the one hand, Jesus was not concerned with directly proclaiming himself and his own identity. Rather, he announced that definitive revelation and salvation which God's final rule was bringing. On the other hand, however, he knew that divine reign to be making itself felt in his life and teaching. In other words, God's offer was essentially linked to the person of Jesus. Accepting Jesus and his proclamation of the divine rule emerged as *the decisive criterion* of human worth before God: 'Every one who acknowledges me before men, the Son of man also will acknowledge before the angels of God; but he who denies me before men will be denied before the angels of God' (Luke 12:8f. par.). One's relationship to Jesus would decide one's ultimate salvation or ruin: 'Whoever would save his life will lose it; and whoever loses his life for my sake and the gospel's will save it' (Mark 8:35 parr.).

To sum up. Jesus claimed a unique and a uniquely important role in establishing the right final relationship between God and human beings.

All of this at least raises serious questions about Jesus' sense of self-identity. What was the self-awareness involved in authoritatively overriding the Mosaic law and inviting others to 'follow me' even at total cost to themselves? What consciousness of himself lay behind Jesus' practice of forgiving sins and serving the social and religious outcasts of his day? What awareness of personal identity was implied by the parables (with their call to a decisive choice in the presence of Jesus) and by his frank warning that – for good or ill – one's relationship to him would shape one's final destiny before God?

Do the Synoptic Gospels allow us to clarify something of Jesus' basic mind-set? Shaping his consciousness of being sent to communicate and enact with unique authority the divine rule was what has been called his 'Abba-experience'. In calling men and women to conversion, he was proclaiming the rule of the One whom he called 'Abba, Father dear' (Mark 14:36). This distinctive and unusual term expressing simple, deep intimacy with God seems to capture the essential self-understanding of Jesus. He thought of himself and gave himself in terms of this relationship to his Father.

Is there evidence to suggest that Jesus thought of his sonship as *a unique relationship* neither shared nor to be shared by others? In the Old Testament the special relationship to God enjoyed by angels, the king and the Jewish nation allowed them to be called 'sons of God'. Thus the second Psalm portrays God as naming as 'my son' the holy person of the king. As such, 'son of God' was an ambiguous term. Did Jesus think or know himself to be in a uniquely distinctive way *the* Son of God? When he spoke of the coming 'day of the Son of man', Jesus called himself 'the Son', but in the context it was a question of his limited knowledge, not of his unique identity: 'Of that day or that hour no one knows, not even the angels in heaven, nor the Son, but only the Father' (Mark 13:32). Above (under 2(b)) I cited a logion which some scholars interpret to mean that Jesus here at least presented himself as *the* Son: 'All things have been delivered to me by my Father; and no one knows the Son except the Father, and no one knows the Father except the Son and anyone to whom the Son chooses to reveal him' (Matt 11:27 par.). Other scholars, who also agree that we have here an authentic saying, interpret its meaning in a 'lesser' sense. Jesus drew on some common maxim about fathers and sons knowing each other intimately. Hence 'the Son' of the saying could be understood in a general and not in an absolute way: 'No one knows any son except his father, and no one knows any father except his son and anyone to whom his son chooses to reveal him'. Granted that this could well be the background of the saying, in the context of Jesus' ministry the saying at least strongly hints at a consciousness of being related to the God whom he called 'Father' in a way that was qualitatively distinct and set Jesus apart from others ('anyone to whom the Son chooses to reveal him').

That impression is confirmed by Jesus' consistent practice of *distinguishing between 'my Father' and 'your Father'*. It is only in Matthew 6:9 (where he is teaching the disciples how to pray) that he says 'Our Father'. Moreover, it is more likely that Matthew (or some source of his) had modified an original 'Father' by adding 'our' than that Luke omitted an original 'our' when he simply begins the Lord's Prayer with 'Father' (Luke 11:2). Apart from Matthew 6:9, Jesus is reported as speaking of (i) 'my Father' (seventeen times in Matthew) and (ii) 'your Father' or 'your heavenly Father' when he talks to other people about (their) God. This practice appears to go back to the historical Jesus and supports the conclusion that he claimed at least implicitly a different (unique?) relationship to One he called Father – a relationship which others could not or at least did not share.

To sum up. Even if the Gospels make it difficult to say much about Jesus' inner life, he clearly *experienced* God in a *special* way. It is quite certain that in his proclamation and behaviour during the ministry he *claimed* a *special* relationship to God. It is harder to find knockdown evidence that *he experienced and claimed a unique relationship* to the Father, a unique identity as divine Son of God which others could not share. But certainly there were hints of such a claim in the way Jesus acted with an authority and a compassion which can only be called divine.

(e) THE MISSION. To fill out this basic sketch of Jesus' ministry, we should move on from the self-understanding (implied by his words and attitudes) to those who formed his chosen audience.

Beyond question, Jesus directed his prophetic appeal to his own nation. According to Matthew's account, Jesus told the Canaanite woman: 'I was sent only to the lost sheep of the house of Israel' (15:24). He had a similar instruction for the twelve when he sent them on their trial mission: 'Go nowhere among the Gentiles, and enter no town of the Samaritans, but go rather to the lost sheep of the house of Israel' (Matt 10:5f.). The very call and sending of *twelve* disciples expressed the intention to gather again the twelve tribes (Matt 19:28; Luke 22:30). We catch Jesus' sense of his mission when we (rightly) translate his remark: 'I was sent only to the lost sheep *who are* the house of Israel'. (We can be sure that this saying came from the historical Jesus. It stands in such manifest discontinuity with the early Church's sense of her universalist mission [Acts 11:19f.; 13:1–3] that, far from being invented in the post-Easter situation, the saying was fortunate not to be suppressed.) Whatever the precise meaning of his statement about the rebuilding of the Jerusalem temple (Mark 14:58; 15:29 parr.), it also spoke of an intention to reform and restore the Jewish nation at its centre.

However, if Jesus saw his own people as the primary beneficiary of the final revelation and salvation of God, his vision was universal. Although he directed his preaching to the chosen people, he called humanity as such to decision. He addressed his Jewish audience as human beings, not as Jews and still less as a holy remnant, some special group of the saved within Judaism. He spoke to them in parables, the language of everyday and a language which has proved itself capable of communicating to the whole human race. He demanded a realistic love towards other human beings in need, a love which was willing to cross racial frontiers (Luke 10:25–37). He called for a new brotherhood and sisterhood which denied any sacrosanct value to family or tribal bonds within Israel: 'Whoever does the will of God is my brother, and sister, and mother' (Mark 3:35 parr.). There was a universal ring to this statement, just as we find in the parable of the tax-collector and the Pharisee (Luke 18:9–14). There Jesus asserted that the extent of God's generosity had been hitherto ignored: the divine pardon was offered to all.

Hence Jesus' vision of Israel's future entailed 'many coming from east and west to sit at table with Abraham, Isaac and Jacob in the kingdom of heaven' (Matt 8:11 par.). The restoration of Israel to come through Jesus' ministry would bring salvation to the nations.

(3) *The miracles.*   (a) Did Jesus work miracles as part of his mission in the service of God's rule? Some would dismiss the miracle stories as a secondary accretion, a somewhat unfortunate product of the fervid imagination of the early Christians. Those first believers worshipped Jesus as their risen Lord. What could have been more natural and inevitable than that they should have looked back through the golden haze of Easter and glorified his human life by attributing to him all kinds of wonderful deeds? Was not this, after all, standard practice in those ancient times? Legends of healings and other miracles gathered quickly around the names of great religious leaders.

This part of the record about Jesus' ministry, however, cannot be repudiated as easily as that. To begin with, *in Mark almost half of the treatment given to the public life is concerned with miracles.* Many of these miracle stories are inextricably bound up with other elements in the narrative. In particular, they are remembered as essentialy linked to Jesus' powerful preaching of God's coming kingdom. These deeds of power anticipated the full divine rule and complete salvation that Jesus proclaimed. If the miracle stories are to be removed from Mark's account of Jesus' ministry, a great deal would have to be ripped away with them. To put matters mildly, it would be very difficult to take all the miracle stories out of Mark and still recognize that Gospel as a substantially reliable guide to the history of the ministry. Either we accept Mark with the miracle stories, or we dismiss this book as being an unsound historical source for the activity of Jesus.

Second, here if anywhere, *the criterion of multiple attestation* applies. Besides the actual miracle stories themselves, Mark also records sayings concerning one class of extraordinary deeds, the exorcisms (3:14f.; 3:22ff.; 6:7). Then Matthew and Luke add material from Q which attests that the earthly Jesus was a worker of miracles (Matt 11:5 par.; 12:27f. par.). An interesting point from Q comes from the woes pronounced on certain Galilean towns: 'Woe to you, Chorazin! woe to you, Bethsaida! for if the mighty works done in you had been done in Tyre and Sidon, they would have repented long ago in sack-cloth and ashes' (Matt 11:21 par.). Here Jesus speaks of miracles done in two towns, but while the Gospels report the working of miracles in Bethsaida (Mark 8:22–26; Luke 9:10f.), they have none to report from Chorazin. We have a saying about miracles in Chorazin but no matching story or stories. It appears that this saying went back to the earthly Jesus and that the Gospels and/or their sources did not feel free either to invent stories of miracles worked in Chorazin or to locate in that town unattached miracle stories found in the tradition. Further, Luke includes a warning against Herod which is generally agreed to come from Jesus and which affirms that he worked miracles (13:32). Finally, summary accounts of Jesus' activity include his miracles (for example, Matt 4:23; Acts 2:22f.). In short, the criterion of multiple attestation points to the fact of Jesus' miraculous activity. If we wish to widen the scope of this criterion, we can also include the witness of ancient Jewish sources. They accepted the fact that Jesus worked miracles but explained it all as sorcery.

As regards the view that in the first century legendary miracles were spontaneously attributed to religious heroes, it is instructive to remind ourselves of John the Baptist. The four Gospels have much to say about the forerunner of Jesus. This great prophet had played a pre-eminent role in preparing the people for the ministry of Jesus, and later he was remembered with honour in the emerging Church. The Baptist had been 'there' as a trail-blazer when the Christian movement began. And yet no miracles were ascribed to him – a point which John's Gospel explicitly notes (10:41). The case of the Baptist shows clearly that at least in first-century Palestine it was by no means inevitable that as a way of enhancing their memory, traditions of supposed miracles should gather around the name of John, Jesus or some other religious leader.

To sum up. There exists no convincing evidence for the case that Jesus was remembered first as a preacher, and that only later a miracle-tradition got attached to him. Here it is instructive to recall Bultmann's main historical conclusion about the miracles of Jesus: 'Undoubtedly he healed the sick and cast out demons' (*Jesus and the Word* [ET: New York, 1958], p. 173). In subsequent works Bultmann argued that miracles are offensive and even inconceivable to modern persons.[3] But as such that is another question.

Once we agree to the general reliability of the miracle-tradition, we should also acknowledge that in the course of the tradition and through the work of the evangelists some adjustment, heightening and even multiplying of Jesus' miracles seem to have taken place. Just as the *words* of Jesus were not preserved and transmitted with rigid exactness, so it appears that the tradition of his miraculous *deeds* underwent some change before the Gospels took shape.

Between Mark and Matthew, for instance, we can detect not only some toning-down of the miraculous but also at times a certain enlarging of details. Let me cite two small examples. The 'five thousand men' who are fed in the desert by the multiplication of the loaves and fishes (Mark 6:44) become 'about five thousand men, besides women and children' (Matt 14:21). In Mark 6:45–52 Jesus alone walks on the water, whereas in Matthew 14:22–33 he empowers Peter also to walk across the water. Admittedly the point here is to illuminate the person of Peter rather than to heighten the miraculous. Nevertheless, whatever the motive, the story has in fact become more remarkable.

If such growth in the miracle-traditions took place between the earliest and a later Gospel, we can suppose similar trends to have obtained in the course of the oral tradition between the ministry of Jesus himself and the time Mark wrote his Gospel. First, some miraculous actions correctly attributed to Jesus could have been elaborated in transmission. Second, it is conceivable that some popular legends may have become attached to his name. One instance of this second trend could be the story of the fish with the coin in its mouth (Matt 17:27). Some scholars have interpreted this unusual miracle as a folk story that strikes them as alien to the normal pattern of Jesus' miraculous activity.

Hence we may reasonably concede that the tradition of Jesus' miracles grew and changed at least a little in the thirty-five years or so between his ministry and the composition of the first Gospel. At the same time, it remains an essentially true part of the New Testament report that he was a miracle-worker. To deal with Jesus simply as a preacher and eliminate his miracles altogether undercuts our right to take Mark and the other evangelists as substantially reliable guides. If we decline to accept their testimony that Jesus worked miracles, we can scarcely give any credence to the rest of their reports about him.

(b) Very often the challenge to Jesus' miracles comes in the name of *historical method, scientific knowledge*, or *theological conviction*. Cherished principles in the areas of history, science or theology rule out the very possibility of such *special* interventions of God.

It is claimed that *historians* must suppose human history to be a closed system of causes and effects, in which historians should expect things to follow similar patterns (the principle of analogy) and not even allow for the possibility of religious wonders which could express special divine interventions and concerns. To maintain that human history is such a closed system is to accept a presupposition – prior to any particular historical investigation – and to maintain something which can never as such be proved historically. Further, analogy means some degree of similarity, but not identity. So far from ruling out different, even strikingly different events, the principle of analogy rules them in, inasmuch as it entails both likeness *and difference*. A miracle, in fact, manifests both a likeness to other (ordinary) religious events and a difference (in being a religious 'marvel' which points to God's special intervention). So far from flouting the historical principle of analogy, a miraculous event would maintain it.

Science, in general, has become rather more open to the possibility of miracles, in that it has come to allow for what is unexpected and downright extraordinary. If science seeks at every level to describe and explain the phenomena of our world, it has relinquished something of that former rigidity which dismisssed the miraculous as impossible. Here, however, one point should be added. A miracle differs from an event which appears scientifically unusual, indeterminate or arbitrary. A miracle is not, so to speak, a 'laboratory marvel', but an event which stunningly conveys God's loving mercy and invites the appropriate human response.

Theologically, some exclude miracles in principle because they believe that God operates and is disclosed only through normal, everyday events. This is to rule out any *special* interventions and activities of God, including miraculous events. Logically such a position has implications far beyond the particular issue of miracles. As we shall see in Chapter 6, the denial of special divine interventions leads or should lead to a rejection of that uniquely special divine presence and activity in the person of Jesus.

(c) Let us return to the Gospel record of Jesus' miracles. I suspect that it is the *significance* rather than the *fact* of these miracles which poses a problem for some people. Traditional apologetics simply used the miracle stories as direct proofs of Jesus' divinity. These stories were interpreted as supernatural deeds that broke the laws of causality and thus demonstrated his claims, in particular his status as Son of God. Neither Jesus himself nor the evangelists, however, regarded his miracles as breaking or going beyond natural laws. Talk about fixed laws of nature was simply foreign to the mind-set of first-century Palestine. Neither Jesus nor the Gospels focused on his miracles as extraordinary events which demonstrated in a marvellous fashion his power to make exceptions from the ordinary laws of causality. Not only the evangelists but also Jesus himself shunned such exhibitionism. As Q reports matters, Jesus saw the preaching of the gospel to be the climax of his miraculous deeds: 'The blind receive their sight and the lame walk, lepers are cleansed and the deaf hear, and the dead are raised up, and the poor have good news preached to them' (Matt 11:5 par.). When asked to do so, Jesus refused to legitimate his claims by performing some clear and decisive 'sign from heaven' (Mark 8:11f.). Even though the saying is only found in Luke, what Jesus is reported as saying to the seventy disciples on their return from their trial mission coheres perfectly with that reluctance to exaggerate the importance of the miraculous which is attested elsewhere:

> Behold, I have given you authority to tread upon serpents and scorpions, and over all the power of the enemy; and nothing shall hurt you. Nevertheless do not rejoice in this, that the spirits are subject to you; but rejoice that your names are written in heaven (Luke 10:19–20).

At least something is clear about the way Jesus himself and the evangelists thought his miracles functioned. They were *not* overwhelming arguments which should *force* people to believe that he was Son of God, Messiah or anything else. It remained open to his audience to disqualify these deeds as evidence by attributing them to Satanic influence (Mark 3:22). Those who refused to be touched in the depths of their existence by Jesus' words were not going to be persuaded by his miraculous deeds.

Positively, Jesus seems to have understood his miracles as deeds of power that expressed and proclaimed the way in which anti-God forces were being overcome as the divine power was finally and effectively saving human beings in their whole physical and spiritual reality: 'If it is by the Spirit of God that I cast out demons, then the kingdom of God has come upon you' (Matt 12:28 par.; cf. Mark 3:23–27).

(d) Much more could and should be said about the miracles of Jesus. For instance, what are particular ways in which the four Gospel-writers interpret these stories and seek to apply them to the needs of the communities for which they wrote? What do his miracles say to contemporary readers in the different cultural contexts of the twentieth-century world? Before leaving the topic I would like to add a few reflections on what one might call *the personal style of Jesus as miracle-worker.*

In the middle and late first century Christians were not distinguished from non-Christians, whether Jew or Gentile, by the fact that they believed that miracles could occur. At that time it was widely taken for granted that there were miracles. In Greek literature miraculous healings were held to take place at famous places of pilgrimage like Epidaurus (with its god of healing Asclepius). Miracle stories were attached to such wandering preachers and wise men as Apollonius of Tyana (born c. A.D. 3). Jewish rabbis were sometimes credited with working miracles through their prayers to God. Matthew 12:27 implies that Jewish exorcists drove out demons and did so by the power of God, even though these exorcisms were not signs of the coming divine rule as were the works of Jesus.

Frequently the Hellenistic miracle stories, in particular the healing stories, followed a certain pattern which went something like this. First, the story depicted the severity and long duration of some sickness or suffering. It might be noted that others had unsuccessfully tried to heal the disease in question – which was a way of stressing the greatness of the cure to follow. The miracle-worker then met the sick person, prayed and through mysterious words and/or physical contact conveyed new strength to the patient. Once the healing took place, its success would be demonstrated. Thus formerly lame persons might throw away their crutch and walk. Finally, the episode would conclude with the public expressing their astonishment and praise for the miracle-worker.[4]

Undoubtedly this scheme for describing healings can remind us of details found in various miracles worked by Jesus. But despite a certain similarity in the way of telling the stories, Jesus was remembered as having a radically different 'style'. His miraculous deeds were dramatically unlike those found in the Hellenistic and Jewish sources. To begin with, he did not in the prescribed way call on God but in his own name and with authority healed people and expelled demons. His miraculous deeds are not described as the results of his prayers being heard. Usually the miracle occurred at a straight word of command. Apart from one or two cases where simply spittle was involved (Mark 7:33; 8:22ff.), Jesus never applied anything. Unlike other ancient miracle-workers, Jesus never punished people in a miraculous way, never worked miracles for profit, and refused to work miracles for show. Whereas Asclepius was believed to come to people in dreams and cure them, Jesus healed the sick when they were awake. Most significantly, the miracles of Jesus were closely connected with the faith of those to be healed and/or the faith of their companions. Over and over again Jesus associated his miraculous deeds with his call to a faith which would believe in his power to forgive human sin and save people from the powers which afflicted them. No less than his preaching, his miracles manifested the reign of God and the divine promise to deliver them from the grip of evil.

JESUS' SELF-DESIGNATIONS

This treatment of Jesus' ministry would remain patently incomplete if I failed to raise the questions: How did he speak about himself? Whom did he believe himself to be? We have already noted that when Jesus proclaimed (through his words and deeds) the divine reign, *he was not so much concerned with directly proclaiming himself* and his own identity. If he experienced and claimed a special relationship to the One he called Father, he did not announce himself to the world as the Son. Nevertheless, can we say something about possible ways in which Jesus assessed and designated himself?

He spoke of himself as a 'physician' in his work of calling sinners (Mark 2:17). He obviously thought of himself as a shepherd sent 'to the lost sheep of the house of Israel' (Matt 15:24; cf. Luke 19:10). During his ministry some or perhaps many people interpreted Jesus as a prophet (Mark 6:15; Luke 7:16; John 6:14; etc.). Apparently that was also *part* of the way he thought of himself and his mission (Luke 13:33). But he knew that merely to be called 'one of the prophets' did not adequately account for the secret of his person (Mark 8:27–33).

Did the earthly Jesus in fact claim and/or accept for himself other designations like 'Servant of the Lord', 'Son of man', and 'Messiah'? Here I prefer to speak of 'designation' or 'self-designation' rather than use the more specific term 'title'. Inasmuch as it denotes or implies some clearly defined 'office' which we can readily describe (like Queen of England, Mayor of Rome or President of India), 'title' could mislead us into thinking that in the early first century 'Messiah', 'Son of man' and 'Servant of the Lord' *already* indicated certain clearly recognized roles and offices which Jesus himself (and then others) either did or did not assign to him. At the time of Jesus the use of these designations does not seem to have been as sharply defined as that. It is misleading here to speak of *clear* Jewish concepts and expectations. Moreover, when Jesus (and/or others) associated such designations with himself, their content became focused and defined through his activities, fate and known characteristics. It is at least as true to say that Jesus identified these designations as that they identified him.

(1) *The Servant of the Lord.* The second part of Isaiah contains four poems about the Servant of the Lord: 42:1–4; 49:1–6; 50:4–9; 52:13 – 53:12; Even if these four poems speak often enough of the Servant in an individual way, they appear to be presenting an ideal picture of Israel as such. The people are the chosen Servant of God with a vocation to expiate human sin through their sufferings and bring the divine blessings to others.

In the Acts of the Apostles in several places Luke includes traditional material in which Jesus is represented as the Suffering Servant whom God has vindicated for the salvation of his people. Peter speaks in these terms to the crowd which has gathered in Solomon's portico:

> The God of Abraham and of Isaac and of Jacob, the God of our fathers, glorified his servant Jesus, whom you delivered up and denied in the presence of Pilate . . . God, having raised up his servant, sent him to you first, to bless you in turning every one of you from your wickedness (Acts 3:13–26).

Here and there the Gospels and the letters of St Paul also interpret Jesus as the (Suffering) Servant of the Lord. But did the earthly Jesus interpret himself and his mission in this way? Did he understand and designate himself as the Servant of the Lord?

It is difficult to find convincing direct evidence that Jesus explicitly understood himself as the Servant and applied to himself the songs from Second Isaiah. Some scholars see a reference to a verse of the fourth song (Isa 53:12) in the words 'This is my blood . . . which is to be *poured out for many*' (Mark 14:24). In Mark 10:45 Jesus says: 'The Son of man also came not to be served but to serve, and to give his life as a ransom for many'. In both cases the words may not have gone back to Jesus – at least not in the precise form in which we have them.[5]

Nevertheless, Jesus consistently *behaved* like one who identified himself as the Servant – as one utterly subject to his Father's will and completely available for the service of those who needed mercy and healing. Even if Jesus never literally said that he had not come 'to be served but to serve', he certainly acted like that. Given this pattern of Jesus' behaviour, it would be strange that he never understood and identified himself as the Servant of the Lord. Of course, whatever conclusion we reach about this self-designation, it entails humility. The more vigorous debates have arisen around designations which involve or could involve lofty dignity.

(2) *The Son of man.* It is quite clear that the evangelists and the early Church understood Jesus to be 'Son of man', a term that occurs about seventy times in the Synoptic Gospels and a dozen times in John. But did the earthly Jesus also identify himself in that way? If so, what did he mean by such a self-designation?

(a) In the mother tongue which Jesus spoke, Palestinian Aramaic, *bar nash(a)* (or 'son of man') served as a generic term for 'man' and as a roundabout way of referring to oneself ('I', 'me' or 'this man'). In the Hebrew psalms we find a well-known example of the first usage where 'son of man' parallels 'man':

> What is man that thou art mindful of him,
> and the son of man that thou dost care for him
> (8:4).

In the Greek Gospels 'Son of man' clearly functions at times in the second sense – as a means of referring to the speaker (Jesus himself). Thus Jesus warns a would-be disciple: 'Foxes have holes, and birds of the air have nests; but the Son of man has nowhere to lay his head' (Matt 8:20). In the context 'Son of man' is a circumlocution for Jesus himself: 'I have nowhere to lay my head'. It is the same with the statement 'the Son of man has authority on earth to forgive sins'. It is tantamount to claiming 'I have authority on earth to forgive sins' (Mark 2:10).

In Jewish apocalyptic literature 'son of man' denoted a judge and deliverer who was hidden but who would come at the end to destroy the wicked and establish God's holy people in their final state. The classic passage comes from Daniel, in a passage apparently written about 167 B.C.:

> I saw in the night, and behold, with the clouds of heaven there came one like a son of man, and he came to the Ancient of Days [= God] and was presented before him. And to him [= son of man] was given dominion and glory and kingdom, that all peoples, nations, and languages should serve him; his dominion is an everlasting dominion, which shall not pass away, and his kingdom one that shall not be destroyed (7:13–14).

Where Psalm 8 referred to the destiny of an individual human being, our passage from Daniel 7 presented a human figure who would redeem Israel and all nations – an individual figure with a collective function.

(b) In the Synoptic Gospels Jesus habitually speaks of himself as 'Son of man' and does so in sayings which fall into three groups. First, there is the Son of man on earth forgiving sins (Mark 2:10), deciding authoritatively about the observance of the Sabbath (Mark 2:28), being derided as 'a glutton and a drunkard' (Matt 11:19 par.), united with humble human beings, and having 'nowhere to lay his head' (Matt 8:20 par.). Second, 'the Son of man' turns up in a context of total humiliation and vindication – in the passion predictions when Jesus announces his suffering, death and resurrection (Mark 8:31; 9:31; 10:33–34). Third, Jesus speaks of the Son of man as a glorious figure coming at the end like the mysterious redeemer-judge of Daniel 7: 'You will see the Son of man seated at the right hand of Power, and coming with the clouds of heaven' (Mark 14:62). Thus the use of the term 'Son of man' spans three classes of sayings which, respectively, portray this figure as serving human beings, being rejected by them, and coming in future glory to judge them.

Do any or all of these three classes of Son of man sayings go back to the earthly Jesus? Waves of debates have flooded across this issue. At times scholars with nerves of steel have taken up extreme positions, a few even attempting to prove that none of these sayings came from Jesus himself. But there remain strong and convergent reasons for maintaining that the Jesus of history did use the designation 'Son of man' to speak of himself in these three ways.

(i) *The criterion of multiple attestation* can be appealed to. Class one (those Son of man sayings in which Jesus referred to his activity in his earthly ministry) is attested both by Mark (for example, 2:10, 28) and Q (Matt 8:20; 11:19 parr.). The second class of Son of man sayings (the passion predictions in Mark), however, do not occur in Q, and hence the criterion of multiple attestation does not apply to them. But for the third class (the sayings dealing with the coming Son of man) the criterion can be pressed into service. Such sayings turn up in Mark (8:38; 13:26; 14:62) and Q (Matt 10:32; 24:27, 44 parr.).

(ii) Apart from one or two marginal cases (Acts 7:56; Rev 1:13; 14:14), we do not find *others* addressing or describing Jesus as the Son of man. In the Gospels themselves other people address and speak about Jesus in a variety of ways (as 'prophet', 'the Christ', 'Son of God' and so forth), but *never* as 'Son of man'. Now *if* the early Church had freely created the Son of man sayings, it is puzzling that this designation for Jesus is not found on the lips of others. The puzzle disappears only if we agree that we have here a genuine historical recollection: *only* Jesus used the term, and the evangelists and their sources faithfully recorded that fact.

Here *the criterion of dissimilarity* at least partly comes into play. If there was some Jewish background to Jesus' Son of man sayings, there was no follow-up in the emerging Church. This designation does not appear to have been useful for preaching the good news, particularly to the Gentile world. The term was too flexible or even vague. As we have seen, it ranges from the mysterious heavenly being of Daniel 7 to simply being a circumlocution for 'I'. The fact that the designation was unsuitable for the early Church's life and ministry points to another source for the Son of man sayings, Jesus himself.

(iii) The *future* Son of man sayings sometimes suggest a certain different-iation between him and Jesus. Thus Luke reports Jesus as declaring: 'Every one who acknowledges *me* before men, *the Son of man* also will acknowledge before the angels of God' (12:8). Matthew modifies this Q saying to read: 'Every one who acknowledges *me* before men, *I* also will acknowledge before my Father who is in heaven' (10:32). But apparently Luke has preserved the original form of the saying which may entail a certain unity of *function* between Jesus himself and the Son of man, but at the same time introduces some differentiation between the two figures.

This differentiation makes sense once we recognize that it genuinely recalls a turn of phrase used by Jesus to distinguish his present (preaching) function and his future (judging) function. The distinction made sense in the historical context of his ministry but not later in the post-Easter situation where believers acknowledged the personal unity of the risen Jesus and the glorious Son of man. Matthew's modification reflects precisely that shift.

(iv) There are some unusual features about *the preservation* of the Son of man sayings. The three classes are not blended together. Thus the passion predictions about the Son of man (class two) never go beyond the death and resurrection to include statements about the future coming of the Son of man (class three). Further, the sayings about God's kingdom (and, specifically, the parables) never bring in the Son of man. As some wit put it, 'the kingdom has no Son of man, and the Son of man has no kingdom'.

What are we to make of this curious independence of the three classes of Son of man sayings and separation of the kingdom sayings from the Son of man sayings? It can be explained if we see the Gospel tradition accurately preserving here distinctions which were genuine features of Jesus' actual preaching. If early Christians, however, were the real authors of the Son of man sayings, why did they not also feel free to blend the different classes of such sayings and also combine them with sayings about the kingdom of God? If they happily created the Son of man sayings, why did they stop short in the way they used and combined them?

(c) Nowadays the tide seems in fact to have turned against any who would interpret the Son of man sayings as all being inventions of the early Church rather than sayings coming from Jesus himself. It seems reasonable to hold that, despite some additions and modifications, the three classes of Son of man sayings are substantially derived from Jesus himself. But *what did Jesus intend by designating himself as the Son of man?*

It is striking that according to the Synoptic Gospels Jesus never expressly said 'I am the Son of man'. Apart from Matthew 16:13, he consistently spoke of the Son of man in the third person (see, for example, Mark 8:38) and in some way differentiated between himself and the Son of man (see, for example, Matt 19:28). Although 'Son of man' was an habitual and characteristic self-designation, Jesus used it in such a way as not to bring his own person into prominence. Much more was at stake than mere reserve and modesty. Nor is it enough to think of a proper prudence which counselled both an indirect way of speaking about himself and the choice of a mysterious self-designation that conveys a lofty as well as a lowly meaning. Seemingly Jesus spoke indirectly and deliberately exploited the possibilities and ambiguities of the term 'Son of man' to make statements about himself and his mission, while still maintaining his Father's reign (and not self-witness) at the centre of his public proclamation.

As we shall see in the next chapter, at some point in his ministry Jesus began speaking more directly to the inner group of his disciples about his impending suffering and future vindication. Here I believe scholars like F. J. Moloney and C. F. D. Moule are correct in holding that Jesus expressed his vocation against the background of Daniel 7. For a people enduring severe trials, that representative figure 'one like a son of man' is associated with their sufferings and collective vindication. In similar terms Jesus presented himself as the Son of man who represented the new Israel in obediently suffering and trusting that he would be vindicated beyond death and thus bring God's judgement and kingdom. As the Son of man, Jesus invited others to join him in this destiny.

(3) *Messiah.* In English and other languages 'Messiah' means the liberator of some oppressed country or, more specifically, the promised deliverer of the Jewish people. In these two senses in which we habitually use the word – and, particularly, in the second case – the notions of suffering, promise and deliverance bulk large. A suffering people through a divine promise will be blessed with the presence of a deliverer.

Originally, however, the term 'Messiah' (in Greek 'Christ') began as a Hebrew adjective *mashiach* ('anointed'), used especially of the anointed king (1 Sam 24:6) and the anointed priest (Lev 4:3). In both cases the term indicated a person invested by God with special functions and powers. Nathan's promise to David (2 Sam 7:12ff.) and other influences (see, for example, Isa 9:5–7; Ezek 34:23f.; 37:24f.; Ps 89:35f.) meant that eventually 'the Messiah' came to indicate 'the promised king from the line of David who would deliver his people'. However, alongside this line of usage which gave prominence to *kingly* status, there also persisted the theme of an agent of salvation who was *not kingly* but was all the same *anointed* by God. A classic example of this theme occurs in the second part of Isaiah:

> The Spirit of the Lord God is upon me, because the Lord has *anointed* me to bring good tidings to the afflicted; he has sent me to bind up the brokenhearted, to proclaim liberty to the captives, and the opening of the prison to those who are bound (61:1).

Whether understood as a king from the house of David or simply as an agent empowered by God, the 'Anointed One' would be a deliverer coming to the people because of divine promises.

Clearly early Christians thought of Jesus not only as (a) the anointed agent of salvation, but also as (b) the kingly Messiah. To begin with, they believed him to be such as presently reigning in heaven (Acts 2:36; 5:31) and to come in power and glory (Acts 3:20f.). But they also thought him to have already been invested with such functions during his ministry (Luke 4:17ff.; Mark 8:29; etc.) and even in his infancy (Luke 1:32f.; 2:11; Matt 1:23; 2:6). As a comprehensive designation for Jesus and his powers, 'Messiah' or (from the Greek *Christos*) 'Christ' was so frequent that by the time of Paul's first letter it had become a (second) proper name (1 Thess 1:1) – as is usually the case when people speak today of 'Jesus Christ'.

But to go back to the earthly Jesus. Did he think of himself in messianic terms, designate himself as 'the Christ' or accept such a designation from others? At the very least he understood himself as a unique agent invested with the mission of bringing God's final rule. What was pointed out earlier in the chapter about Jesus' authoritative and compassionate proclamation of the divine reign necessarily implies that his self-identification went as far as sense (a) above. But on his mission of deliverance to his people did he *also* understand himself to be the promised *kingly* deliverer *from the house of David*? Notoriously the evidence at this point is somewhat elusive. It is speculation to maintain that his baptism revealed to Jesus his status as royal Messiah (Mark 1:9–11). Then if we agree that Peter's identification of Jesus in Mark 8:29 ('You are the Christ') reaches back to an historical episode at Caesarea Philippi, it is noteworthy that Jesus made no direct answer, ordered silence on the point, and went on to speak of the suffering destiny of the Son of man (Mark 8:30f.). Again if we do accept John the Baptist's question from prison ('Are you he who is to come?') as being concerned with Jesus' identity as the promised kingly Messiah, at best Jesus offered only an indirect response to John's disciples: 'Go and tell John what you hear and see' (Matt 11:2ff.). Apparently Jesus discussed the Davidic descent of the Messiah (Mark 12:35–37), but that passage does not report Jesus as openly identifying his own role with that of the royal Messiah. Neither here nor elsewhere is there evidence that Jesus took up the notion of messiahship to purify and reinterpret it. Jesus' identification of himself as the awaited Christ is clear enough in John 4:25f. But does that interchange with the Samaritan woman authentically derive from the earthly ministry of Jesus or is it part of a narrative constructed by the fourth evangelist and/or his sources? In Matthew 23:10 Jesus implicitly identifies himself as Messiah, but this does not appear to be an authentic saying coming from the earthly Jesus. The situation envisaged seems to be that of the post-Easter Church.

Perhaps on the occasion of his entry into Jerusalem Jesus, recognizing in himself the goal of the messianic prophecies, deliberately set out to fulfil those prophecies (Mark 11:1ff.). Nevertheless, at his trial in his answer to the High Priest's question, 'Are you the Christ, the Son of God?', Jesus may have given only the somewhat non-committal response indicated by Matthew 26:64: '*You* have said so', 'the words are yours', 'I do not say so'. But conceivably the meaning could be: 'It is as you say'. According to Luke's account, Jesus was reserved and did not commit himself. Mark reports him as having replied to the question ('Are you the Christ, the Son of the Blessed?') quite openly: 'I am' (14:61f.). But then according to all three accounts Jesus dropped the term 'Messiah' or 'Christ' and went on at once to speak of the Son of man coming with the clouds of heaven. As at Caesarea Philippi the notions of Messiah and Son of man were juxtaposed, albeit differently. At Caesarea Philippi the messianic confession was linked to the *suffering* Son of man, but in the reports of the trial the Messiah was associated with the glorious Son of man to come in judgement at the end.

Further, in trying to reach the historical facts we should recognize a general difficulty at this point. Did the early Christians have any accurate information about the events which followed Jesus' arrest? How did they know precisely what transpired, for example, in the hearings before the High Priest and Pilate?

Nevertheless, we are not simply pulling at broken strings. Some conclusions can be plausibly drawn. At the trial before the High Priest, although Jesus did not simply dissociate himself from 'the Messiah', the designation was not one positively chosen by Jesus himself. Yet the inscription attached to the cross read 'The King of the Jews' (Mark 15:26 parr.). It seems very unlikely that Jesus would have been put to death on the charge of being a messianic pretender, if he had in no sense made that claim. Second, it also appears unlikely that Jesus would have been universally acclaimed as Messiah in the emerging Church if early Christians remembered that during his lifetime he had simply refused that self-designation. Let me make the same point in another way. Unless Jesus had at least implicitly associated himself with the figure of the Messiah, it would be very strange that the appearances of the risen Jesus at once brought the disciples to the conclusion: 'He really is God's promised Messiah'.

Finally, can we describe in even a little detail how Jesus seems to have related to the messianic question during his ministry? Clearly his activity raised for his disciples and others the persistent question: 'Who is he?' Although Jesus did not relentlessly conceal from the public his messianic identity, he did not directly proclaim his messiahship. Of course, by announcing God's final and imminent *kingdom*, he could hardly have been unaware of the fact that this proclamation would also encourage people to think of an anointed kingly agent who would bring about this reign of God. Furthermore, if I am correct in maintaining that Jesus consciously linked himself with the 'one like a son of man' in Daniel 7, he was relating himself to a figure who *delivers* his people and receives *kingly dominion*. In other words, an appeal to Daniel 7 meant that Jesus made a messianic use of the self-designation 'Son of man'.

All in all, apparently Jesus took up a certain 'yes/but' attitude towards his messianic identity. Perhaps the sequence in Mark 8:29ff. reaches back to the history of the earthly Jesus. He qualified Peter's messianic confession by announcing the Son of man's suffering destiny, thus reinterpreting the Messiah as a suffering figure. He could well have been (or become) aware that it was only through his suffering, death and vindication that he would effectively function as a messianic deliverer.

EVALUATING JESUS' HISTORY

Many other items could have found a place in this chapter: for instance, Jesus' *Jewishness*. Here I am thinking not so much of levels at which he fulfilled Old Testament expectations but much more of his thoroughly Jewish way of life: from his circumcision, through his daily practices of prayer, worship in the Temple, participation in synagogue services, and all the other items right up to his final appearance in Jerusalem for the festival of the Passover and Unleavened Bread. As Joachim Jeremias, W. D. Davies and other scholars have shown, Jesus was deeply and faithfully Jewish in his behaviour, language and piety.

The name of Jeremias recalls a feature of the ministry which stunningly illustrates Jesus' sense of authority. In his *New Testament Theology* Jeremias lists 118 sayings under the heading of 'antithetic parallelism'. Through these sayings Jesus authoritatively declared that God's will radically disrupts the world's outlook. The divine order of things startlingly reverses the human order of things: 'Whoever seeks to gain his life will lose it, but whoever loses his life will preserve it' (Luke 17:33 parr.). These antithetic parallelisms, which disclose that extraordinary authority with which Jesus stated the divine view of things, fill out the picture of his preaching presented earlier in this chapter.

Here I want to complete this treatment of the ministry by returning to a theme discussed at the beginning of this chapter and introducing a further theme. Then in Chapter 6 I plan to include three issues connected with the life and ministry of Jesus: the virginal conception, the scope of his knowledge, and the nature of his faith.

(1) *Christian faith and Jesus' history.* Some scholars like Oscar Cullmann and Joachim Jeremias have held or at least implied that Christian beliefs about Jesus' person and mission simply stand or fall with the way Jesus identified himself and his work.

The other extreme would be to maintain doctrines about Christ *irrespective* of whether the earthly Jesus considered himself Messiah, intended his death to have saving effects and so forth. In such a view Jesus *was* in fact Son of God and Saviour, even if he was never aware of being such. Where Cullmann and Jeremias would maximalize the significance of Jesus' earthly life for Christian faith and theology, this other extreme would minimalize it. But as so often is the case the truth is to be found in a mediating position.

Against the maximalizers we should insist that Christian doctrine cannot and does not *totally* rest on what we can establish to have been taught by the earthly Jesus. Other sources contribute to a valid interpretation of his person and work: the divine revelation already communicated in the Old Testament period, Jesus' death and resurrection, all that the Holy Spirit led the first Christians to see implied in that death and resurrection, and the whole ongoing life of the Church guided and illuminated by that same Spirit. In short, what came *before* and *after* the ministry of Jesus also essentially fills out a full understanding of his person and mission. Thus even if John sits more lightly to the historical facts of the ministry than the Synoptics, nevertheless, the experiences from decades of Christian living validly guarantee the way that Gospel evaluates and presents the ultimate truth about Jesus. Against the minimalizers we should recall that the risen Christ of the post-Easter Church is identical with the earthly Jesus. There are not two persons: the Jesus of the then and the Christ of the now. There is only one Jesus Christ whose total past is very much part of his present. Even more than is the case with others we cannot really know him now, unless we appreciate and understand something of his past. Thus the story of the ministry belongs essentially to the Christ we experience and believe in. If we neglect the concrete history of Jesus, we may finish up over-spiritualizing Christianity and turning it into a religion of ideas. Jesus Christ is more than the Word; he is the Word made flesh (John 1:14). Hence his 'fleshly' history enters essentially into Christian faith and theology. A serious disconcern for the concrete details of Jesus' history undercuts any sincere proclamation of him as true God *and true man*.

To sum up. The Gospel record of Jesus' ministry is an important source for Christian faith and theology. His earthly claims and activities laid some basis for what followed. The crucifixion, resurrection, gift of the Holy Spirit and experience of the early Church were to reveal the full truth about his person and mission. But during his brief ministry something had already been disclosed about his personal status as Son of God and Saviour. We can rightly talk about an implicit Christology and Soteriology recorded by the Synoptic Gospels unfolding into the explicit Christology and Soteriology of the post-Easter Church. This was *not* a movement from a low to a high Christology and Soteriology, as if Jesus made only minimal and modest claims which were later maximized. Rather the shift was from something indirectly implied to something directly proclaimed.

(2) *Jesus' significance for us.* Christian (and also non-Christian) experience shows that the story of Jesus' life speaks to different people and cultures in almost endlessly different ways. Let me quickly point out a few examples.

Some people notice the extraordinary blend of strong and tender characteristics in his teaching and behaviour. If he courageously and angrily drove out those who bought and sold in the Temple (Mark 11:5ff.), he also took little children in his arms (Mark 10:13–16) and told his disciples: 'Do not resist one who is evil. But if anyone strikes you on the right cheek, turn to him the other also' (Matt 5:39).

The Declaration on Religious Freedom (*Dignitatis Humanae*) from the Second Vatican Council noted how Jesus never used his freedom to limit, let alone destroy, the freedom of others but only to enhance it (n. 11). His authority revealed no dominance or lurking desire to promote his self-interest at the expense of others. The freedom which he respected and encouraged in others was in function, not of property and power, but of genuinely human responsibility before God.

As I briefly recalled above, Jesus was deeply conditioned by the religious culture of the Jewish people. Yet he also challenged and broke at times with that culture. For instance, women travelled in the company of Jesus and his male disciples (Luke 8:1–3) – something that no religious teacher of his day would have risked or tolerated.

The word 'culture' reminds me of some features of the Gospel story which bear a special significance for certain societies today. Neither the genealogy provided by Matthew 1:1–17 nor the one provided by Luke 3:23–38 may provide us with accurate information about Jesus' family tree, but they do underline an important fact about his origins. He did not arrive, as it were, from heaven, but was born from the tribe of David and enjoyed a *kinship* that reached back to the beginnings of the Jewish race. This is highly significant for cultures in which kinship forms an essential part of their vision of humanity: '*Cognatus ergo sum homo*' (I have kin and therefore I am a human being). The fact that Jesus was *initiated* into his people through circumcision and later acted as a master of initiation in training his disciples is also important for some societies in expressing Jesus' authentic humanity.

In a thousand ways the character and story of Jesus have proved themselves compellingly attractive and distinctively human. Over and over again the process of discovering things from his history has involved people in *self-discoveries in their own history*. Let me develop this point.

Knowing and appreciating the concrete humanity of Jesus' life inevitably brings a deeper self-knowledge and a new appreciation of personal ways of being human in our own specific environments. Faith in Jesus' humanity carries with it faith in our own humanity.

Here we run up against the basic intention of the Gospel-writers. They tell stories about Jesus' human life because they want to change their readers through the telling of those stories. In their passion narratives they describe Jesus' suffering, which is *the* story of human suffering, and appeal to their readers to behave similarly under present or impending persecutions.

Finally, in their differing but complementary pictures of Jesus, the four evangelists invite us to carry forward a process which in fact began during his ministry. Let me explain what I have in mind. A totally uninterpreted grasp of anyone or anything is impossible. Hence from their earliest contacts with Jesus the first disciples were taking him in through their own ears and eyes. Later the evangelists did the same. While respecting the tradition about Jesus, they could only interpret and express him in their own individual ways. In our turn we must see Jesus with *our* own eyes and hear him with *our* own ears, if we are to absorb him at all. No one, not even John, has ever adequately grasped the mystery of Jesus' life. But the record of that mystery constantly challenges our lives and calls forth our devotion. No less than earlier Christians we bear the responsibility for remembering, interpreting and expressing in our societies something of what the mystery of Jesus' history can mean.

NOTES

1 R. Bultmann 'The Primitive Christian Kerygma and the Historical Jesus', *HJKC*, p.17.
2 Here I am referring to the unusual way Jesus used 'Amen' at the *beginning* of various affirmations. The Jewish practice had been to add 'Amen' at the *end* of a phrase or sentence, as was to happen with the congregation's response in Christian liturgies. As regards 'Abba', we find it used in Rom 8:15 and Gal 4:6, but that is all.
3 'It is impossible to use electric light and the wireless and to avail ourselves of modern medical and surgical discoveries, and at the same time to believe in the New Testament world of spirits and miracles' (R. Bultmann, 'New Testament and Mythology', *Kerygma and Myth*, ed. H. W. Bartsch [ET: New York, 1961], p. 5).
4 R. Bultmann, *History of the Synoptic Tradition* (ET: Oxford, 1963), pp. 209–244, esp. pp. 220ff. For further material on Jewish and pagan miracle stories see D. R. Cartlidge and D. L. Dungan, *Documents for the Study of the Gospels* (Philadelphia, 1980), pp. 151–165.
5 Mark 10:45a ('The Son of man also came not to be served but to serve') most likely does come from Jesus himself. As an authentic saying it receives support from Luke 22:27 ('I am among you as one who serves') and from the washing of the disciples' feet in John 13:4–17). Mark 10:45b ('and to give his life as a ransom for many') looks like a community translation, a theological counterpart to Jesus' saying. See 1 Tim 2:5f., where we find a less Semitic and more Greek equivalent of Mark 10:45b.

QUESTIONS FOR DISCUSSION

(1) What features of Jesus' character appeal most to you?

(2) In what ways do you think our interpretations of Jesus are influenced by contemporary culture, especially by our social, economic and political systems?

(3) How significant are Jesus' miracles in your environment?

(4) Make out a list of the designations and titles given to Jesus in the Gospels and the rest of the New Testament. Which ones are the most significant and important to you?

(5) What does the story of Jesus' ministry have to say to the life of the institutional Church?

(6) How can Jesus' solidarity with sinners, the poor and socially marginalized persons be imitated in your environment?

(7) What questions does the example of Jesus raise *both* about the social and political structures of our world *and* about our own commitment to effect change and improvement?

(8) What do the Synoptic Gospels indicate about the role of the Holy Spirit in Jesus' ministry?

ADDITIONAL READING

Besides the works already indicated in the text and notes, the following works could be consulted:

(1) *On the Ministry of Jesus*:
G. Bornkamm, 'Jesus Christ', *EncBrit* 10, pp. 145–155.
G. Bornkamm, *Jesus of Nazareth* (ET: London, 1973). This is a classic study by a leading post-Bultmannian.
H. Conzelmann, *Jesus* (ET: Philadelphia, 1973). Another (shorter) work by a post-Bultmannian, which also indicates the significance of the historical Jesus for Christian faith.
C. H. Dodd, *The Founder of Christianity* (London and New York, 1971). A simple but profound account of Jesus' life.
J. D. G. Dunn, *Jesus and the Spirit* (London and Philadelphia, 1975), pp. 11–92. Dunn uses the theme of experience and presents accurately the ministry of Jesus.
W. R. Farmer, 'Teaching of Jesus', *IDB* supplementary vol., pp. 863–868.
F. C. Grant, 'Jesus Christ', *IDB* 2, pp. 869–896.
W. Kasper, *Jesus the Christ* (ET: London and New York, 1976), pp. 65–112.
H. Küng, *OBC*, pp. 145–318.
X. Léon-Dufour, 'Jesus Christ', *DBT*, pp. 265–272.
J. P. Mackey, *Jesus the Man and the Myth* (London, 1979), pp. 121–172.
H. K. McArthur, *In Search of the Historical Jesus* (London and New York, 1970). A superb survey of scholarly approaches to the history of Jesus.
W. Pannenberg, *JGM*, pp. 53–66.
E. Schillebeeckx, *Jesus*, pp. 41–102, 105–271.
J. Sobrino, *Christology*, pp. 41–78.

(2) *On form and redaction criticism*:
L. Alonso Schökel, 'Form Criticism, Biblical', *NCE* 5, pp. 1017–1023.
K. Grobel, 'Form Criticism', *IDB* 2, pp. 320f.
E. V. McKnight, *What Is Form Criticism?* (Philadelphia, 1969).
N. Perrin, *What Is Redaction Criticism?* (Philadelphia, 1969).
R. Pesch and S. Lyonnet, 'Form Criticism', *SM* 2, pp. 337–344 (= *EncTh*, pp. 525–533).

(3) *On miracles*:
S. V. McCasland, 'Miracle', *IDB* 3, pp. 392–402.
J. B. Metz and L. Monden, 'Miracle', *SM* 4, pp. 44–49 (= *EncTh*, pp. 962–967).
W. Mundle and others, 'Miracle', *DNTT* 2, pp. 620–635.
L. Sabourin, *The Divine Miracles Discussed and Defended* (Rome, 1977).
C. Sant and T. G. Pater, 'Miracles', *NCE* 9, pp. 886–894.
P. Ternant, 'Miracle', *DBT*, pp. 360–365.
R. J. Zwi Werblowsky, 'Miracle', *EncBrit* 12, pp. 269–274.

(4) *On the Servant of the Lord*:
C. Augrain and M.-F. Lacan, 'Servant of God', *DBT*, pp. 531–533.
M. A. Gervais, 'Servant of the Lord Oracles', *NCE* 13, pp. 126–130.
O. Michel and H. Marshall, 'Servant of God', *DNTT* 3, pp. 607–613.
C. R. North, 'Servant of the Lord', *IDB* 4, pp. 292–294.

H. Wansbrough, 'Jesus of Galilee: The Servant of the Lord', *Clergy Review* 51 (1976), pp. 136–142.

(5) *On the Son of man*:

J. Bowker, 'The Son of Man', *Journal of Theological Studies* 28 (1977), pp. 19–48.

C. Colpe, '*Ho Huios tou Anthrōpou*', *TDNT* 8, pp. 400–477.

J. Delorme, 'Son of Man', *DBT*, pp. 563–565.

J. D. G. Dunn, *Christology in the Making* (London, 1980), pp. 65–97.

J. Jensen, 'Son of Man', *NCE* 13, pp. 431–433.

S. E. Johnson, 'Son of Man', *IDB* 4, pp. 413–420.

O. Michel and H. Marshall, 'Son of man', *DNTT* 3, pp. 613–634.

N. Perrin, 'Son of Man', *IDB* supplementary vol., pp. 833–836.

B. Vawter, *This Man Jesus* (New York: Image Book ed., 1975), pp. 117–134.

(6) *On the Messiah*:

P. E. Bonnard and P. Grelot, 'Messiah', *DBT*, pp. 354–357.

M. J. Cantley, 'Messiah', *NCE* 9, pp. 714–721.

E. Jenni, 'Messiah, Jewish', *IDB* 3, pp. 360–365.

S. E. Johnson, 'Christ', *IDB* 1, pp. 563–572.

K. H. Rengstorf, 'Christ', *DNTT* 2, pp. 334–343.

E. Rivkin, 'Messiah, Jewish', *IDB* supplementary vol., pp. 588–591.

B. Vawter, *This Man Jesus*, pp. 91–115.

Note: C. F. D. Moule's *The Origin of Christology* (Cambridge, 1977) contains material on 'The Son of Man', 'Christ' and other designations of Jesus (pp. 11–46). D. M. Stanley and R. E. Brown, 'Aspects of New Testament Thought', *JBC* 2, pp. 768–799, provide relevant sub-articles on 'Titles of Christ', 'The Kingdom of God', 'The Gospel Miracles', etc. There are various articles in *ODCC*: 'Form Criticism', 'Jesus Christ', 'Messiah', 'Miracle' and 'Son of Man'. See also J. M. McDermott, 'Jesus and the Son of God Title', *Gregorianum* 62 (1981), pp. 277–318.

3
The death of Jesus

While we look for him among priests, he is among sinners. While we look for him among the free, he is a prisoner. While we look for him in glory, he is bleeding on the cross.

CARLOS ALBERTO LIBANIO CHRISTO

The cross was not only a stumbling block to the Jews and foolishness to the Gentiles. It is a permanent mystery for Christians.

JÜRGEN MOLTMANN

'Jesus uttered a loud cry, and breathed his last' (Mark 15:37). With these words the earliest Gospel gives us a relatively bare statement of Jesus' death. Literally it was a death by a criminal's execution at the hands of an occupying army. According to the same Gospel, however, this appallingly painful and utterly disgraceful death manifested Jesus' own true identity as Son of God (15:39) and effected salvation for others (10:45; 14:24).

The crucifixion brought Jesus' life and ministry to a brutal finish. He who had proclaimed God's reign with divine authority and compassion now became silent and inactive in death. After gaining a certain popularity and gathering some followers, Jesus was finally to be found not with society's winners but crucified between two of society's failures.

Why and how did the crucifixion happen? What forces and intentions converged to produce this death? *Did Jesus anticipate his violent death and evaluate it in advance?* Did he, for instance, intend his crucifixion to atone representatively for the sins of human beings and bring in a new covenant with God? Then did he expect that his death would be quickly followed by a divine vindication?

In the previous chapter I recalled the way in which a certain knowledge of the earthly Jesus essentially enters into Christian faith and theology. The historical record of what he proclaimed, did, intended and suffered provides some legitimizing basis for the subsequent Christian proclamation of Jesus as Son of God and Saviour of the world. Apropos, then, of his death it is clearly relevant in principle to investigate what can be glimpsed of Jesus' intentions as the opposition closed in. Those intentions suggest some of the grounds for holding that the crucifixion was in fact redemptive and could be known to be such.

But before examining Jesus' own concept of his death, I want to look first at the hostile forces which interacted to bring about the crucifixion.

THE OPPOSITION

(1) *The opponents.* It is clear that by the time of Jesus' arrest no major religious group of his society was willing to intervene and save him. On the contrary, enough powerful leaders were ready to see him executed.

Jesus' inner group of followers may have included one ex-Zealot (Luke 6:15). But Jesus did not preach armed revolt and a war of national liberation. His response to the issue of paying taxes ('Render to Caesar the things that are Caesar's') conflicted with the Zealots' uncompromising refusal to accept Roman taxation.[1]

The Pharisees led a more popular movement to transform Israel by strictly observing an elaborate range of traditional and written laws. Clearly the relations between Jesus and the Pharisees were by no means uniformly bad. For instance, Luke reports a number of occasions on which Jesus was entertained as a guest by leading Pharisees (7:36ff.; 11:37; 14:1; etc.). Nevertheless, what Jesus said about handwashing (Mark 7:3, 5), tithing (Luke 18:12; Matt 23:23 par.) and a casuistry that perverted the divine will (Mark 7:8ff.) provoked hostility among the Pharisees. His association with sinners and unclean persons (Mark 2:16) also contributed to the tension. He was seen to tamper with the proper prohibition of work on the Sabbath (Mark 3:1–5), and to challenge rules for interpreting the Sabbath obligations was to touch something which lay at the heart of national identity and religion. Although Jesus' religious zeal led him to drive out those who defiled the Temple, he attached no absolutely sacred value to the place. The Temple and its cult were soon to be replaced by something better (Mark 14:57f.; cf. Acts 6:13f.). It is admittedly difficult to establish just what the original point. was in Jesus' Temple-saying. But at least it entailed the claim that his mission to Israel was to bring a new relationship between God and the people which would relativize the central place of their present relationship, the Temple of Jerusalem. These and other features in Jesus' public message and activity roused the misgivings and antagonisms of pious and learned Pharisees.

In the event the deadly opposition came as such from the Sanhedrin, the highest court of justice and supreme council in Jerusalem. Its seventy-one members formed three groups: the chief priests (including the current high priest and retired high priests), the elders (laymen drawn from the leading families of the capital), and the scribes or scholars (who were either Pharisees or Sadducees). The members of the Sadducean party (who denied not only the traditional oral law but also the resurrection of the dead) were particularly strong among the priestly and lay aristocracy. At the time of Jesus the Sadducees held the balance of power in the Sanhedrin.

Mark never wavers in holding 'the elders and the chief priests and the scribes' (8:31) – that is to say, the members of the Sanhedrin – responsible for initiating the passion of Jesus. At an early stage that Gospel notes how some Pharisees and followers of Herod Antipas conspired to kill Jesus (3:6). But this murderous plot came to nothing. Some of them were 'sent' (by whom?) to trap Jesus over the issue of Roman taxation (12:13–17), but as such, neither Pharisees nor Herodians turn up at the end among those who arrest, try and condemn him.

The Jewish opponents who immediately contributed to Jesus' death were the clergy and lay aristocracy of Jerusalem, Sadducees who identified with the interests of the capital and the Temple worship. They mediated between the people and the Roman forces of occupation. The fact that one of them, Caiaphas, managed to retain his office right through Pontius Pilate's years as governor of Judaea (A.D. 26–36) testified to the high priest's political sense. The hostility of Caiaphas and other Sadducees to Jesus was plausible. In general there was much in Jesus' activity to provoke them: his initiatives towards sinners, reinterpretation of the Sabbath obligations, claims to unique religious authority, and promise of salvation to the Gentiles. Then he not only staged a demonstration when he entered Jerusalem (Mark 11:1ff.), but also 'cleansed' the Temple – a symbolic action which involved much more than a righteous anger against those who profaned the sacred precincts by their business activities. Jesus came as master and judge to confront the nation and call it to a radical renewal. All of this endangered the public order in the capital, and threatened to disrupt working arrangements with the occupying army.

In brief, the Sadducees had good religious and political reasons for a deep antagonism towards Jesus. As I noted in the last chapter, if John's Gospel is correct in reporting that during his ministry Jesus made repeated visits to the capital, that longer exposure to the Jerusalem public would account more readily for the Sadducean hostility.

Historically the Gospel record supports at least this minimal reconstruction. For reasons that are unclear, Judas turned informer and led a party of Temple police to arrest Jesus. After some kind of hasty hearing before members of the Sanhedrin, Jesus was condemned as a despiser of the law and a blasphemous messianic pretender, and then handed over to the Roman authorities. Pilate found Jesus to be a sufficient threat to the public order to have him executed by crucifixion with the charge of being a messianic pretender attached to the cross.

(2) *The significance of the opponents.* It might seem odd to include in a Christology some treatment of the Sadducees, Pilate and other human agents connected with the passion and death of Jesus. But they belong in this book, inasmuch as they formed an essential part of what Jesus faced and experienced. If his history enters into any adequate Christology, that history was not lived in a vacuum. Other human beings must be recalled and reflected on. What theological meaning can we uncover in the roles played by Caiaphas, Pilate, Judas and the rest?

(a) It is significant that after Jesus was arrested some legal proceedings intervened before he was executed. Unlike John the Baptist, Jesus did not simply experience the sequence: arrest, imprisonment, execution. Whatever precisely happened in the hearings before the Sanhedrin and Pilate, these human agents injected an extra element of deliberateness into the story by putting Jesus on trial. Both sides could confront one another to challenge, reply and offer their final words of interpretation before Jesus was taken off to Golgotha. Both sides could claim the right to say and do what they did. God must decide where the truth and falsity lay in these conflicting statements.

(b) In dealing with Jesus' trial(s), it is quite unsatisfactory to list and discuss the various charges against him, as if they were *either* political (for instance, crimes against the public order or attacks on the taxation system) *or* religious in character (for instance, false claims to unique divine authority or offences against the Mosaic law), but no single charge could be both political and religious. In his *The Execution of Jesus* (New York, 1970) William R. Wilson sets up such an alternative from the start: 'Was he [Jesus] convicted of violating Jewish religious laws or Roman civil laws or both?' (p. 2). The presupposition comes through clearly. Religion and politics are distinct. Secular indictments will split off neatly from accusations of religious aberrations. Roman charges will be merely civil and Jewish will be religious. Wilson correctly notes that he does not stand alone in making such a sharp distinction: 'A great many scholars have called attention to the fact that the Roman trial is political, not religious, in character and that Jesus died as a political criminal' (p. 200).

However, not only today but even more in the ancient world such a division between secular politics and religious realities will not work. Given the sacred role of the emperor, Roman trials could never be 'merely political'. State religion was a potent force then and continues to be such today, albeit under different guises. An execution to maintain national security and further the public good is never a purely secular affair. Here I would still stand by everything I wrote on this topic in *The Theology of Secularity* (Cork, 1974). There was a religious dimension to the hearing before Pilate no less than there were political aspects to Jesus' trial by the Sanhedrin (as we saw above).

(c) Finally, those who joined forces to kill Jesus acted as *representative sinners*. This point calls for some elaboration.

At least some writers who produce studies on the passion of Jesus come perilously close to explaining away or even exonerating Pilate, the members of the Sanhedrin and even Judas. They speak of the Temple officials being afraid of Jesus' impact in the capital, where they were intent on preserving some residue of national rule and maintaining at least a relative peace. In a situation of political turmoil Pilate made an error in taking Jesus to be a dangerous messianic pretender. The desire to further some interests wrongly led Judas to co-operate in the arrest which then, to his horror, was rapidly followed by Jesus' conviction and execution. In these and similar terms one can come up with 'justifications' for Jesus' trial and condemnation. But I find a deeply disturbing parallel between such explanations and the arguments used by countless men of power and privilege to justify their moral outrages. Throughout human history a certain moral indifference can impel people to misuse their power, protect their national interests and seek their own goals, even when it involves co-operating in murder. At the end Jesus was extremely vulnerable, as have been the victims of countless other atrocities. Pilate and the rest hardly had to ignore any traditional safeguards or ordinary defences before killing him.

If we refuse to rationalize away what Judas, Caiaphas and Pilate did, what is our relationship with those who actively took the life of Jesus? Many sermons, hymns and prayers have described these men as representatives of the human race. A Roman governor, a Jewish priest and a disciple of Jesus stood in for us and did the deed. Thus the Good Friday liturgy addresses its reproaches to contemporary congregations, evokes their common experience of guilt, and associates them with the historical persons who two thousand years ago literally put Jesus to death. We share the responsibility with our representatives from the first century. The liturgy presents the crucifixion as a public enactment of destruction, which involves all social groups and every individual. Yet what sense does it make to allege some collective guilt, and maintain that *we all* somehow had a hand in the crucifixion?

The disturbing reproaches of the Good Friday liturgy rightly imply that we are all spiritually interconnected with Pilate, Caiaphas and Judas. These men played out a psychodrama, in which we can recognize our archetypal sins of self-concern, greed and misuse of power. We have no inbuilt guarantee that we could not be as ruthless, treacherous and uncaring. Given their chance, even our laziness and cowardice could produce as much evil as the greedy force and cunning of others. Of course, each of us has no conscience to examine but his or her own. But do I recognize in myself degrading flaws that – given the required circumstances – could even make me join forces with those who directly killed Jesus?

We share in the irrational evil of those who killed Jesus. If the *good effects* of Calvary spread to all generations, the *moral malice* that struck Jesus down wore a common face. In his death, as we will see, Jesus acted for the good of all human beings. The human agents responsible for his death also acted larger than life. Their Roman and Jewish identities were no more than a thin veil through which our mysterious passion for evil was plainly visible. They represented us *in* our moral indifference, as much as Jesus represented us *for* our ultimate good. We share in the *Sin* of Pilate, Caiaphas and Judas, even though it may flare up into a variety of personal *sins*. Only one Roman soldier drove a spear into Jesus' corpse, but the words John quotes from Zechariah aim at everyone: 'They shall look on him whom they have pierced' (19:37). Only those Romans and Jews directly involved bore the guilt for the crucifixion. Yet universal solidarity in the radical disorder of sin allows us to speak of a collective guilt shared by all. The crucifixion has all the appearance of an event for which particular persons took responsibility, but which at the same time was outside their control. It was under the power of that primal lust for evil which lays its hand on everyone.

JESUS AND HIS OWN DEATH

In Mark's account Judas leads a paramilitary force to arrest Jesus, who surrenders himself with the explanation 'let the scriptures be fulfilled' (14:43–50). The passage expresses clearly enough the sense that the plan of God and the plans of certain human beings (members of the Sanhedrin acting through their agents) converge to initiate the passion. But what of the earthly Jesus himself? What were his own intentions as death loomed up? It is not that these intentions (and what we can establish about them) provide the *only* criterion for acknowledging that Jesus died to save sinful human beings. There could have been much more meaning in his death than he fully and clearly realized when he accepted that death. Nevertheless, we normally expect at least part of the value of important human actions to stem from the conscious intentions of the primary agent.

In the case of Jesus' crucifixion things would rapidly turn confused and confusing if we failed to distinguish five basic questions: Did Jesus in fact anticipate and accept his violent death? When did he start doing so? Did he trust that his death would be followed (quickly) by a divine vindication? Did he see his death (and resurrection) as positively bringing salvation to others? Lastly, did he understand the beneficiaries of his suffering and death to extend beyond his own nation and include everyone? These five questions will be presupposed in what follows.

For a long time the academic theology and popular piety of many Catholics (and other Christians) found little difficulty in crediting Jesus of Nazareth with having anticipated – right from the outset of his human existence – all the historical details and the full redemptive force of his crucifixion. Then the rise of biblical criticism led some writers to minimize drastically Jesus' expectations about his coming death. At times they even declared this death to be something which simply overtook him without being accepted and interpreted in advance. But in recent years a consensus appears to be growing that recognizes how Jesus viewed his execution as what Kasper calls 'a representative and saving service to many' (*Jesus the Christ*, p. 120). I want to outline first the maximizing and minimizing views before describing the moderate consensus which is taking over.

(1) *The maximal view.* Until fairly recently many theologians and popular writers regularly attributed to the earthly Jesus more or less unlimited knowledge. From the first moment of his conception he was alleged to have enjoyed the beatific vision and so-called 'infused' knowledge: as if the beatific vision needed to be supplemented! This meant not only a clear consciousness of his own identity as the Word of God incarnate, but also precise information about everything that was to happen, including his violent death and all its saving consequences.

Thus books of meditation invited readers to reflect on the circumcision as the time when the week-old Jesus pledged with his blood his intention to save the human race. Preachers and retreat directors portrayed the boy Jesus as being from time to time reminded of his coming crucifixion when Joseph gave him wood to shape. Jesus saw the cross casting its shadow over the workshop at Nazareth. To judge from his *Jesus Christ*, Ferdinand Prat felt sure that 'Jesus knew in advance, to the smallest detail, all the atrocious vicissitudes of his own death' (ET: vol. I, Milwaukee, 1950, p. 318).

On the eve of the crucifixion, part of the suffering in Gethsemane was supposed to have stemmed from an exact foreknowledge of the ways in which this death would fail to have its full results for human salvation. Thus Prat wrote of 'the frightful spectacle' which assailed Jesus' imagination:

> He sees heaping up in the course of centuries the iniquities of men, those men for whom he is about to shed all his blood. How many souls, through negligence or malice, in every case through their own fault, will still hold aloof from the fruits of his redeeming death! Even in the Church, how many schisms, how many heresies, what scandals and apostasies and sacrileges!

The major cause for Jesus' agony was alleged to have been the clear presence to his consciousness of all the sins committed by human beings in the whole sweep of history. This Prat called 'the most fearful trial' which Jesus suffered: 'He feels all the sins of man weighing down upon him . . . . Under the blows of divine malediction which he accepts, he experiences what we ourselves ought to experience when confronted by sin' (pp. 319f.). Widely-read writers like Prat not only interpreted the agony in the garden as entailing such a universal vision of sin, but also frequently represented Jesus on the cross as dying quite consciously for every single human being in particular.[2]

Prat, of course, was only one among many writers and preachers who attributed to Jesus such an utterly full knowledge of his coming death and all its implications in the history of salvation. One motive that seemed to have lurked behind such maximal views was a certain fear that, unless the earthly Jesus himself explicitly intended such an interpretation of his death, we would not be entitled to hold it for ourselves. Hence the maximizing writers credited Jesus in his adulthood or even in his babyhood with a comprehensive knowledge of his redemptive death.

Moreover, a straight line led from maximal views about the earthly Jesus' knowledge of his *identity* to maximal views about his foreknowledge of his *atoning death*. Logically a clear perception of his divine personhood was understood to entail an equally clear perception of his saving work. But at both levels, theologians have pulled back from such extreme positions.

It is not too much to speak of a Copernican revolution having taken place in the general approach to Jesus' knowledge: and that for two reasons. First, the classic formulations have kept tugging at theologians' coat-sleeves. It is after all orthodox faith to believe that Jesus Christ was (and is) true God and true man. Being limited in knowledge and foreknowledge is precisely part of being human, and not an ugly imperfection from which Jesus must be miraculously freed. Among other things, some limitation in knowledge makes it possible *for human beings* to act freely. Genuinely free acts mean entrusting oneself to situations and a future which are to one degree or another unknown. Hence in the name of Jesus' true humanity and genuine liberty theologians defend real limitations in his knowledge and fore-knowledge.

Secondly, instead of (or as well as) arguing for what 'must have been the case', theologians have turned to the evidence which the Gospels offer about the character of Jesus' knowledge and foreknowledge. A critical study of Mark, Matthew and Luke allows us at least to glimpse Jesus' sense of his identity and understanding of his impending death. Contemporary biblical scholarship shows that the maximalists overstated their case for the earthly Jesus' knowledge both as regards his personal identity (Christology) and the salvation effected through his ministry, death and resurrection (Soteriology).

In Chapter 6 I come back to the issue of the extent of Jesus' knowledge. In this chapter I want only to put together the evidence for Jesus' attitude towards his coming death. But before outlining the growing consensus on that point, let me outline the position of those who have minimized Jesus' acceptance and interpretation of his suffering and crucifixion.

(2) *The minimal view*.   Rudolph Bultmann has been quoted a thousand times as a classic exponent of those who minimize the redemptive value which Jesus attached to his coming death. But to quote him once again will do no harm. Bultmann flatly maintained that 'we cannot know how Jesus understood his end, his death'. He dismissed the predictions of the passion (Mark 8:31ff.) as simply prophecies after the event – later Christian formulations placed on the lips of Jesus. Bultmann also rejected as 'an improbable psychological construction' the widely-held thesis that 'Jesus, after learning of the Baptist's death, had to reckon with his own equally violent death'. Bultmann's reason? 'Jesus clearly conceived his life in an *entirely* [italics mine] different fashion than did the Baptist from whom he distinguished himself.' Bultmann refused to recognize the crucifixion as 'an inherent and necessary consequence' of Jesus' religious activity. 'Rather it took place because his activity was misconstrued as *political* [italics mine] activity. In that case it would have been – historically speaking – a meaningless fate. We cannot tell whether or how Jesus found meaning in it. We may not veil from ourselves the possibility that he suffered collapse' (*HJKC*, p. 23).

There is much to be challenged here. For instance, Jesus invoked the violent death of prophets as illuminating his own threatening fate: 'O Jerusalem, Jerusalem, killing prophets and stoning those who are sent to you!' (Luke 13:34 par.). He saw his mission, at least partially, as standing in continuity with the prophets, right down to John, his prophetic precursor from whom he had received baptism. Even if, for the sake of argument, Jesus had 'clearly conceived his life in an *entirely* different fashion than did the Baptist', the violent death of this man who was close to Jesus threateningly exemplified how dangerous was a religious ministry, prophetic or otherwise, in the Palestine of that time. It is no 'improbable psychological construction' to hold that Jesus saw the point. Anybody would have been extraordinarily naïve not to have done so. Hans Küng rightly calls the execution of John the Baptist 'an extremely serious warning to Jesus' (*OBC*, p. 321).

Second, Bultmann slipped over in silence the Last Supper and the agony in the garden. As I will argue, those two events say something about the way Jesus understood his imminent death. Third, in Bultmann's thesis we bump up against an unjustified separation of politics and religion. A *purely* political mistake on the part of the Romans is alleged to have led to Jesus' execution. And from a religious point of view such a political death can only be 'meaningless'. Such a thesis fits snugly into the sharp (and quite unacceptable) separation between the world and religion which characterized Bultmann's theology.[3]

This last point reminds me that we should not debate Bultmann's minimizing view of Good Friday on merely historical grounds. In the very essay from which I have quoted he himself emphasized just that. After raising his historical objections, he remarked: 'However much we may glean from a historical-critical evaluation of the "features" of Jesus, and even if the traditional interpretation of his path to suffering and death should be correct, what is to be gained by it?' (*HJKC*, p. 24). Ultimately it was not historical scepticism but theological conviction which generated Bultmann's position. No matter what our historical findings might prove to be about Jesus' intentions in the face of death, for Bultmann they always remained theologically insignificant. In Bultmann's view, only the sheer existence (the 'that') of the earthly Jesus mattered for theology and faith. Everything else which scholarship might or might not critically establish about the history of Jesus was decreed to be irrelevant for the believer and the theologian.

As we saw in the last chapter, squads of scholars (not to mention other believing Christians) rejected this severe division between faith and history. Günther Bornkamm, Ernst Käsemann and other notable ex-students of Bultmann's eventually disagreed with him, partly over this issue. They came to see how their former teacher had intolerably trivialized the earthly existence of Jesus. In short, any debate with Bultmann over Jesus' understanding of his death sweeps us off to a larger theme, the whole significance for Christian faith of Jesus' historical existence.

In the last two decades, Wolfhart Pannenberg has proved perhaps the most damaging critic of Bultmann's separation of history and faith. He argues that the ascertainable events of past history can and should yield objective grounds for faith. However, when it comes to the earthly Jesus' expectations and intentions about his coming death, Pannenberg lapses back into a relatively minimal view. He plays down the voluntary obedience of Jesus. His classic *Jesus – God and Man* remains silent about the agony in the garden. The way Pannenberg explains matters, Jesus was so seized by his mission that he was hardly left with any genuinely human choice about accepting or refusing his fate on Calvary (p. 350). Pannenberg also fails to scrutinize carefully Jesus' possible interpretation of his coming death. Where *Jesus – God and Man* discusses the Last Supper, it is only to examine whether the first Christians understood the crucifixion as a covenant sacrifice, and *not* to investigate how the earthly Jesus might have viewed and defined his death in advance (pp. 248f.).

Pannenberg broke new ground when he first published *Jesus – God and Man* back in 1964. But Christology and biblical scholarship have moved on since then. The lines of a fairly well-defined consensus about Jesus' interpretation of his death seem to have emerged, and were reflected by the International Theological Commission's 1980 statement, 'Select Questions on Christology' (IV. B). If both the maximizing and the minimizing views have proved unsatisfactory, what does the moderate consensus have to say in answer to the two key questions: Did Jesus anticipate and accept his execution? What value did he attach to it?

(3) *The moderate view*. Did the Jesus we know from the Gospels of Matthew, Mark and Luke expect that he would suffer and lose his life violently? Did he – at least from some point in his public ministry – begin to move consciously towards such a death? Küng persuasively marshals the evidence for an affirmative answer. First the ministry:

> Would he [Jesus] have been so naive as not to have had any presentiment of what finally happened to him . . . No supernatural knowledge was required to recognize the *danger of a violent end*, only a sober view of reality. His radical message raised doubts about the pious self-reliance of individuals and of society and about the traditional religious system as a whole, and created opposition from the very beginning. Consequently Jesus was bound to expect serious conflicts and violent reactions on the part of the religious and perhaps also the political authorities, particularly at the centre of power. Accusations of infringing the Sabbath, contempt for the law and blasphemy had to be taken seriously (*OBC*, p. 320).

Then the move of Jesus and his disciples to Jerusalem for the Passover, his entrance into the city, and his actions and statements in the Temple inevitably increased the conflict with the forces opposing him. Küng writes:

> The move of the heretical 'prophet' from the province to the capital, confusing and upsetting the credulous people, in any case meant a challenge to the ruling circles . . . Anyone who was suspected of working miracles by demonic power, of being a false prophet or a blasphemer, had to reckon with the possibility of the death penalty . . . Jesus' sensational entry into Jerusalem could only increase the danger. And the prophetical act of cleansing the temple – which certainly has a core of historical truth – likewise put his life in danger, since it was an act of arrogance in the sanctuary itself (*OBC*, pp. 320f.).

The evidence that – sooner or later in his ministry – Jesus came to foresee his violent death is cumulative and persuasive. At some point he recalled the murder of prophets as prefiguring his own fate:

> Woe to you! For you build the tombs of the prophets whom your fathers killed . . . The Wisdom of God said, I will send them prophets and apostles some of whom they will kill and persecute, that the blood of all the prophets, shed from the foundation of the world, may be required of this generation (Luke 11:47, 49f. par.).

When warned of threats from Herod Antipas, Jesus apparently named Jerusalem as the setting for his end: 'It cannot be that a prophet should perish away from Jerusalem. O Jerusalem, Jerusalem, killing the prophets and stoning those who are sent to you!' (Luke 13:33f. par.). At least some of his audience knew that his parable of the wicked husbandmen (who murder the vineyard-owner's messengers) was directed at them. Just as the final killing of the son provoked the owner's intervention against the tenants, so the killing of Jesus would provoke a divine intervention (Mark 12:1–9). In the light of such material from the Gospels, Küng can reasonably conclude that Jesus both anticipated and accepted his coming death in obedience to his Father:

> Whatever attitude we adopt to the authenticity of any particular saying, we may take it as certain that Jesus . . . must have reckoned with a violent end . . . . And he accepted death freely, with that freedom which united fidelity to himself and fidelity to his mandate, responsibility and obedience, since he recognized in it the will of God (*OBC*, p. 322).

On the eve of his death, the agony in the garden strikingly exemplified this free obedience to the Father's will. There are, of course, difficulties in settling the details of that episode. The Synoptic Gospels do not provide uniform evidence. Nevertheless, it seems reasonable to accept a historical basis for the story of that agonizing decision.

All in all, unless we revert to a relentless but unjustified scepticism about our sources, it should be easy to agree that death was much more than something which simply overtook Jesus out of the Judaean blue. Besides, a completely unexpected and unwanted death would make Calvary look too much like a meaningless catastrophe turned to the divine purposes by an outsider God. It is not that we need to assert that the value of the crucifixion resided wholly – or even principally – in the conscious intentions behind what Jesus did and suffered. Nevertheless, if we strike out any deliberate purpose on his part, we make him into a totally passive or even unwilling victim, whose execution God picked to serve for the redemption of human beings. Such a thesis maintains an extreme separation between (a) the order of being and (b) the order of knowledge. On the level of what is and what is done, Jesus' death brought salvation to the world. Yet he neither knew nor intended anything of this in advance! Even St Paul, although he usually bypasses any reference to Jesus' mind-set before the crucifixion, cannot confine himself simply to the order of being and cries out: 'He loved me and gave himself for me' (Gal 2:20). It seems both historically correct and theologically sound to acknowledge that Jesus went willingly and to some extent 'knowingly' to his death.

How far, then, did Jesus intend his crucifixion? Was it a totally premeditated death which he directly aimed at as the only possible way of realizing the kingdom? At the end, did he deliberately go to Jerusalem precisely in order to provoke the religious establishment and political authorities into killing him? Rather it appears that Jesus went up to the capital both to make one last effort at bringing his people to their senses and to keep the Passover like any good Palestinian Jew of that time. He did not wish some of his audience to react by rejecting and killing him, but utter loyalty to his vocation prevented him from escaping, even though his actions set him on a deadly collision course. By continuing his ministry, going to Jerusalem and facing his opponents, Jesus indirectly brought about the fatal situation. *He willed his death by accepting it* rather than by deliberately and directly courting it.

Granted the truth of this reconstruction, what did Jesus hope to achieve through his martyrdom and what did he expect would follow that death? It was one thing to accept death. But it was another to find and give meaning to his being repudiated and killed. Did he understand his death to be salvific? If so, in what sense and for whom? Here we need to scrutinize the evidence with care.

(a) To begin with, some of the material which supports the conclusion that Jesus anticipated a violent death says little about what he expected to follow it. Thus the sayings in which he aligned himself with *the fate of prophet-martyrs* say nothing either about his own vindication after death or about the saving significance of his martyrdom (Luke 11:47ff.; 13:33f.). Likewise the parable of the wicked vine-growers expresses a claim to special authority, associates Jesus with the violent fate of prophets, but offers no interpretation of the redemptive value of his coming martyrdom (Mark 12:1–9).

(b) A circumstantial argument, coupled with the passion predictions, can help us at this point. It would seem almost unaccountably odd if Jesus had never reflected on and applied to himself the Jewish conviction that *the righteous are bound to suffer but God will vindicate them* (Pss 27; 37; 38; 41; 55; 69; 109). In fact Jesus was remembered as having used in prayer the opening words of Psalm 22, perhaps the classic expression of this theme of the righteous sufferer (Mark 15:34). It is important to observe, incidentally, how in Psalm 22 (and the other psalms) the righteous person does *not* die, but after severe sufferings is delivered and vindicated by God in the course of this life. Wisdom (2 – 5) testifies to a further development in the theme which apparently had taken place by the time of Jesus: the just man who suffers would be vindicated by a blessed life beyond death.

The three predictions of the passion which Matthew and Luke took over from Mark associate 'the Son of man' with suffering, death and a vindication through resurrection. These predictions suggest how *the earthly Jesus applied to himself the theme of the righteous sufferer*: after a violent death he would be vindicated through resurrection.

The Son of man must suffer many things, and be rejected by the elders and the chief priests and the scribes, and be killed, and after three days rise again (Mark 8:31).

The Son of man will be delivered into the hands of men, and they will kill him; and when he is killed, after three days he will rise (Mark 9:31).

The Son of man will be delivered to the chief priests and the scribes, and they will condemn him to death, and deliver him to the Gentiles, and they will mock him, and spit upon him, and scourge him, and kill him; and after three days he will rise (Mark 10:33f.).

We noted above how Bultmann flatly dismissed these predictions as prophecies after the event. Kasper picks his language more carefully:

> All these show Jesus as having foreknowledge of his death and stress the voluntary character of his acceptance of his fate. In addition, they treat Jesus' passion as a divinely ordained necessity. . . . *In their present form* at least [italics mine] these prophecies are prophecies after the event. They are post-Easter interpretations of Jesus' death and not authentic sayings. That applies particularly to the third prophecy, which gives very precise details of the actual course of the passion (*Jesus the Christ*, pp. 114f.).

Here Kasper allows for a distinction between the *content* of the predictions and their *formulation*. This means that, even if they were formulated by later Christians, they are not necessarily simply statements retrospectively attributed to Jesus during his ministry. Some of the content could well derive from the earthly Jesus.

In fact Kasper will argue that 'the second of the three announcements of the passion definitely has a historical core' (*Jesus the Christ*, pp. 120f.). Up to a point Küng agrees: 'Even if we maintain a critical reserve, we cannot deny a historical core to what is perhaps the shortest, most vague and linguistically the oldest variant of the prophecies of the passion: that Jesus will be delivered up to men' (*OBC*, p. 321).

Two further items call for attention here. If the predictions are 'post-Easter interpretations' of Jesus' death and resurrection, one early and pervasive piece of interpretation is missing in these predictions as such. It is *not* stated that 'the Son of man must suffer and be killed *for us and for our sins*, and then rise again'. That standard reflection from the very early Church which Paul endorses repeatedly does not turn up in the three passion predictions. Further, the third prediction may give some 'details of the actual course of the passion', but they are hardly 'very precise', if they omit one enormously important detail, the killing by *crucifixion*. What hangs upon these two omissions? Just this. The omissions should encourage the view that the passion predictions are by no means totally free inventions which simply incorporate both the actual course of historical events and later theology. The Church tradition and the evangelist Mark, here as elsewhere, knew their limits in attributing material retrospectively to the earthly Jesus.

Let me pull matters together. We can conclude that (at least to his core group of disciples) Jesus announced his imminent death and affirmed that his Father would quickly vindicate him through resurrection. Such a conclusion says something about Jesus' view of what that death entailed *for himself*. But what did he expect it would bring *to others*?

(c) The theme of God's *kingdom* can help us here. It would take a sceptic with nerves of steel to deny the centrality of this theme in Jesus' preaching. From the outset he announced the divine rule to be at hand. It would be false to separate sharply his proclamation of the kingdom from his acceptance of his own victimhood. Kasper and others have endorsed the true aspect of Albert Schweitzer's original insight into the ministry: Jesus saw suffering and persecution as characterizing the coming of that kingdom which he insistently preached. The message of the kingdom led more or less straight to the mystery of the passion. That message entailed and culminated in the suffering ordeal to come: a time of crisis and distress which was to inaugurate and move towards the day of the Son of man (Mark 13 parr.), the restoration of Israel (Matt 19:28 par.), the banquet of the saved and the salvation of the nations (Matt 8:11 par.). Thus his arrest, trial and crucifixion dramatized the very thing which totally engaged Jesus, that rule of God which was to come through a time of ordeal.

At the Last Supper Jesus linked his imminent death with the divine kingdom: 'Truly, I say to you, I shall not drink again of the fruit of the vine until the day when I drink it new in the kingdom of God' (Mark 14:25). It is widely agreed that this text has not been shaped by the eucharistic liturgy of the early Church but comes right from Jesus himself and his last meal with his friends. The argument is this: *Since Jesus interpreted his death in terms of the coming kingdom, he saw that death as a saving event*; for he had consistently presented the equation: the kingdom = human salvation.

Is it enough to maintain here a lesser explanation – Jesus announced that his imminent death would not prevent the coming of the kingdom which he had preached? Despite his death, the kingdom was still to come. This lesser version, however, fails to match a feature of Jesus' message which was noted above: the kingdom was to come *through* a time of ordeal. Against that background it seems reasonable to conclude that Jesus viewed his death as somehow salvific. He not only integrated it into his surrender to his Father but also into his offer of salvation to human beings. Through those words about the kingdom (Mark 14:25) Jesus wanted to help his disciples grasp some meaning in his death: it was to effect, and not jeopardize, the coming of that kingdom.

It is hardly surprising that Jesus would have made such a positive integration between the coming kingdom and his death. As we saw in the last chapter, the message about the divine reign might be distinguishable but was not separable from the person of Jesus. This essential connection between the message of Jesus and his person meant that the vindication of his person in and through death entailed the vindication of God's kingdom, and vice versa.

Together with the kingdom saying from the Last Supper we can usefully consider the intentions conveyed by an episode which took place shortly before Jesus' death: the cleansing of the Temple. Beyond question, it is difficult to settle all the details of that action. Likewise the different versions of his saying about the destruction of the Temple (Matt 26:60ff.; Mark 14:57ff.; John 2:19ff.; Acts 6:13ff.) make it hard to state with any kind of assurance all that he originally said. Nevertheless, it seems that the point of both his symbolic action and his Temple-saying was to call for a radical break with the past. As his death drew near, he announced that the new age of God's kingdom was dawning. At the very heart of their religious existence he would refashion God's people. Jesus' mission in life and death was to replace the Temple and its cult with something better ('not made by hands').

(d) To return to the Last Supper. The 'words of institution', if taken at face value, show Jesus defining his death as a *sacrifice* which will not only representatively *atone* for sins but also initiate a new and enduring *covenant* with God. But here we must reckon with the question: How far have the sources of Paul, Mark and the other evangelists been shaped by liturgical usages in early Christian communities? In 1 Corinthians 11:23–26 we read:

> The Lord Jesus on the night when he was betrayed took bread, and when he had given thanks, he broke it, and said, 'This is my body which is for you. Do this in remembrance of me.' In the same way also the cup, after supper, saying, 'This cup is the new covenant in my blood. Do this, as often as you drink it, in remembrance of me.'

In Mark's version of the Last Supper, however, the repeated instructions to perform the Eucharist ('Do this in remembrance of me' and 'Do this, as often as you drink it, in remembrance of me') are missing. And – what is more significant for the issue under discussion – the qualification of 'my body' as being 'for you' is also missing. However, unlike the Pauline tradition, Mark describes the blood as being 'poured out for many'. His version runs as follows:

> He took bread, and blessed, and broke it, and gave it to them, and said, 'Take; this is my body.' And he took a cup, and when he had given thanks he gave it to them, and they all drank of it. And he said to them, 'This is my blood of the covenant, which is poured out for many' (14:22–24).

Confronted with the differences between the Pauline tradition (to which Luke 22:19–20 approximates) and the Markan tradition (which is more or less followed by Matthew 26:26–28), some writers back away from relying too much on the words of institution as accurate sources for settling the way Jesus understood his death – at least the night before it happened. Whom did Jesus believe to be the *beneficiaries* of his death? The 'for you' of the Pauline and Lukan tradition indicates the companions of Jesus at the Last Supper. Of course, in that case he might well have intended the twelve to represent others. Mark (followed by Matthew) has Jesus speaking of his blood 'poured out for many' (= all). But in that case did Jesus mean not merely all Jews but also all Gentiles? Some modern writers, however, have not let the difficulties stop them from reaching firm conclusions. Hans Küng, for example, believes that the evidence from the Last Supper accounts points to Jesus' intention to establish a new covenant through the sacrifice of his death:

> In the face of his imminent death he interpreted bread and wine – so to speak – as prophetic signs of his death and thus of all that he was, did and willed: of the sacrifice, the surrender of his life. Like this bread, so would his body be broken; like this red wine, so would his blood be poured out . . . . And as the head of the family gives a share in the blessing of the meal . . . , so Jesus gives to his followers a share in his body given up to death . . . and [a share] in his blood shed for 'many' . . . The disciples are thus taken up into Jesus' destiny. The meal becomes a sign of a new, permanent communion of Jesus with his followers: a *new covenant* is established (*OBC*, pp. 324f.).[4]

(e) Ultimately, the pressure on us to establish precisely what Jesus said and intended at the Last Supper can be eased in three ways: by recalling his *characteristic attitudes*, pointing to *contemporary ideas* and noting *an implication* of early Christian convictions about Jesus' atoning death.

In general the characteristic ways in which persons act and speak can fill their deaths with meaning, even when they have no chance at the end to express their motivation and make an explicit declaration of intent. Archbishop Oscar Romero, for instance, was abruptly shot dead when celebrating the Eucharist. He had no last-minute opportunity to blurt out some statement evaluating and interpreting the death which confronted him. Nevertheless, all that he had been saying and doing during his three years as Archbishop of San Salvador served to indicate his basic intentions and fill his martyrdom with significance.

In the case of Jesus, even if he did not explicitly designate himself as 'the Servant of the Lord', he consistently behaved as one utterly subject to his Father's will and completely available for the service of all those who needed mercy and healing. As we saw in the last chapter, his words and actions brought divine pardon to those who felt they were beyond redemption. He never drove away the lepers, children, sinful women, taxation agents and all those anonymous crowds of 'little people' who clamoured for his love and attention.

Now it would be strange to imagine that the threat of the passion abruptly destroyed Jesus' resolution to show himself the servant of others. Rather, a straight line led from his serving ministry to his suffering death. There *was* a basis in his life for the saying 'The Son of man came not to be served but to serve, and to give his life as a ransom for many' (Mark 10:45). He who had shown himself the servant of all was ready to become the

suffering servant of all. And – as Kasper, Küng, Moltmann and many others
have insisted – that service was offered especially to the outcasts and the
religious pariahs. Part of the reason why Jesus' ministry led to his crucifixion
stemmed from the fact that he faithfully served the lost, the godless and the
alienated of his society. The physician who came to call and cure the
unrighteous eventually died as their representative. His serving ministry to
the reprobate ended when he obediently accepted a shameful death between
two reprobates.

In these terms the passion of Jesus became integrated into his mission as a
final act of service. In death, as in life, he served and sacrificed himself for
others. Luke 22:27 ('I am among you as one who serves') is an authentic
pointer to this basic pattern in Jesus' behaviour.

Whom did Jesus take to be *the beneficiaries* of his suffering and death? In
the last chapter I argued that at some point in his ministry he did in fact
present himself to the inner group of his disciples as the Son of man who was
to represent the new Israel in suffering and bringing God's judgement and
kingdom. We saw also that, while Jesus did see his own people as the
primary beneficiary of divine salvation, his vision was universal. The
restoration of Israel would bring salvation to the nations. It seems reasonable
to maintain that at the end Jesus in some sense accepted that he would die for
all people.

Secondly, *contemporary ideas* also serve as pointers to Jesus' intentions in
the face of death. The experiences of the Maccabean martyrs in the second
century B.C. helped to give rise to an idea which was then in the air at the
time of Jesus. The suffering and violent death of a just person could expiate
the sins of others. The martyrdom of even one individual could representatively atone for the sins of a group (2 Macc 7:37f.; 4 Macc 6:27–29; 17:12;
18:4). In *The Atonement* (ET: London, 1981) Martin Hengel marshals the
evidence to show how earlier Greek (and Roman) literature, history and
customs supported the notion that someone could *die for* his city or people
and so atone for their sins. In fact the Jewish conviction to this effect which
we find in the Maccabean texts could well have been taken over from Greek
sources.

But my point here is not to discuss questions of provenance, but rather to
recall a relevant belief found at the time of Jesus. Once the threat of violent
death loomed up, it would have been strange if Jesus had never applied to
himself that religious conviction of his contemporaries. Through his
martyrdom he could vicariously set right a moral order disturbed by sin.

Here I should add a parenthesis on the fourth poem about the Servant of
the Lord from the book of Isaiah (52:13 – 53:12). Although this material
dates from the sixth century B.C. and could obviously support reflections on
vicarious atonement, the text is never *quoted* either by later works of the Old
Testament or by non-canonical books of the inter-testamental period. Even

where *allusions* to this poem about the Suffering Servant can be detected in later texts, we do not find the notion of a death which representatively atones for others. Nevertheless, Isaiah 52:13 – 53:12 helped to shape early Christian preaching. Eventually the New Testament was to include ten literal quotations from this poem and around thirty-two allusions to it.

What conclusion does this parenthesis point to? We should be cautious about invoking the fourth poem on the Lord's Servant to establish contemporary ideas of vicarious atonement which Jesus could have easily applied to himself. The Maccabean literature shows that the Palestinian Judaism of the first century A.D included the belief that the death of a martyr could representatively atone for the sins of others. But, curiously enough, this case cannot be so simply proved for the current interpretation of Isaiah's fourth song of the Suffering Servant. Certainly we have no clear text from pre-Christian Judaism which speaks of the Messiah's vicarious suffering in connection with Isaiah 53.

Finally, Paul's letters abundantly document the pre-Pauline tradition that Jesus' crucifixion was a death 'for us', which representatively atoned for human sin (1 Thess 5:10; 1 Cor 15:3; Rom 4:25; 8:32; etc.). As Hengel has rightly argued, we meet in these formulations from the earliest Christian tradition a conviction that ran clean counter to the predominant Jewish beliefs. At the time of Jesus the popular messianic hopes did not include a *suffering* Messiah. And to talk of a *crucified* Messiah was real blasphemy. Hence the early Christians defended something utterly offensive when they proclaimed that the crucifixion of someone who was executed precisely as a messianic pretender was in fact a sacrificial death which atoned representatively for the sins of all.

How can we account for this understanding of Jesus' crucifixion as 'the universal vicarious atoning death of the Messiah' (Hengel, *The Atonement*, p. 71)? Would the disciples' encounters with the risen Jesus *alone* have been sufficient to trigger off this interpretation? It would have been enough to have taken the resurrection simply to mean that Jesus had been vindicated by God as a prophetic martyr or an innocent sufferer (Wis 2 – 5; Rev 11:11f.). But the early Christians went much further than that in recognizing Jesus' crucifixion to be the representative death of the Messiah which atoned for human sin. They could hardly have done so, *unless the earthly Jesus had already in some way claimed to be Messiah and indicated that his coming death would have such an atoning value.*

CHRISTIANS AND THE CRUCIFIXION

Much of this chapter has been an attempt to retrieve the motivation and intentions of the earthly Jesus when faced with death. His interpretation of his coming fate served as a basis for subsequent Christian reflections on the meaning of the crucifixion and resurrection. I want to complete this chapter by briefly dealing with several related themes: some early Christian interpretations of Jesus' death, the Trinity and Calvary, the necessity of Jesus' death, the symbolism of Calvary, and the Shroud of Turin.

(1) *Early Christian interpretations.* So far we have discussed whether and how the earthly Jesus associated himself with various given themes: the prophets who die because of their prophecies, the suffering righteous man who is vindicated by God, the suffering Son of man, the martyrs whose sufferings can atone for the sins of others, and the Servant of the Lord who suffers for others.

(a) In their attempt to understand Jesus' death and cope with the horror of his crucifixion, early Christians and the New Testament authors took up and developed some of these themes. Jesus, for instance, had already linked himself with the suffering righteous man by his cry of abandonment taken from Psalm 22 (Mark 15:34 par.). We find that the Synoptic tradition built on this interpretation by echoing further verses from Psalm 22 (Mark 15:24, 29 parr.).

Another example. The theme of prophets who died because of their prophecies (along with other such themes which went back to the historical Jesus) obviously implied that suffering and death occurred because of *obedience* to the divine will and one's vocation. It comes then as no surprise to find the passion and death of Jesus being interpreted by early Christians in terms of obedience. Thus Paul, for example, cites a hymn to this effect (Phil 2:8), and introduces the same theme in his masterpiece (Rom 5:19).

Since Jesus freely chose the time of *the Passover* for his final confrontation with the Jerusalem authorities and then died after celebrating the festival with his close followers, it was natural that this commemoration of liberation from the Egyptian bondage would also be developed as an interpretative key. By the time Paul wrote 1 Corinthians, he could simply take the association for granted. He did not need to argue for it when he wrote: 'Christ, our paschal lamb, has been sacrificed' (5:7). A few years later, Mark three times noted the link between Jesus' death and the Passover, the feast when 'they sacrificed the passover lamb' (14:12, 14, 16). At the end of the first century John apparently endorsed the same motif when that Gospel presented 'the Lamb of God, who takes away the sin of the world' (1:29, 36), and at the end observed that like the Passover lamb the bones of the dead Jesus were not broken (19:36).[5]

Originally the Jews understood the feast of the Passover to commemorate their deliverance from Egypt. But by the time of Jesus some may *also* have begun interpreting it as a sacrifice of atonement. There were clear reasons for extending the significance of the feast. The lambs' blood was shed before

they were roasted and eaten. The killing of the lambs took place in the sacred
precincts of the Temple. When Christians acknowledged the crucified and
risen Jesus as 'our paschal lamb', they believed his sacrificial death to have
both *delivered* them (and others) and *expiated* their sins.

(b) Besides continuing lines of interpretation which derive from Jesus
himself, early Christians added fresh motifs to elucidate further the basic
belief which in its essence came from the earthly Jesus: his crucifixion was a
representative, atoning, sacrificial death which brought a new covenant for
the benefit of all. The Letter to the Hebrews made an interpretative leap
when it connected the death of Jesus not only with the daily sacrifices offered
in the Temple (7:26ff.) but also with the annual ceremony of *the Day of
Atonement* (9:6ff.) – in both cases to point out the superiority of Christ's
sacrificial death. For several reasons this was not an immediately obvious
connection to make. Jesus was not born into a priestly family and hence by
ordinary reckoning did not count as a priest. His death took place outside
the Temple and the city of Jerusalem (Heb 13:12), and occurred around six
months before the time for celebrating the Day of Atonement
(September/October). Nevertheless, Hebrews drew from that feast and
Jewish liturgical life to illuminate Jesus' role as priest and victim in his own
redemptive death. Incidentally, it should be remarked that even before the
writing of Hebrews St Paul's Letter to the Romans had already briefly
linked the crucifixion with the rites performed in the Holy of Holies on the
Day of Atonement. Like the 'mercy-seat' in the Holy of Holies the crucified
Jesus was the place where God's mercy was revealed (3:21–26).

These should be enough examples to show how early Christians reflected
on the crucifixion both by taking up themes which went back to Jesus
himself and by developing fresh approaches. What has been sketchily
indicated here will be filled out by the treatment of the models of
redemption in Chapter 5.

(2) *The crucifixion and the triune God.* The cross of Jesus stands between
heaven and earth. What it says about heaven is more fundamental than what
it says about earth. Christian teaching, writing and preaching have very
often been engrossed with the human, earthly side of things and fashioned
their primary questions accordingly: What does the cross say *about us*? What
is the saving value of the cross *for us*? But, as Moltmann, Sobrino and others
have insisted, we need to go beyond the anthropological ('about us') and
even the soteriological ('for us') perspectives to take a more *theo*logical view
of the cross. What does the cross say about God? What does the cross
indicate about the revelation of the Trinity?

We can spot this kind of shift of perspective in the writings of St Paul. In
his first letter he refers to the death of Jesus in human terms and interprets it
as the result of men's wickedness (1 Thess 2:15). By the time he writes to

the Romans Paul thinks of the crucifixion in terms of the Trinity (5:5ff.; 8:32).

Admittedly it is hard to bring the Trinity and the cross together. Frequently atheists have pointed to the kind of senseless suffering of innocent people symbolized by Jesus' death as *the* proof that God does not exist. They see the cross as the place where God is absent and any belief in an all-powerful, all-loving God should decently end. If there is a God, how can one explain such evil (*si Deus, unde malum*)? This persistent and radical difficulty brought up by theoretical and practical atheists serves to illustrate the truth of St Paul's words: 'We preach Christ crucified, a stumbling block to Jews and folly to Gentiles' (1 Cor 1:23).

Nevertheless, our New Testament witnesses, so far from becoming anxiously nervous over the difficulty, associate the cross, God and the self-revelation of God. In that classic passage where he develops 'the word of the cross' (1 Cor 1:18–25), Paul nine times speaks of God – that God whose 'foolishness is wiser than men' and whose 'weakness is stronger than men' (1 Cor 1:25). In Mark it is precisely the moment of death by crucifixion which allows a Roman soldier to break through the divine incognito and become the first human being in that Gospel to recognize the full identity of Jesus: 'When the centurion, who stood facing him, saw that he thus breathed his last, he said, "Truly this man was the Son of God!" ' (15:39). The Letter to the Hebrews begins by acknowledging that God 'has spoken to us by a Son . . . through whom he created the world' (1:2), and ends by recalling the unholy, profane place of Jesus' crucifixion (13:12). Public execution 'outside' the holy city was the last place that we would expect for the death of God's Son.

Often Christian artists have appreciated better than theologians that the brutality and seeming silence of Calvary formed the historical event in which the triune God was revealed as a loving, saving God. Here I am thinking especially of the 'mercy-seat' paintings and carvings of the crucifixion. The Father receives the cross which bears the dead body of the Son, or else simply holds the corpse in his arms. Above or below the Holy Spirit appears under the form of a dove. This art maintained a fully Trinitarian vision of Calvary which theology has at times lost.

Such a Trinitarian understanding of the passion should be taken beyond the first Good Friday. When crucified between two criminals, Jesus ended as he had lived – in solidarity with society's victims rather than with society's successes. He had proclaimed his Father's coming kingdom to the poor, the mourners and the hungry. Jesus' crucifixion not only dramatized the beatitudes which he had preached, but also disclosed a privileged place where we should expect the self-revelation of God – among the world's failures and victims. Among those who *are* forsaken (and even mercilessly destroyed) by their fellow human beings and *look* forsaken by God, we can expect to find in a special way the presence and power of Father, Son and Holy Spirit. As the setting for the self-communication of the triune God, the passion of God remains a piece of unfinished business. It continues in the whole history of human suffering.

(3) *The necessity of the crucifixion.* When they reflect on the passion of Jesus, many Christians feel obliged to ask, 'Did Jesus have to suffer and die?' Perhaps they recall that reproach to the disciples on the road to Emmaus, 'Was it not necessary that the Christ should suffer these things and enter into his glory?' (Luke 24:26). The passion predictions spoke in somewhat similar tones: 'The Son of man *must* suffer many things . . . and be killed, and after three days rise again' (Mark 8:31). St Paul cited an early Christian creed which also struck the note of necessity: 'Christ died for our sins in accordance with the scriptures' (1 Cor 15:3). Those who knew their sacred texts could see that the crucifixion *had* to be. The first Christians discerned in the event of Calvary much more than the cruel killing which just happened to put a violent end to Jesus' life. They acknowledged that in the divine plan of salvation it needed to be so.

What sense can we discover in this 'must' of Jesus' death by public execution? St Thomas Aquinas and other theologians mitigated the 'absolute necessity' of the crucifixion by arguing that at least in theory Jesus could have saved the human race by undergoing any act of suffering, even by shedding one drop of his blood. Nowadays it appears more helpful to leave behind speculations about alternative possibilities in God's design of redemption for humanity. If we take up the 'must' of Calvary on the *historical* level, we can readily appreciate how it was unavoidable in human terms.

At all times in the history of the human race prophets have been persecuted for refusing to be moderate and accommodating and for faithfully transmitting some message from God. Jesus' fidelity to his mission inevitably brought him into conflict with the ruling classes. In such a conflict he was – humanly speaking – bound to lose. Even a moderately astute analyst of politico-religious affairs in first-century Palestine would have reached that conclusion. Human malice made Jesus' suffering and death inevitable.

Back in the fourth century B.C. Plato suggested in the introduction to Book II of his *Republic* the kind of fate which a perfectly just man could expect:

> The just man, then, as we have pictured him, will be scourged, tortured, and imprisoned, his eyes will be put out, and after enduring every humiliation he will be crucified.

Christians, of course, found this to be a remarkable, pagan prophecy of what happened to Jesus himself. Prophecy or not, Plato's words have been fulfilled with depressing frequency. Society continues to make uncompromisingly good individuals suffer both for what they are and for what they try to do. In the case of Jesus the wonder is not so much that he was struck down so quickly as that he lasted as long as he did.

Besides human malice, something else on the historical scene fed into the 'must' of Jesus' passion: his own unswerving fidelity to his mission and the service of others. In these terms Calvary became the inevitable consequence of a commitment which he refused to abandon even at the cost of his life.

(4) *The cross as sign and symbol.* Christians put crosses (or crucifixes) in their churches, on altars, on buildings, in cemeteries and on flags. They wear crosses on their clothes and make the sign of the cross during public worship or at private prayer. This universal Christian use of the cross which constantly reminds believers and others of the way Jesus died calls for some reflection in this chapter on the crucifixion.

Not only is the frontier between signs and symbols blurred and imprecise, but also their nature cannot be adequately handled in any brief treatment. Nevertheless, something must be said before taking up some symbolic functions of the cross.

Signs may be effects from which we infer causes (for instance, smoke as a sign of fire), conventional gestures or objects conveying some information or directions (as in the case of sign language or signposts), or things used to represent something else (for example, sacraments as outward signs of inward grace). *Symbols* go further and prove richer than signs. The *Concise Oxford Dictionary* in the first place defines a symbol as follows:

> Thing regarded by general consent as naturally typifying or representing or recalling something (esp. an idea or quality) by possession of analogous qualities or by association in fact or in thought.

Among the examples given is the lion as a symbol of courage. Something more needs to be added about the *power* and *meaning* of symbols.

By making things present, symbols enter our imagination, affect our feelings and influence our behaviour. Symbols are felt to be powerful and important before we consciously perceive their possible meanings. Then over and above those meanings which society generally associates with given symbols, different people will recognize and appreciate different meanings. Cultural and historical conditioning brings it about that the perception of symbols will vary from period to period and from place to place. In all cases rational explanations will always fall short of the potential range of meanings expressed by given symbols. Particularly when we take up religious symbols which point to ultimate, transcendent realities, we can expect these symbols to prove inexhaustible.

What then should be said about the power and meaning of the cross? One can identify two sides to the symbolism of the cross. As the most shameful death known to Jews and Gentiles, it represents degradation and destruction. But it also expresses order and redemption. The masters of Jesus' world regularly used crucifixion to execute runaway slaves and rebels. Not everyone who looks today at a cross or crucifix cares to think of the ancient Romans as sadists who liked to degrade people and inflict frightful cruelties with sheer delight. Nevertheless, crucifixion happened within the regular framework of their society. As a form of execution it gets close to being unbearable in its horror. A man pinned to a cross symbolizes the weakness of unspeakable pain, an extreme and shameful case among pointless atrocities.

If degradation and destruction form one range of meanings, order and redemption gather up another set of meanings when we reflect on the symbolism of the cross. Various Fathers of the Church, Thomas Aquinas, Carl Jung and others have noted this second range of meanings. The cross expresses a totality and order which readily suggest universal redemption. The crucified Christ forms a kind of axis of the universe. He hangs impaled between heaven and earth, his body stretched out in four directions and his arms open to the world. Day by day people experience this symbolic power when they visit churches. Great crosses and crucifixes at the end of the buildings instantly seize their attention and produce order within the space enclosed by walls and roof.

St Paul's theology matches this double-sided symbolism of the cross, when he writes of 'power being made perfect in weakness' (2 Cor 12:9). The language of 'weakness' could lead us astray into thinking of moral weaknesses. But for the apostle the crucifixion was the supreme example of what he meant by 'weakness' (2 Cor 13:4) or 'vulnerability', as we might say. We catch his meaning by talking of order being made perfect in degrading disorder and redemption taking place in destruction. It sounds paradoxical. But this paradox parallels the peculiarly double-sided nature of the cross as symbol.

There is another way of stating this double-sided effect. In general symbols may function to resolve contradictions or at least to deal with incoherent elements in our human situation. Thus national symbols, for example, work to reconcile divisions in a country. In the case of the cross this symbol deals with the seeming contradiction between the universal fact of human suffering and the existence of an all-loving, all-powerful God. Nothing other than the cross has helped believers to cope more with this radical 'incoherence' between their experience of apparently senseless suffering and their faith in God.

One could add theme after theme which belong to a full discussion of the cross as sign and symbol. For instance, the horizontal thrust of the cross represents that suffering human existence conditioned by space and time in which Jesus fully participated. The vertical thrust suggests how his identity as Son of God and redemptive work as Saviour of the world broke through the limits of space and time. Second, the other two crosses flanking Jesus' cross speak of his solidarity in the whole history of human suffering. His cross was not an isolated cross; he died in the company of two others.

Third, this solidarity gets expressed in another way. On the cross we see a *suffering body*. Suffering and bodies are two things in which every human being shares. They create a kind of universal language. Through his suffering body on the cross Jesus can speak and has in fact so spoken to millions of men and women that we might adapt Paul's opening theme in 1 Corinthians and talk of 'the universal language of the cross'.

To complete this chapter I want to give a few pages to that extraordinary representation of our suffering Saviour, the Shroud of Turin.

(5) *The Shroud of Turin.* Through the 1950s, the 1960s and well into the 1970s, I dismissed as ridiculous any claims that the fourteen-foot-long piece of cloth kept in Turin Cathedral could actually be the shroud in which Jesus was buried. My attitude was supported by that Catholic work of fourteen volumes on theology and Church history which Karl Rahner and other German scholars prepared, *Lexikon für Theologie und Kirche* (1957–68). It simply ignored the Shroud of Turin, except for a brief reference in an article on Ulysse Chevalier (1841–1923). Among his other achievements he had gathered 'weighty arguments' to disprove the authenticity of the Shroud. Like the English Jesuit who was his contemporary, Herbert Thurston, Chevalier maintained that it was a fourteenth-century forgery.

The classic Protestant theological dictionary, *Die Religion in Geschichte und Gegenwart*, however, took a different view. Volume VI of the revised, third edition which appeared in 1962 included an article on the Shroud by H. -M. Decker-Hauff, '*Turiner Grabtuch*'. The author summarized some of the major reasons in favour of its authenticity. In its material and pattern the Shroud matches products from the Middle East in the first century of the Christian era. In the mid-fourteenth century the prevailing conventions of Church art would not have allowed a forger or anyone else to portray Jesus in the full nakedness that we see on the Shroud. In any case no medieval painter could have anticipated modern science and made the image on the Shroud a 'negative' – as Secondo Pia discovered when he photographed it in 1898. Further, the many small wounds around the head and the great perforation in the right side do not fit the normal methods of crucifixion but strikingly correspond with particular details of Jesus' passion reported by the Gospel-writers – the crowning with thorns (Matthew, Mark and John) and the piercing of the side (John). Then medical experts judge that the corpse and the Shroud were in contact for only thirty-six to forty hours. On the basis of these and other arguments, Decker-Hauff concluded that we cannot 'scientifically rule out' the hypothesis that 'the dead man was the historical Jesus'. He hoped that further scientific tests would finally settle matters one way or another.

Since Decker-Hauff's article appeared, the Shroud of Turin has undergone many more scientific tests in a way that no other relic has – down to five days of intensive examination by scientists in October 1978. Often this research has been carried on by non-Catholics like Max Frei, a Swiss criminologist. He took pollen samples from the Shroud and discovered that some of the pollen came from plants which grow only around the Dead Sea and elsewhere in the Holy Land. Layers of sediment in the Lake of Galilee which date from the time of Jesus have also yielded types of pollen found on the Shroud. The conclusion from the pollen analysis is clear. At some point in its history the Shroud was exposed to the air in Palestine.

Even before Decker-Hauff published his piece in 1962, photographic evidence had already excluded the view that the Shroud was a painting. Since then techniques developed by the National Aeronautic and Space Administration (NASA) for use on satellite photographs have been applied to it. The results were startling. The optic intensity of the body images on the cloth stands in a regular relation to the third dimension. Thus NASA scientists have been able to plot a true-to-life relief and reproduce in three dimensions the face on the Shroud. This is normally impossible with ordinary paintings and photographs.

The remarkable photographs which illustrated the *National Geographic*'s June 1980 article, 'The Mystery of the Shroud', showed the two kinds of images on the Shroud. There are the photographically positive 'blood' images which penetrate the Shroud, spreading through the threads and being trapped in the crevices. Some scientists have identified these as haemoglobin, the oxygen-carrying substance containing iron which is present in red blood-cells. Then there are the 'body' images: those photographically negative images which are found only on the top fibrils of the threads and which have stained each fibril an identical shade of yellow. Whatever created these images acted at a distance and not by direct contact. Scientists have discussed at length and speculated about the process which caused these images. Were they produced by sweat, body oil and the spices which Nicodemus supplied for the burial (John 19:39f.)? Some scientists are convinced that no liquid or vapour could have caused the 'body' images. The scorch-like nature of these images has prompted the hypothesis that they were produced by a moment of intense radiation from within.

Some readers will have seen the BBC film *The Silent Witness*, which documented the history of research on the Shroud – from Secondo Pia's first photographs through to the use of computer technology. Like many other studies that film focused on the question: Is the relic in Turin really the burial

cloth of Jesus? But by now the converging evidence has accumulated to the
point that in a 1977 article in *Theology* John Robinson could admit:

> For me the burden of proof has shifted. I began by assuming its inauthenticity until
> proved otherwise and then asking how one explained it. On the hypothesis of a
> medieval forgery, or any other I could think of, this was very difficult. I now find
> myself assuming its authenticity until proved otherwise.

It is high time then that we moved on from the question of historical
authenticity to face issues which belong to Christology. What significance
could the Shroud have for Christian belief in Jesus Christ as Son of God and
Saviour? What theological implications does it carry? The theme of *faith*
offers a convenient way in.

(a) Ever since I read Newman's *Grammar of Assent* I have been convinced
that it is much more helpful to examine how *in fact* people *do* come to believe
rather than start pontificating on how we think they *should* come to faith. In
a BBC television discussion on Holy Thursday 1979 John Robinson called
the Shroud 'a trigger of faith'. He was on particularly safe ground that
evening, as the discussion followed a screening of *The Silent Witness*. The
producer and director of that film, David Rolfe, began his three-and-a-half
years of investigation of the Shroud as an agnostic and then moved to belief
in Jesus Christ. Like others he saw on the burial cloth the image of the dead
Jesus and believed in the living Christ.

'Trigger' was a well-chosen word. A gun needs a barrel, a stock and other
features over and above the trigger mechanism itself. Likewise, no matter
what finally triggers off faith in Christ, a wide range of elements gets
involved in its making: personal needs, questions about the ultimate issues of
life, the influence of the Christian community, contact with the Gospel
story and the rest. Rolfe himself, as he indicated in an interview in the
Catholic Herald of 1 June 1979, neither wishes nor claims 'to base faith purely
on the Shroud'. But he does recognize that some people in their path to faith
'need a form of underpinning in twentieth-century scientific terms'.

How strong is this underpinning? Granted that Jesus was actually buried
in the Shroud now kept in Turin, what does this suggest or even establish?
Like the empty tomb itself this fourteen-foot-long and three-and-a-half-feet-
wide piece of cloth does not *prove* the resurrection. But there would have
been no empty tomb nor would we now have the Shroud unless Jesus had
been raised from the dead. Here it is important to note that the Shroud was
separated from the corpse before decomposition set in. Yet it bears no traces
of the kind of tearing which we could expect if it had been pulled away from
the body. Further, as we saw above, the body left its image by some
mysterious process. Nevertheless, it would be wrong to go looking for some
knock-down proof for the resurrection that we cannot and will not get.

If scientific study of the Shroud were somehow to provide full, 'objective' evidence for the truth of the Christian message, faith would be ruled out. Such a mass of evidence that to everyone's satisfaction totally supported the Christian confession about Jesus of Nazareth would reduce faith to the necessary conclusion of an argument and forget that it is a free commitment to a personal relationship. If faith were merely a matter of scientific reason alone, we could run the data through a computer and have our assured result. However, unless it remains a free and fundamental option, faith is no longer faith. Thus absolutely tangible guarantees from the Shroud or any other source would rule out, not rule in, real Christian belief in Jesus as our risen Lord.

Furthermore, the four Gospels provide *the* access to the passion of Jesus, as well as to the story of his life and post-resurrection appearances. The Shroud cannot match in value those texts. In that sense we should protest against any enthusiasm for the Shroud or other items from the ancient world which would brush aside the canonical Gospels.

However, a both/and rather than an either/or attitude describes more accurately many of those three million pilgrims who visited Turin to see the Shroud in 1978. I put the question to a number of them: 'In what way does the Shroud support your faith?' The fullest answer came from one Italian pilgrim. He responded emphatically: 'My faith results from hearing God's word. I believe in Jesus Christ.' But then he added: 'The Shroud makes the Jesus I know through the Gospels very concrete. When we want to meet someone, we all like to see his face or at least a picture of him.' He ended by reflecting on the threat of doubt: 'We can always argue about the truth of Jesus and Christianity. But people fall silent when they see the face on the Shroud.'

(b) The Shroud triggered faith for David Rolfe when he found the scientific proofs for its authenticity convincing. These proofs come from a wide range of specializations. In a remarkable way *the Shroud stands at the cross-roads of human science and technology*. Here we might fairly adapt the words of Jesus in John's Gospel: 'When I am lifted up in death and resurrection, I will draw all sciences to myself – through the relic I will leave behind, my burial cloth' (12:32).

I have already noted how photographic techniques developed by NASA have recently contributed to the study of the Shroud. For a long time medical scientists have pointed out the correctness of various anatomical and physiological details of the imprint on the Shroud. The markings correspond exactly not only to what doctors would expect from the corpse of a crucified man, but also to those special features of Jesus' crucifixion which the Gospels attest.

Experts in ancient coins (numismatologists) have noted that Roman coins from around the time of Jesus (54 B.C. to A.D. 70) show Jewish prisoners of war with beards and hair falling to the shoulders. At that time in the Roman

Empire other men were beardless. No Greek, Roman or Egyptian portrait of the period shows a man with the full beard and long hair which we see on the Turin Shroud. Thus we can be sure of this. The man whose image remains on the Shroud was a crucified *Jew* and not some other victim of that atrocious Roman method of execution.

After studying the material and weave of the Shroud, specialists in the history of textiles admit that it could be a first-century product from the Middle East. That type of linen was commonly used in ancient Palestine for grave cloths. The Shroud also contains traces of cotton of a Middle East variety. Then art experts have pointed to the way depictions of Christ changed in the sixth century. Instead of being young and beardless, he was portrayed as a more mature man with a forked beard and long hair parted in the centre. Did the impact of the Shroud lie behind that familiar and standard Byzantine image of Christ?

Historians also have played their part in investigating the Shroud. On the one hand, they point out that the Emperor Constantine abolished crucifixion as a method for executing people sentenced to death. That suggests that the man on the Shroud was put to death some time before the early fourth century. On the other hand, however, because historians concentrate on documentary evidence, it concerns them that the available records do not allow them to trace *clearly* and *fully* the whereabouts and history of the Shroud before 1353. There are some hints and indications on which Ian Wilson builds in *The Turin Shroud* (Penguin, 1979) to track the earlier history of the Shroud. But no compelling documentary evidence is so far at hand.

Another scientific speciality which still retains a 'yes-but' attitude towards the Shroud is biblical scholarship. By now some professionals in the field are satisfied that a long-standing difficulty from the Fourth Gospel does not count against the authenticity of the Shroud. John tells us that when Simon Peter went into the empty tomb of Jesus, 'he saw the linen cloths [*othonia*, plural] lying, and the napkin [*sudarion*], which had been on his head, not lying with the linen cloths but rolled up in a place by itself' (John 20:6f.). The plural ('cloths') seemed to rule out a single piece of cloth like the Shroud. If a 'napkin' covered the face of Jesus, how could its features have been imprinted on the Shroud along with the rest of his body? John Robinson and other exegetes now explain *othonia* as a generic plural for grave cloths and hence compatible with a single piece of cloth like the Turin Shroud. The *sudarion* they interpret as a band slipped under the chin of dead persons to keep the mouth closed. Such a band would not have interfered with the imprinting of Jesus' face on the burial Shroud.

Nevertheless, some modern studies on John's Gospel both continue to create difficulties and also reveal a certain conflict between medicine and exegesis. For their part, medical scientists have recognized as correct the detail about the flow of 'blood and water' from the side of the dead Jesus (John 19:34). Such an effect would occur *only* if a crucified man were so pierced *after* his death. The Shroud bears the traces of just such a wound inflicted on the right side of the corpse. Leading commentators on the Fourth Gospel, however, have dismissed any such medical discussion about that blood and water. It wrongly supposes that John here intended to describe some 'objective' episode. Thus Rudolf Schnackenburg called such a discussion 'misleading' and Rudolf Bultmann described it as downright 'comic'. But perhaps what we have here is yet another example of the way in which John's Gospel has been found to contain more details from actual history than biblical scholars have been inclined to admit.

All in all, despite some conflicts (like the one between medical scientists and exegetes over the blood and water which flowed from the side of the dead Jesus), various sciences and technologies intersect at the Shroud. They each have something to say, but by itself no speciality proves decisive in establishing that the piece of cloth preserved in Turin is genuinely the burial Shroud of Jesus. The different specialities complement one another in reaching this conclusion. This modern research prompts two reflections.

First, such scientific research encourages a proper humility. A specialist in one field has to trust or at least respect the specialists in other fields. Second, research on the Shroud and its impact on people like David Rolfe illustrate remarkably how scientific reason – in its many fields – can help to bring about for thoroughly 'modern' people faith in Jesus crucified and risen from the dead.

(c) Finally, what special contribution does the Turin Shroud make to this study of Jesus Christ as Son of God and Saviour of the world? Obviously it provides some information about his physical appearance. He was bearded, wore long hair, weighed about 175 pounds, stood almost six feet tall, and – as the marks of the body indicate – was right-handed. Then for some Christians the Shroud pacifies certain doubts and strengthens their faith in Jesus. We have the Shroud because he rose bodily from the dead. It decisively checks the temptation to take a falsely 'spiritual' view of the resurrection.

However, the particular contribution of the Shroud lies elsewhere. It is a dramatic reminder of the suffering and death of Jesus – something which many Christians and non-Christians have played down or even denied. Many authors of the Apocryphal Gospels simply omitted the Passion story. Basilides, a second-century Alexandrian theologian of Gnostic tendencies, held that Simon of Cyrene was crucified instead of Jesus. According to Sura 4 of the Koran, someone else took Jesus' place on the cross. It seems that John was concerned to counter this tendency, which had already set in at the end of the first century. Even more than the Synoptics, the Fourth Gospel emphasized the reality of Jesus' death by including such details as the blood and water coming from his pierced side. Of course, this particular detail in the narrative carries further meanings, but it also belongs to the Johannine insistence on the fact that Jesus truly died.

The Shroud encapsulizes the passion of Jesus. On that piece of cloth Jesus wrote the story of his suffering and death. In a way that Zechariah and John never imagined, the Shroud has fulfilled for millions of people those words: 'They shall look upon him whom they have pierced' (Zech 12:10; John 19:37). It expresses with terrible directness man's inhumanity to the Son of man. The Shroud reveals what Jesus looked like when human beings had finished with him. The marks of the scourging – to mention just one horrifying detail – show around a hundred wounds inflicted very systematically by two men on almost every part of the body. They each used a whip (*flagrum*) tipped with bits of lead or bone. The scourging proves to be much more atrocious than what we might have supposed from the concise Gospel reports (Mark 15:15 parr.). Ian Wilson (*The Turin Shroud*) and other writers run through the physical details on the Shroud which show how much worse the passion was than we might have cared to imagine.

Let us suppose then for a moment that the man on the Shroud was not Jesus but another crucified Jew from the first century whose wounds – by some extraordinary coincidence – just happened to have matched exactly the special details reported by the Gospels, as well as the marks left by a 'normal' crucifixion. In that case the Shroud would still depict for us a victim of human brutality. It would portray for us someone violently done to death who, whether he knew it or not, suffered together with the man who came from Nazareth 'to give his life as a ransom for many' (Mark 10:45).

Of course, if the Shroud spoke to us only of human brutality, it would be enough to make us despair. But the picture on the Shroud says more. People sense the extraordinary majesty and peace of that ravaged face. In death it seems as if Jesus sees us and blesses us through his closed eyes. He may be completely naked and horribly battered, but the divine beauty shines through. John's Gospel foreshadows this reaction and interpretation: 'They shall *look on* him whom they have pierced' (19:37). Here seeing and looking are understood as leading to belief. In fact many people have looked at the face on the Shroud and come to recognize the exalted Son of God in the crucified Jesus.

What we have in the Shroud is a pictorial counterpart to St Paul's message about Christ who 'was crucified in weakness, but lives by the power of God' (2 Cor 13:4). As we have seen, 'vulnerability' catches better what the apostle means by 'weakness'. Who is more vulnerable than a crucified man? And yet through the crucifixion of Jesus the divine power comes to heal and help us. By its impact on viewers the Shroud of Turin illustrates and re-enacts the mystery of the passion. In his utter vulnerability and seeming powerlessness the man on the Shroud acts to save us.

NOTES

1   It should be added that recent scholarship has suggested that it was not till ten years or more *after* Jesus' ministry and crucifixion that strong opposition to the Roman rule in Palestine really began (H. Guevara, C. Perrot etc.).

2   Matthew, Mark and Luke (who report Jesus' agony in the garden) all agree on Jesus' fearful distress at his approaching suffering and death, but provide no support for the kind of speculations we find in Prat and other such authors. See D. M. Stanley, *Jesus in Gethsemane* (New York, 1980).

3   See my *EJ*, pp. 95, 97.

4   See also J. Jeremias, *The Eucharistic Words of Jesus* (ET: London, 1966), and *New Testament Theology*, I (ET: London, 1971), pp. 288–292.

5   It should be noted, however, that John 1:29 and 36 do not describe Jesus as the *Passover* lamb. The reference might be to the Suffering Servant (Isa 53:7). Just possibly, John 19:36 could refer to a Jewish belief that breaking the bones of the dead might be an impediment to resurrection.

QUESTIONS FOR DISCUSSION

(1) What does Jesus' crucifixion say to you about the Trinity?

(2) Do you agree with the explanation given for the 'necessity' of Jesus' death? Have you further reflections to add?

(3) What groups and events in the history and present situation of your country speak to you most powerfully of the continuing presence of Jesus' passion? What reasons have you for your choice?

(4) Does the religious painting and sculpture which you know suggest further thoughts on the cross as sign and symbol?

(5) Why do we invoke the Trinity as we make the sign of the cross?

(6) Do you believe that people sometimes exaggerate the theological significance of the Turin Shroud? Would you agree with the way I have expressed the Shroud's implications for faith?

ADDITIONAL READING

Besides the items already indicated in the text and footnotes, the following works could be consulted.

J. P. Galvin, 'Jesus' Approach to Death', *Theological Studies* 41 (1980), pp. 713–744.

J. Jeremias, *New Testament Theology*, I (ET: London, 1971), pp. 276–299. His knowledge of the Jewish background always makes Jeremias rewarding reading.

W. Kasper, *Jesus the Christ* (ET: London and New York, 1976), pp. 113–123.

H. Küng, *OBC*, pp. 328–342.

J. P. Mackey, *Jesus the Man and the Myth* (London, 1979), pp. 52–85.

J. Moltmann, *The Crucified God* (ET: London, 1976). Moltmann rightly links the crucifixion with the revelation of the Trinity, even if he draws unwarranted conclusions from Jesus' cry of abandonment.

C. F. D. Moule, *The Origin of Christology* (Cambridge, 1977), pp. 107–126. A classic study of the New Testament by a great Cambridge scholar.

G. O'Collins, *The Calvary Christ* (London and Philadelphia, 1977). This book examines the death of Jesus in terms of story, history and the theology of redemption.

G. O'Collins (ed.), *The Cross Today* (Dublin and New York, 1977).

E. Schillebeeckx, *Jesus*, pp. 294–319.

J. Sobrino, *Christology*, pp. 179–235.

B. Vawter, *This Man Jesus* (New York: Image Book ed., 1975), pp. 57–89. Vawter studies the historical and theological significance of Jesus' death.

H.-R. Weber, *The Cross* (ET: Grand Rapids, 1978). One of the best accounts of the crucifixion in terms of history and theology.

For further material on the Shroud of Turin see:

M. Hebblethwaite, 'The Shroud and the Cross', *Theology* 84 (1981), pp. 266–274.

M. Hebblethwaite, 'The Shroud of Turin and Faith', *Doctrine and Life* 31 (1981), pp. 416–425.

G. O'Collins, 'The Shroud of Turin', *The Way* 20 (1980), pp. 140–147.

K. E. Stevenson and G. R. Habermas, *Verdict on the Shroud* (Ann Arbor, 1981).

4

The Resurrection of Jesus

God has made him both Lord and
Christ,
this Jesus whom you crucified.

THE ACTS OF THE APOSTLES

Resurrexit in eo mundus,
resurrexit in eo caelum,
resurrexit in eo terra.

ST AMBROSE

It has been repeatedly said that Christian faith in Jesus as Son of God and
Saviour of the world stands or falls with the truth of Easter. Thousands of
sermons have appealed to those words, 'If Christ has not been raised, then
our preaching is in vain and your faith is in vain' (1 Cor 15:14). Yet even
more is at stake here than Christian proclamation and faith. St Paul saw
clearly that *to be wrong about the resurrection was to be wrong about God*: 'If
Christ has not been raised . . . we are even found to be misrepresenting God
because we testified of God that he raised Christ' (1 Cor 15:14f.).

It would be bad enough to preach and believe 'in vain' (1 Cor 15:14), to
be still in our sins (1 Cor 15:17) and to 'perish' once we fall asleep in death (1
Cor 15:18). But there could be no more serious religious error than to 'misrepresent God'. It is understandable why St Paul shows himself to be so
negative about a Christian 'faith' which leaves aside or denies the
resurrection of Jesus and others (1 Cor 15:19, 32).

We are dealing here with a profound revolution in the very notion of
God. By the first century B.C. belief in resurrection was reflected in Jewish
prayer-life. The second of the eighteen Benedictions praised 'the God who
makes the dead live'. Many Jews — including the Pharisees but not the
Sadducees – believed that history would end with a *general* resurrection and
judgement. Then Christians introduced an unexpected element by
announcing that God had already raised the crucified Jesus to new and
glorious life, even though the world and its history had not yet ended.[1]

Paul reveals this development in belief about God by adopting the early Christian formula which described God as the One 'who raised Jesus from the dead'. At the beginning of the Letter to the Galatians the apostle uses this formula when he appeals to 'God the Father who raised him [sc. Jesus] from the dead' (1:1). He introduces the same divine attribute to warn the Corinthians against fornication: 'God raised the Lord and will also raise us up by his power' (1 Cor 6:14). In Romans the formula turns up as the basic element in the brief Christian creed which Paul quotes: 'If you confess with your lips that Jesus is Lord and believe in your heart that God raised him from the dead, you will be saved' (Rom 10:9).

In short, the first Christians identified and worshipped their God as a God of resurrection. But what precisely were they claiming at this point? And how did they come to know about, accept and interpret the resurrection of Jesus?

THE CLAIM

Every now and then, even before they begin to speak, lecturers on the resurrection get asked 'Well, did *it* happen?' But no one can be reasonably expected to answer that question without some clarification of what *it* was that is supposed to have happened. What then did Paul mean by the confession that 'God the Father raised Jesus from the dead'? What kind of thing was being claimed? And how far back did this claim go in the history of Christianity?

(1) *The antiquity of the claim.* Our earliest Christian document, St Paul's first Letter to the Thessalonians, dates from about the year 50. Nevertheless, his letters and the Acts of the Apostles (probably written after 70) incorporate resurrection formulae which stem from the thirties. What is the evidence for maintaining that texts written after A.D. 50 contain material originally formulated right at the beginning of the Christian Church?

The sermons attributed to Peter in the early chapters of Acts include brief expressions which seem to belong to the first years of Christianity (2:22–24, 32f., 36; 3:13–15; 4:10–12; 5:30–32). These formulations do not match the normal language and thought of Luke. For instance, the assertion during an address situated on the day of Pentecost that 'God *has made him both Lord and Christ*, this Jesus whom you crucified' (Acts 2:36) stands in tension with the angel's message to the shepherds which indicated that at birth Jesus was *already* 'Christ the Lord' (Luke 2:11). Apparently Acts 2:36 faithfully reports an early way of speaking of Jesus' messianic Lordship, even though Luke himself (and other later Christians) had come to recognize that one could speak this way of the infant Jesus. The messianic status was there from the start.[2]

The old formulations from Acts are built around an antithesis between an (evil) human action and God's action: 'You crucified and killed Jesus . . . but God raised him up' (2:23f.). Men condemned and crucified Jesus as a messianic pretender, blasphemer and threat to the nation's peace. But God then vindicated him by raising him from the dead and making him 'both Lord and Christ' (2:36). The scheme of these expressions is simple and 'primitive': a human condemnation and a divine vindication (through resurrection).

At times the formulations add the apostolic witness: 'This Jesus God raised up, and of that we are all witnesses' (2:32; see 3:15; 5:32). These early formulations do not, however, qualify the crucifixion as a 'dying *for us* and for our sins'. In Acts 2:23 it is simply stated that Jesus was 'delivered up according to the definitive plan and foreknowledge of God'. To say that the crucifixion happened according to the divine will is, of course, about as minimal a theological 'explanation' as could be imagined. One formula in Acts affirms something of the resurrection's saving consequences: 'God exalted him [sc. Jesus] at his right hand as Leader and Saviour, to give repentance to Israel and forgiveness of sins' (5:31). But in general the formulations lodged in the early chapters of Acts indicate neither the expiatory nature of Jesus' death nor the salvific value of his resurrection. Their minimal theological content points to their antiquity.

When Paul wrote his letters *before* the composition of the Acts of the Apostles, he also used formulae from early Christian preaching and confessions of faith – 'so we preach and so you believed' (1 Cor 15:11). These kerygmatic and credal expressions cited by Paul no longer identify as *crucifixion* the brutal and scandalous way Jesus was executed, as do some of the formulae in Acts (for example, 2:23, 36; 4:10). The traditional expressions picked up by the apostle have already begun to soften matters by simply announcing that Jesus 'was put to death' (literally, 'was handed over'; Rom 4:25), 'died' (1 Cor 15:3; 1 Thess 4:14) and was raised 'from the dead' (Rom 1:4).[3] Moreover, the fact that the formulations adopted by St Paul are more theologically developed suggests that they were fashioned slightly later than those which turn up in the opening chapters of Acts. In the formulations which are taken over by the apostle the expiatory quality of Jesus' death is regularly noted: 'Christ died *for our sins*' (1 Cor 15:3). This same is true of traditional expressions concerned with the resurrection. They affirm its redemptive nature: Jesus 'was put to death for our trespasses and raised for our justification' (Rom 4:25). Nevertheless, the resurrection formulae adopted by Paul also go back to the early years of Christianity (1 Thess 1:10; 4:14; Rom 1:3f.; 10:9; etc.). This summary treatment should be completed by briefly noting the most famous resurrection formula in the New Testament, 1 Corinthians 15:3–5:

3 For I delivered to you as of first importance
  what I also received,
      that Christ DIED   for our sins
                               in accordance with the scriptures,
4   *that* he was buried,
  that he was RAISED   on the third day
                               in accordance with the scriptures,
5   and *that* he appeared to Cephas [= Peter],
                               then to the twelve.

St Paul here introduces his testimony to the resurrection with technical
terms clearly indicating that he had handed on an early Christian tradition ('I
delivered to you what I also received'). Even without this introduction it
would have been obvious that he is quoting a community formulation.
Various terms are foreign to Paul's normal usage: 'sins', 'in accordance with
the scriptures' and 'the twelve'. The apostle speaks of 'sins' in the plural
only where he adopts traditional phraseology. In his own usage 'sin' appears
in the singular, as a personified force which invades and enslaves human
beings (see Rom 5 – 8). Elsewhere Paul introduces the Jewish scriptures with
such rubrics as 'it is written' (1 Cor 14:21), 'as God said' (2 Cor 6:16) or
simply 'it says' (Gal 3:16). 'In accordance with the scriptures' is no Pauline
expression. Lastly, the apostle nowhere else refers to 'the twelve'.

The literary shape and style of 1 Corinthians 15:3b–5 also point to a fixed
formulation. The phrases are concise and the various affirmations parallel
each other closely. Two verbs ('died' and 'was raised') provide the central
statements and give this early creed its basic structure. Three secondary
affirmations are attached to each of the primary statements, and provide
both historical and scriptural evidence for this death and resurrection.
Historically, the burial establishes the truth of Christ's death, the
appearances that of his resurrection. Further, both death and resurrection
occurred 'in accordance with the scriptures' – that is, according to the will
of God. The death took place 'for our sins' (= its expiatory value), the
resurrection 'on the third day' (= the biblical day for decisive divine
interventions in the history of salvation).

When and where did this traditional formulation about Christ's death
and resurrection reach Paul? It may have been transmitted to him during his
first visit to Jerusalem where he met Peter and James (Gal 1:18f.). Or
perhaps he learned it from the community which he met in Damascus
immediately after his conversion, or later when he visited the Christians in
Antioch (Acts 11:25f.; see 9:27). Whatever the circumstances, Paul received
the formulation contained in 1 Corinthians 15:3b–5 in the thirties or early
forties. It may be derived from an Aramaic original composed in Palestine.
An alternative view holds that Jewish Christians (perhaps in Antioch)
created this formula in a Greek which betrays Semitic influences. The

arguments for a Jerusalem origin have a certain plausibility: the references to 'Cephas' and 'the twelve' tie the formulation to that city. It is only here that Paul mentions 'the twelve', who enjoyed great significance for the Jerusalem community but beyond that circle were not so significant. A Jerusalem origin would not necessarily rule out composition in Greek. In any case the formula and the traditional material Paul adds about appearances to 'more than five hundred brethren', to James and to 'all the apostles' (1 Cor 15:6f.) imply an early origin, in that individual witnesses themselves – and not the Church as such – guarantee the truth of the Easter message.[4]

We could range beyond the Acts of the Apostles and Paul's letters to examine the early kerygmatic and credal formulae which also turn up in the Gospels and other New Testament books (for instance, Mark 16:6; Luke 24:34; 1 Pet 1:21). But the evidence from Acts and Paul is enough to support this conclusion. At the very origins of Christianity we do not find some general truth ('God is the Father of us all') or some basic moral injunction ('Let us love one another as brothers and sisters'), but a specific message proclaimed by Peter and the other apostles: the crucified Jesus had been raised from the dead. But what did this claim mean?

(2) *Merely a new commitment?*   Did the resurrection language of Paul and the other early Christian preachers simply function to declare their personal commitment to a new way of life? In that case they would have been *merely* expressing an intention and not making a fact-claiming statement at all when they spoke of resurrection.

The basic argument against this line of interpretation comes from the ordinary use of words. The general conventions governing language clearly suggest that the formula 'God raised Jesus from the dead' was offering some factual information. In uttering such a sentence early Christians did make a fact-claiming statement. To be sure, a commitment to 'walk in newness of life' (Rom 6:4) was associated with this claim. But primarily they were communicating and maintaining some fact.

(3) *Merely a matter of meaning?*   Other interpretations – or rather under-interpretations – of the original Easter message maintain that the proclamation of the resurrection simply expressed and expresses some inner meaning of Jesus' earthly history.

Thus to announce that 'God raised up Jesus' would be no more than a way of detecting retrospectively and claiming the real value of Jesus' life and death: he had truly shown himself to be the Messiah. In a similar way Bultmann tended to reduce the message of the resurrection to a mere expression of what Jesus' death meant.[5] The Easter proclamation was a value-judgement which did no more than interpret and communicate the true significance of the crucifixion.

Once again such interpretations do violence to the terms in which the New Testament proclaims the resurrection. Ordinary conventions of language and general linguistic usage indicate that *two* actions and events are intended by the statement 'You crucified Jesus but God raised him up'. The speaker is not shifting the level of discourse from event ('you crucified Jesus') to mere meaning ('but God raised him up'). Clearly these early Christian formulations claim some new event which followed Jesus' death and are not *simply* expounding the significance of that death when they talk of resurrection. Beyond question, the second event (resurrection) *also* throws light on the significance of the first (crucifixion). In fact this is a commonplace in ordinary human affairs, where later events very frequently clarify the deeper significance of earlier ones. But this interpretative function of such later events rests upon and in no way tampers with their status as actual events.

We can properly conclude that in announcing Jesus' resurrection, the early Christian witnesses intended to make a factually informative statement about something new which God had brought about after Jesus' death. But what was the content of this new event distinct from and subsequent to the death of Jesus?

(4) *The object of the divine intervention?* Granted that there was new content in the message of resurrection, what was it claimed that the divine activity had done? (a) Were the early Christian preachers *merely* stating something which had happened to themselves and other believers? After the crucifixion God had intervened to raise *them* from spiritual death and brought them to respond finally in faith to Jesus' appeal. In this view statements about the resurrection were *no more than* dramatic ways of reporting divinely caused changes in the spiritual lives of the disciples. They spoke and eventually wrote of Jesus' 'resurrection', but this was only a way of speaking about the emergence of their faith under the impact of divine grace. (b) Or did the Easter message of primitive Christianity make fact-claiming statements about Jesus himself? In this interpretation the resurrection proclamation first claimed something about the dead Jesus. God had intervened to raise him to a new and glorious life. The subsequent appearances of the risen Lord then dramatically changed the existence of the disciples. *Eventually* the New Testament spoke of this change in the believers as a resurrection *with Christ* (Eph 2:5f.; Col 2:12; 3:1). But the original and essential point of the Easter message centred on this: God had done something to and for the dead Jesus, raising him from the dead to a transformed and definitive life of glory. I can illustrate these two interpretations of the resurrection message as follows:

(a) God the Father

                          → The disciples remember Jesus and are

    The dead Jesus ←————brought to faith (= their 'resurrection')

(b) God the Father

    The dead Jesus raised——→ Jesus appears and through the Spirit brings
                           the disciples to faith

The decisive argument against (a) comes to this. Choosing resurrection language for such a purpose would have been extraordinarily odd. It would have caused great confusion to Jewish audiences and been incomprehensible to Gentile audiences. If the early Christians had primarily wanted to state something about the rise of their own faith, they could easily have done just that. They had appropriate terms available for such purposes. 'Faith' (*pistis*), 'to believe' (*pisteuein*) and their synonyms were to be among the commonest words in the New Testament: *pistis* turned up 243 times and *pisteuein* 241 times.

The Easter formulations which go back to the first Christians state something which happened to Jesus himself. In the same breath they reported the crucifixion and the resurrection. For them the resurrection affected Jesus just as personally as did his crucifixion. We misrepresent their witness if we take it to mean simply that God raised them to faith in the aftermath of Jesus' life and death. Their primary purpose was to announce what God had done to Jesus, not to relate fundamental religious changes in themselves.

To sum up. The general usage of biblical language and the conventions governing the recognition of words should lead us to conclude that the early Christian preachers (and later the New Testament writers) meant just what their words about Jesus' resurrection said. God had intervened to rescue him from the dead. In a new and glorious existence the crucified Jesus had presented himself alive to those who had known him to die by crucifixion. The first Christians used resurrection language primarily to communicate such information about Jesus.

(5) *The resurrection event.* No author in the New Testament reports any claim to have witnessed the resurrection of Jesus as such. Various individuals and groups met him gloriously alive and/or discovered his tomb to be empty. In the light of these and other experiences, they believed and proclaimed him to be risen from the dead. But what did they understand this resurrection to involve?

We draw together much of the New Testament claim by speaking of *the passage of Jesus himself from the condition of death to that of new and definitive life.* The Jesus who now lives in a transformed and glorious state maintains, on the one hand, a personal continuity with his prior earthly, bodily existence. On the other hand, his risen condition definitively anticipates the end of all things to come with God's new creation.

A double set of affirmations are involved. Historical elements enter into the picture, inasmuch as it was 'this Jesus . . . crucified and killed by the hands of lawless men' whom God 'raised up' (Acts 2:23f.). At the same time, the resurrection makes Jesus transcend space and time (= the sphere of history), and – as 'the first fruits of those who have fallen asleep' (1 Cor 15:20) – brings him to actualize now in anticipation the ultimate future of human beings and their world. As much as anything else, this eschatological aspect of the resurrection turns it into a unique event, which is qualitatively different from all events within history, including the greatest miracles.

Since it has truly inaugurated the new and final creation, the resurrection of Jesus eludes any adequate description and explanation. Asking how this resurrection occurred is 'harder' than asking how creation itself occurred. The final mystery exceeds even the mystery of the world's origins.

In the next two chapters we shall see how the resurrection (with the crucifixion) effectively communicated redemption and identified Jesus with the being of God. But before moving to those matters, I should raise the question: How did the disciples come to know that Jesus was gloriously alive? What led them to accept and proclaim his resurrection?

THE EASTER EXPERIENCES

No approach to the origin of faith in Jesus' resurrection promises very much unless it recognizes just what a shattering blow his crucifixion was for his followers. Chapter 3 indicated the horror and crisis of faith generated by such an execution. If anything, Paul understated matters when he described 'Christ crucified' as 'a stumbling block to Jews and folly to Gentiles' (1 Cor 1:23). Even without any evidence from the Gospels (for example, Luke 24:17ff.), we could only expect the disciples to be in a state of shock and spiritual disillusionment over the crisis of the crucifixion. It required new events (the appearances of the risen Jesus and the discovery of the empty tomb) to reveal the resurrection and catalyse the disciples' robust faith in the risen Lord.

Of course, there have been attempts to explain belief in Jesus' resurrection simply in terms of the disciples' preparation before his death and reflection after it. They knew he had risen, because they were somehow prepared for it and through reflection found the clue to the tragedy of Calvary in the conviction that God must have raised and exalted Jesus. Certainly the elements of preparation and reflection should not be passed over. But any view that appeals merely to these elements and postulates a relatively easy continuity between the disciples' commitment to Jesus during his earthly

ministry and their faith in him risen from the dead must play down the
atrocious disgrace of his crucifixion.

(1) *The appearances.* St Paul and the Evangelists nominate the appearances
of the risen Christ as *the* major catalyst which led the first Christians to
accept and proclaim his resurrection. What was the nature of their
experience of the risen Jesus? Can we probe these post-resurrection
encounters and specify many, or even any, details? How did the Easter
witnesses perceive the risen Christ?

According to a classical saying, 'there is nothing in the intellect which
was not first found in our sense knowledge' (*nihil est in intellectu, quod prius
non fuerit in sensu*). We can properly apply this to the knowledge of believers.
There is nothing in the intellect and the confession of faith which has not
first been communicated through the senses. In what way(s) was the
presence of the risen Christ made known to and through the sense
knowledge of the Easter witnesses?

(a) In reporting the encounters with the risen Christ, the New
Testament shows a massive preference for *the language of sight*. In a key
passage Paul four times uses the technical term *ōphthē* (1 Cor 15:4–8), which
could be taken to mean 'he was seen by' (the witnesses) or even 'he was
made manifest' by God (= God revealed him). However, rather than
adopting these versions which express, respectively, the activity of the
Easter witnesses and that of God, nearly all translations agree that this
passive form of the verb 'see' (*horaō*) should be taken in terms of the risen
Christ's own (active) initiative: 'He appeared, he let himself be seen'. We
find *ōphthē* also being used occasionally in this sense by Luke to express the
Easter encounters (Luke 24:34; Acts 13:31; see also 9:17; 26:16).

Normally the Gospels prefer the active form 'to see', which as such
emphasizes the activity of the witnesses. This usage predominates from the
promise 'you will see him' (Mark 16:7) right through to Mary Magdalene's
report, 'I have seen the Lord' (John 20:18; see also Matt 28:7, 10, 17; Luke
24:37, 39; John 20:14, 20, 25, 27, 29; 1 Cor 9:1). When Jesus made himself
visible, they saw him.

Other verbs like *phaneroō* ('manifest') and *deiknumi* ('show') occur
sporadically in the Easter narratives and indicate a visible perception of the
risen Christ (John 21:1, 14; Acts 10:40; John 20:20). At the beginning of
the meeting on the Emmaus road we read: 'Their eyes were kept from
recognizing him' (Luke 24:16). At the end 'their eyes were opened and they
recognized him; and he vanished out of their sight' (Luke 24:31). The story
of the ascension speaks of Jesus leaving the disciples and being taken 'out of
their sight' (Acts 1:9).

To be sure, there are many particular issues to be faced in the passages I have cited or referred to. But clearly there is an overall stress on the language of sight.

In Matthew 28, Luke 24, John 20 – 21 and Acts 1 the risen Christ is represented as speaking to his disciples. On the Damascus road Saul *hears* the voice of the risen Jesus (Acts 9:4; see 9:7; 22:7, 9; 26:14). But in our Easter texts, seeing the risen Lord bulks much larger than hearing his voice and words.

This last point, incidentally, imposes a serious qualification on Küng's comparison between the experiences of the Old Testament prophets and those of Jesus' disciples when they encountered him after his resurrection (*OBC*, pp. 376–378). Characteristically the prophets heard the word of God both in their initial callings and later. They were hearers more than seers (of visions). It was exactly the opposite with the Easter witnesses. The New Testament portrays them much more as having seen the risen Lord rather than as having heard his voice or word.

In the resurrection narratives the sense of *touch* is very occasionally involved. Mary Magdalene and the other Mary 'took hold of' Jesus' feet (Matt 28:9). He invited 'the eleven' and 'those who were with them' to 'handle' him (Luke 24:39), but we are not told that they did so. The doubting Thomas was also invited to touch the risen body of the Lord. But once again we are not told that he did so. Rather, he blurted out his confession of faith, 'My Lord and my God!' (John 20:27f.). The risen Jesus told Mary Magdalene, 'Do not hold me' (John 20:17). Here the Gospel is not stressing the condition of the risen Christ and does not portray him as saying 'Do not cling to my feet' or 'Do not cling to my body'. The point at issue is her way of relating to him rather than the state of his risen body (and the possibility of touching it).

(b) When they report the encounters with the risen Christ, our New Testament sources employ primarily the terminology of sight rather than that of hearing or touching. But what did they intend to convey by the claim to have 'seen' the Lord? Was it merely a matter of the witnesses being brought by God to see the truth *about* Jesus, or did they have a vision *of* the risen Jesus himself? If so, was there a genuine visual quality to that seeing, so that the encounter with the Lord entailed a visible component?

At this point we would tamper with the New Testament claim if we took it simply to mean that the truth about Jesus was revealed. St Paul maintains that he saw the risen Jesus (1 Cor 9:1; 15:8). This encounter was not merely a revelation of the truth *about* the Son of God but a revelation *of* the Son himself to Paul (Gal 1:12, 16).

Elsewhere I have summarized the case against those who argue that Peter and other disciples were deceived by their own longings and projections. In *merely subjective visions* – it is alleged – they 'saw' and proclaimed the risen

Christ, simply because they needed his resurrection in order to cope psychologically with the horror of his crucifixion (*EJ*, pp. 30–32). Other reasons could supplement the argument provided in *The Easter Jesus*. For instance, both psychologically and publicly it would have been much easier for the disciples to think of Jesus as another martyred prophet and to proclaim him as such. Admittedly his death on Calvary called into question his claims to speak and act for God. Jesus' opponents may even have decided on and called for this method of execution in order to put a stop to any such claims. Nevertheless, Jesus had aligned himself with the noble company of persecuted and martyred prophets. John the Baptist had recently exemplified once again the fate of such divine envoys. It would have been simpler for the disciples to have adjusted their image of Jesus and proposed him merely in such terms. But they did much more than merely propose him as a martyred prophet. They announced his resurrection. To have accepted and proclaimed the crucified Jesus as risen from the dead and messianic Saviour of the world *neither* matched what we can reasonably presume to have been the psychological state of the disciples, *nor* emerged naturally from the religious possibilities offered by their Jewish faith and environment. Küng correctly points out that 'the idea of a resurrection of the *Messiah* – still more of a *failed Messiah* – was an absolute novelty in the Jewish tradition' (*OBC*, p. 372).

In other words, those who would explain away in merely psychological terms the appearances and subsequent proclamation of the risen Christ rightly recognize the disciples' need to find some way of coping with the awful shock of Calvary. But such merely psychological explanations of the Easter appearances, among other things, fail to take account of the psychological and religious possibilities made available for the disciples by their Jewish faith and historical environment.

It took an objective encounter with the risen Jesus to catalyse the disciples' faith in him and proclamation of his resurrection. But could we understand their 'seeing' him to have consisted of internal visions; that is to say, objective perceptions presenting the risen Christ (*and produced by him*) but which did not involve something 'out there' to be seen? In such a case, supposing that the Jerusalem authorities had been monitoring the upper room and/or the disciples' movements in Galilee, they would have recognized nothing more than a dramatic transformation in the disciples' emotions, activities and patterns of behaviour. However, in biblical Greek 'to see' normally involves some kind of seeing with the eyes.[6] This suggests that the Easter visions included some kind of sense perception of something (or rather Someone) 'out there'. This is not to allege that the risen Christ made himself an external object, available for inspection by neutral observers. Nor is it to specify what the visible component of those Easter visions was like. But we can reasonably take the appearances of the risen Christ to have been objective, external visions of some kind.

It would do no harm to characterize these appearances as 'eschatological visions', in order to remind ourselves that the encounters with the risen Christ were much more than visions that remained totally *within* history and the structures of the present world. Christ manifested himself as one who now transcended the ordinary limits of space and time and already belonged to that final future of God's new creation.

Some might prefer to speak of 'Christophanies'. This term could serve to recall that the Easter encounters depended upon the initiative of the risen Christ. He freely emerged from the divine sphere of his glorified state to show himself where and to whom he wished. Like the divine epiphanies (or theophanies) in the Old Testament, these Christophanies called for the personal involvement of the recipients. They were brought to faith in the resurrection and received the mission to proclaim the resurrection of the crucified Jesus.

It is important to note that the appearances of the risen Christ did not dispense the Easter witnesses from faith. Paul's proclamation of the God 'who raised the Lord Jesus' came out of and was based upon the apostle's own faith: 'Since we have the same spirit of faith as he had who wrote, "I believed, and so I spoke," we too believe, and so we speak' (2 Cor 4:13f.). John's Gospel does not picture Thomas as being exempted from faith through his encounter with the risen Christ. Because he had seen, Thomas came to believe (20:28f.). The believing resulted from the seeing. Obviously Thomas' passage to faith differed from those who do not see and yet believe. Nevertheless, he too was called to faith.

A phrase from Aquinas' *Summa Theologiae* expresses this point as follows: 'the apostles saw the living Christ after his resurrection with the eyes of faith (*oculata fide*)' (III, 55, 2 ad 1). It was the living Christ they saw. Yet their faith in him as risen from the dead was not simply the automatic result of their experience (namely, his appearance to them), still less something forced on them or forced out of them. As John presents the meeting with Mary Magdalene, the mere sight of the risen Jesus did not necessarily lead her to 'know' him and believe (20:14). In general, the disciples were called to put aside doubts, fears and questionings (Matt 28:17; Luke 24:37ff.; John 20:24ff.), to recognize the risen Christ, and freely to believe in him.

Here it could be as well to add that there were other factors beyond the appearances of the risen Christ and the discovery of the empty tomb (a confirmatory sign to which I shall return later in this chapter) that entered into the making of the disciples' Easter faith. *Before* the Easter appearances they had all shared the Jewish faith in the living God. Most, if not all of them, presumably accepted with the Pharisees a belief that at the end of history there would be a resurrection of all the dead together with a general judgement. All the disciples were familiar with the Jewish Scriptures which might have helped them to expect that Jesus would rise from the dead (Luke

24:25ff., 44ff.; John 20:9). Those who were with Jesus during his earthly ministry had heard his proclamation and witnessed his signs.

After the appearances of the risen Christ (and discovery of his empty tomb), personal and social experiences confirmed their Easter faith for the disciples. They received the Holy Spirit, knew themselves to be forgiven and freed from sin, saw the signs of divine power in the life of their communities, and felt in many ways what it was to exist 'in Christ' (St Paul, *passim*). There was much that continued to support, legitimate and interpret their faith in the risen Lord.

In brief, the Easter appearances (together with the discovery of the empty tomb) acted as the major catalyst of faith in the risen Lord. At the same time, we should acknowlege the other factors which *also* contributed to the making and interpretation of that faith.

Here a word about Willi Marxsen's *The Resurrection of Jesus of Nazareth* (London and Philadelphia, 1970) seems appropriate. He takes 'resurrection' to have been no more than one possible way of interpreting the experience of seeing Jesus and finding faith. Undoubtedly the verbal translations of the encounters with the living Christ were conditioned by the thought-forms of the actual recipients (and later by the community traditions of the early Christians and the particular intentions of the New Testament writers). In that sense, 'resurrection' interpreted the experience of meeting Jesus gloriously alive. But surely to encounter him as living again in glory after his shameful death called for such a necessary inference and was not just an optional interpretation? God had raised Jesus from death and vindicated his cause.

(2) The appearances challenged.   Before moving on from the claim that Jesus appeared gloriously alive after his death and burial, it seems useful to discuss two ways in which the testimony to such appearances has been challenged. Schillebeeckx reduces these appearances to no more than verbal expressions of prior events (which he somewhat misleadingly calls 'conversion visions'). Then there are those like Louis Evely who deny anything special about the experience of the Easter witnesses: their encounters with the risen Jesus in no way differ from the encounters which later Christians experience.

(a)   At the outset it would confuse matters not to note that Schillebeeckx clearly accepts the personal, bodily resurrection of Jesus (*Jesus*, pp. 644f.). Any debate concerns the manner in which this resurrection *became known* to the disciples. As Schillebeeckx reconstructs matters, things went like this. After Jesus' death Peter and other disciples had a 'concrete experience of forgiveness', discussed this renewed offer of salvation, underwent a deep conversion, and concluded: 'Jesus must therefore be alive . . . . A dead man does not proffer forgiveness' (p. 391). On the initiative of the risen but invisible Jesus, they were thus converted. They then expressed this experience of forgiveness, faith, conversion and revelation by talking of 'appearances'. But this talk of 'appearances' was no more than a means of expressing what Jesus had already done to them (pp. 354–390).

(b)   With all due respect to Schillebeeckx and his learning, there are serious arguments against this reconstruction.

(i)   What prompted the disciples to conclude from some renewed offer of forgiveness that Jesus was risen and alive? Why not associate such an experience with the God whom Jesus had called 'Abba' (Father dear)? Even though Jesus was dead and gone, God had forgiven the disciples for their lifelong failures and their particular collapse at the time of the passion. Appearances of the risen Jesus clarified his status in a way that no experience of forgiveness could. But Schillebeeckx rejects any actual appearances in the sense of meeting Jesus alive after his death and burial.

(ii)   What is more, I find it hard to make sense of any 'concrete experience of forgiveness' which does not involve a personal encounter with the one who forgives me. Forgiveness takes place in an immediate and (as such) conscious contact with the person who offers forgiveness. By ruling out real appearances of the risen Jesus, Schillebeeckx makes any claim to an experience of forgiveness very questionable.

(iii)   If Schillebeeckx is correct in finding the key to the Easter experience of the disciples in their 'concrete experience of forgiveness', we could surely expect to detect much fuller indications of this in the New Testament texts. However, *forgiveness is a marginal theme when the Evangelists and Paul report the events which followed Jesus' death and burial.* In Mark 16:1–8 and Matthew 28:1–20 there is nothing as such about forgiveness. Luke plays down the disciples' need for forgiveness by omitting their flight at the time of Jesus' arrest. Luke alone reports how 'the Lord turned and looked at Peter' after his threefold denial (22:61). Are we to understand the glance as not only reproachful but also forgiving? At the crucifixion Jesus prays: 'Father, forgive them; for they know not what they do' (23:34). But is there anything on this theme in Luke's resurrection stories? The disciples are to preach 'repentance and forgiveness of sins' (24:47). The Acts of the Apostles reports them as doing just that (2:38 etc.). But there is very little that suggests forgiveness in the first disciples' own Easter experiences. The motif of the risen Christ sitting at table and eating with them may *also* imply that he has forgiven them (Luke 24:30, 41f.; see John 21:9–13). But the main thrust of this theme is to underline the bodily reality of the resurrection, to illustrate their qualification as Easter witnesses (see Acts 10:41), and to indicate that later believers will in their own way recognize the risen Jesus 'in the breaking of the bread' (Luke 24:35).

John's Gospel likewise yields very little on the theme of forgiveness when it comes to the Easter story. Presumably it is also involved in the comprehensive greeting of 'Peace' (20:19, 21, 26). But forgiveness is explicitly mentioned only in the context of the disciples' mission to others (20:23). The interchange between Jesus and Peter probably implies pardon. That disciple's threefold denial is now matched by a triple protestation of love (21:25–27). All in all, however, one can hardly allege that forgiveness bulks large in the two Easter chapters of John's Gospel. But it should, if Schillebeeckx's reconstruction is right.

Paul's letters deal with his Easter experience a number of times (1 Cor 9:1; 15:8; Gal 1:12, 16; probably Phil 3:8; perhaps 2 Cor 4:6). In three of these places the apostle recalls how he had persecuted the Church prior to his encounter with the risen Christ (1 Cor 15:9; Gal 1:13; Phil 3:6). But Paul never interprets his Easter experience as involving forgiveness. He had persecuted Christians through sincere, if misguided, religious zeal (Gal 1:14; Phil 3:6).

(iv) In Paul's case, however, Schillebeeckx reconstructs matters in terms of legitimating the apostle's mission. In 1 Corinthians 15:5–8 Paul is said to provide 'a list of authorities who all proclaim the same thing, namely, that the Crucified One is alive' (*Jesus*, p. 348). This proclamation and mission are *subsequently* legitimated by what 'has come to be called an "appearing" of Jesus' (p. 350). Thus it was not some appearance of Jesus which commissioned Paul for his apostolate. Rather Paul expressed (and legitimated) his mission by speaking of an 'appearance' to him of the risen Lord – even though such an episode never actually took place (pp. 361f.).

To speak frankly, all of this is not what Paul intends to say but what Schillebeeckx wants him to say. The apostle's list of authorities in 1 Corinthians 15:5–8 proclaim that 'the Crucified One' is risen and alive *because he has appeared to them*. Paul himself is an apostle because he has 'seen Jesus our Lord' (1 Cor 9:1). The revelation of God's Son generated Paul's mission to the Gentiles (Gal 1:16). It was not that mission which generated Paul's talk about a revelatory appearance to him of the risen Son of God.

If Schillebeeckx is correct, Paul has shown himself to be an extraordinarily incompetent and confusing writer. For two thousand years, readers have (wrongly) interpreted Paul by the ordinary conventions governing the use of language and taken him to mean that a special revelatory encounter with (or appearance of) the risen Lord effected a conversion to the Christian faith and legitimated a mission to the Gentiles. According to Schillebeeckx, Paul intended to say exactly the opposite! The apostle verbalized his conversion and mission by eventually speaking of an appearance of the risen Christ.

Not only with Paul but also with the evangelists, general usage can normally be expected to clarify their intentions. If they had wanted to say that Peter and other disciples were converted under the impact of grace, the words were available to say just that (*metanoein, charis*). Instead, they reported that the risen Christ appeared to his followers and so brought them to faith. Were the evangelists such confused and confusing writers that they really intended to say that the disciples first believed in the risen Christ, were converted and then later expressed this conversion-experience 'in the form of an appearance vision' (*Jesus*, p. 390)? Surely the ordinary conventions of language indicate the evangelists meant to say that the appearances to the disciples effected their conversion, and not that their conversion was later verbalized by reporting appearances of the risen Christ.

(v)   Schillebeeckx in fact is aware that his 'hypothesis' 'constitutes a break with a centuries-old hermeneutical tradition' (p. 710, fn. 119). But why does he insist on interpreting the evangelists and Paul to say the opposite of what normal conventions indicate them to say? Some theological convictions tucked away *in this footnote* disclose the principles which are in control.

First, Schillebeeckx assures us that 'the appearances as such are . . . not an *object* of Christian faith'. It is worth remarking, however, that at least two New Testament credal passages included appearances (1 Cor 15:5; Luke 24:34). Yet in general it was not like that. Neither in the New Testament nor in our standard creeds have the appearances as such been proposed precisely as objects of faith. Christians believe in the risen Christ rather than in his appearances. Nevertheless, his appearances to the original witnesses proved *the major means* of first bringing about their Easter faith. Today people continue to believe in the risen Christ, at least partly because they accept the testimony to those appearances coming from those apostolic witnesses. Schillebeeckx's comment about the object of faith slides over this point about the means of faith.

Second, he maintains that 'there are always intermediary historical factors in occurrences of divine grace. The appearances form no exception to this scheme of grace.' The key word here is 'always'. Of course, there are *always* intermediary historical factors. In those occurrences of divine grace which were the appearances of the risen Christ many such factors entered in: the spiritual crisis of the disciples, the places they found themselves in, the company they were keeping, and so on. Since the risen Christ encountered human beings *in history*, such intermediary historical factors were present. But were there *only* such factors? Schillebeeckx's doctrine of grace may be slipping from rightly affirming that intermediary historical factors are *always* present to implying that *nothing but* such factors are present. And that is a very different matter. It would rule out in principle the possibility of a trans-historical factor – the special intervention of the risen Christ from his state which lies beyond the normal limits of history.

Third, Schillebeeckx demands: 'What would a straight appearance of Jesus in the flesh prove? Only *believers* see the one who appears; a faith-motivated interpretation enters into the very heart of the event.' I wonder about a number of items here. 'A straight appearance of Jesus' would at least 'prove' that he was risen from the dead and truly living. It is more accurate to say that 'only those who *become* believers' see the one who appears. Mary Magdalene and the other Mary (Matt 28:1–10) are not yet believers when they discover the empty tomb and meet the risen Lord. It took an appearance to prompt the faith of Peter, Cleopas and his companion (Luke 24:13–35). Various New Testament sources agree that Paul was a persecutor and certainly not yet a believer when he saw 'the one who appears'. Lastly, interpretation 'enters into the very heart' of every event we experience. A non-interpreted event is impossible. But that fact neither decides for or against the claim that the risen Christ appeared to a number of disciples. It is simply a universal condition of human knowledge and existence.

Fourth, in the same footnote Schillebeeckx argues that we not only raise all sorts of false problems about the nature of 'seeing' the risen Christ but also 'emasculate' faith if 'we insist on grounding it in pseudo-empiricism'. This raises the whole question about the role of visible signs, empirical evidence and possible grounds of faith. If God provides appearances of the risen Christ to indicate the fact of the resurrection, should we disdain all that as a 'pseudo-empiricism' which threatens to deprive our faith of its integral and virile purity? There is much to discuss and debate here. Let me simply state my concern. It seems that Schillebeeckx is uneasy about two things: empirical grounds of faith, and a God who may also intervene in such a strikingly special way as through appearances of the risen Christ. In spite of my esteem for Schillebeeckx, I strongly suspect that certain prior theological convictions control his interpretation of the New Testament texts which report the Easter appearances.

(3) *The appearances reduced.*   More frequently the appearances of the risen Christ are 'tampered with' by being identified with the experiences of the Lord enjoyed by later Christians. As regards the appearance which Paul lists in 1 Corinthians 15:8, John Macquarrie observes: 'It is not unreasonable to suppose that it is . . . on a par with encounters which subsequent believers may have had with the risen Christ'.[7] Louis Evely maintains: 'The apparitions of which the apostles speak are apparitions that we ourselves can experience'.[8] But do St Paul and the evangelists agree that the Easter encounters were totally the same as later Christian experiences of the risen Lord?

In their Easter stories Luke and John are concerned to indicate the analogies between the experiences of the witnesses to the risen Lord and subsequent Christian experiences of him. He will reveal himself when his people gather for meals and worship (Luke 24:33ff.; John 20:19ff.; 21:12f.). They will know him in the reading of the scriptures (Luke 24:27, 32, 44ff.), the forgiveness of sins (John 20:23) and 'the breaking of the bread' (Luke 24:30f., 35).

Nevertheless, we are dealing here only with analogies and not with a total identity. (a) Paul writes: 'Last of all, as to one untimely born, he appeared also to me' (1 Cor 15:8). Presumably the apostle means to say that with that appearance the series of official Easter encounters came to a close. Paul's later experiences of the Lord (2 Cor 12:1–9) may have been extraordinary, but they were different and did not as such validate his role as apostolic witness. They were simply not on a par with his Damascus road meeting with the risen Jesus. All the more will this hold true of the various ways *later believers* experience the risen Christ. For Paul the Damascus road encounter was not the first of many experiences of the same kind, but the last of a number of experiences of a unique kind.

(b) When writing to his communities, Paul never says to them: 'Christ has appeared to you', or 'Christ will appear to you', or 'Christ should appear to you'. These other believers share with Paul the gift of the indwelling Spirit and like him are also incorporated into Christ through faith and baptism. But they have not experienced that encounter with the risen Christ which made him a founding father of the Church.

Luke introduces a similar distinction when he distinguishes between the experiences (and functions) of that limited number of resurrection witnesses and those of all other persons (believers or non-believers). He presents Peter as declaring that the risen Jesus was 'made manifest' 'not to all the people but to us who were chosen by God as witnesses' (Acts 10:40f.).

(c) John acknowledges how the end of the apostolic age entails the final passing of all those who had seen the risen Christ and believed. From then on Christians could only count as those 'who have not seen and yet believe' (20:29).

(d) Apart from Paul, all the resurrection witnesses we know of *identify* the risen Christ with the earthly Jesus. Like the 'disciple whom Jesus loved' they were in a position to say 'It is the Lord' (John 21:7). Obviously only those who had known Jesus during his ministry could recognize this continuity between his historical and risen existence. This function of the Easter experiences simply could not apply to any later Christians, no matter how direct or intense their experiences of the risen Lord might be.

(e) Finally, the *special mission* received by the apostolic witnesses matches the special nature of their meetings with the risen Christ. They alone are called to testify to that experience and so *found* the Church. In doing this they do not rely on the experience and testimony of others. As resurrection witnesses and Church founders they have a once-and-for-all function, which associates them intimately with the once-and-for-all character of the total Christ-event and which cannot as such be passed on. Later Christians, including Church leaders, can only have the responsibility to proclaim the resurrection and maintain the Church in existence. The Easter appearances brought the resurrection witnesses both a special experience and a special function (which died with them).

(4) *The discovery of the empty tomb.* It was (and is) neither possible nor necessary to turn the discovery of the empty tomb into the decisive motive for faith. By itself, an empty tomb is an ambiguous phenomenon. Simply by itself, it could not and cannot ground Easter faith. So far from being a later legend which acted as a 'proof' for the resurrection, the empty tomb was something which itself required interpretation.

How strong is the evidence that Mary Magdalene alone (John 20:1f.) or with other women (Matt 28:1; Mark 16:1; Luke 24:10) found the tomb of Jesus to be empty?

(a)   We can appeal to the criterion of multiple attestation (see Chapter 2). Different traditions attest both the finding of the empty tomb (Mark 16:1–8; John 20:1, 11–13) and the womens' report to the disciples (Luke 24:10, 23; John 20:18).

(b)   Some have argued that the story of the empty tomb was simply a legend illustrating a conviction of faith. It was elaborated on the basis of a Jewish notion that bodily resurrection was impossible, unless the actual corpse of the dead person were raised. Hence the corpse of Jesus 'must' have disappeared from the tomb. However, the role of women in the Gospel traditions speaks against such a hypothesis and for the historical authenticity of the discovery story. If this story were a legend created by early Christians, they would have attributed the discovery of the empty tomb to male disciples rather than to women, who in that culture did not count as valid witnesses. Legend-makers do not usually invent positively unhelpful material.

(c)   Early Jewish polemic against the resurrection seems to have supposed that the tomb of Jesus was known and known to be empty (Matt 28:11–15). Naturally opponents of the Christians could explain the missing corpse as a case of theft. But there is no early evidence that anyone, believer or non-believer, alleged that the tomb of Jesus was unknown or known to contain his remains.

(d)   Some have argued that at least in Jerusalem the preaching of Jesus' resurrection could not have lasted a day if his tomb were not empty. Opponents could at once have produced his corpse and so put a stop to the apostolic proclamation of his resurrection. The force of this particular argument depends on our answers to three questions. (i) Were the enemies of the Christian movement so strongly motivated that they would have done anything to stop it? Or would even they have been inhibited about opening a tomb to inspect and produce for public display the remains of someone they had executed? (ii) How strongly enforced was Roman legislation against the violation of tombs? Did the presence of the Roman army effectively rule out any opening of Jesus' tomb by outsiders? What is more, Pilate would have had a special reason for preventing and/or severely punishing the violation of *that* grave. To produce the corpse of Jesus in the city of Jerusalem could easily have provoked a riot. (iii) If we suppose that the apostolic proclamation of Jesus' resurrection began only at Pentecost, any remains of someone buried weeks before at the time of the Passover would hardly have been identifiable. Producing a corpse in a more or less advanced state of decomposition would not have worked.

I have developed somewhat the pros and cons of this last argument to illustrate how debates about the empty tomb can go when they remain simply on the *historical* level. As I maintained in *The Easter Jesus* (pp. 38–45), there is a reasonable but not coercive case to be made for the tomb of Jesus having been discovered empty. In that same book I also argued that theological convictions often predetermine one's conclusions. The real demand is not to assess judiciously the force of the historical arguments but to make theological sense of the empty tomb (*EJ*, pp. 90–100).

(5) *The significance of the empty tomb.* Those who reject the empty tomb may do so because they fail to appreciate what it expresses about the nature of redemption, the identity of Jesus, the continuity between his earthly and risen existence, and the challenge of Easter faith.

(a) The empty tomb of Jesus powerfully symbolizes the way God goes about the *redemption* of human beings and their world. Of course, we do not know precisely how Jesus' corpse was raised, transformed and entered into his new, glorified existence. Any such exact details of that mysterious event evade us. But we do know at least this. The corpse of Jesus stood for the ultimate human sin. Certain individuals represented us all in rejecting and crucifying the divine Saviour. Yet God took his corpse and, as it were, used it as the raw material for the new creation. To raise and transform that corpse, which symbolized the climax of deliberate evil, was to announce what redemption finally comes to. It is *not escape from a wicked world, but God's willingness to transform this material world with all its history of sin and suffering.*

In one of her plays, *The Devil to Pay*, which she subtitled *A Faustian Drama*, Dorothy Sayers has the Judge observe to Dr Faustus:

> There is no waste with God; He cancels nothing
> But redeems all.

We might almost paraphrase this remark by saying 'God is no throw-away God'. The wounded corpse of Jesus, no matter how honourable his burial, signified human hatred and injustice. Its transformation in resurrection spoke of the effective desire of God to turn evil into good and raise a fallen world.

One's attitude towards *matter* and its possibilities can prove decisive here. Those who in various ways downgrade the material dimension of human beings and their environment will find it easier to deny the empty tomb. They will reduce Jesus' resurrection to the existence of a separated (and glorified) spirit, or portray his soul as assuming a *totally* new body. The last possibility looks rather like a reincarnation of Jesus' soul, albeit in a heavenly body rather than – as is usually the case with reincarnation views – in an earthly body. Like all theories of reincarnation, the belief that Jesus' soul assumed a totally new (heavenly) body offers an over-spiritual approach to reality which lacks respect for matter.

Those, however, whose attitude towards the material creation is strongly positive will be much more prone to see in the transforming resurrection of Jesus' corpse the supreme example of how matter can be spiritualized and enter the life of God. In creation God produces the material world. In the incarnation matter is personally united to the Son of God. In the resurrection the corpse of Jesus is raised and transformed to become the risen Christ, whose glorified humanity has been divinized in the highest possible way. When risen from the dead, Jesus remains truly human. Yet his resurrected humanity (which is both spiritual *and material*) now enters into the divine life (Rom 6:10) in the most intense manner.

(b)   About the corpse laid in the tomb on Good Friday two things could be said which could never be said about any other corpse in the history of the human race. First, this corpse had been the body which suffered on the cross once and for all and to save all. It would seem appropriate that this corpse which was the means of universal salvation should share in a glorified existence and belong to the enduring work of redemption carried on by the risen Christ through the Holy Spirit.

Second, *this* lifeless corpse had been the body of the Son of God during his earthly life. That fact sets this corpse apart from all other corpses the world has ever contained. It is hardly surprising that the matter of such a corpse should somehow become part of Jesus' speedy resurrection from the dead. Recognizing the past history and personal identity of this corpse would lead us to expect its 'incorporation' into a transforming resurrection.

(c)   It may be hard to refute in principle those who imagine a scenario with a risen Christ enjoying a new, glorified, bodily existence, even though his corpse decays in the tomb. Can we really say that God *could* never bring about such a situation, no matter what? But in fact the empty tomb and what it implies – that the corpse of Jesus has been taken up into the glorified existence of the risen Christ – carries with it something which one misses in that imaginary scenario. The empty tomb very powerfully expresses *the personal continuity* between the earthly Jesus and the risen Christ. Alongside or even despite all the transformation of a resurrection which makes the risen Christ the anticipated beginning of the end of the world, he remains personally identical with the Jesus who lived and died. He does not appear as some kind of replica in his place. There is a genuine identity in transformation.

What then of all those others who will be raised 'in the resurrection of the last day' (John 11:24)? Surely the continuity of each one with some particular person who once lived will not depend on some continuity with a particular corpse which has long since decayed and disappeared? Even here, however, in spite of the gap between the dissolution of the earlier (dead) body and the emergence of the later risen body, there must be some bodily continuity. Otherwise we will not genuinely have the *same* person, but only a duplicate or spiritual successor. In chapter 3 of *What are they saying about the Resurrection?* I have suggested ways of 'getting at' such continuity in transformation.

Nevertheless, there is no reason to suppose that the participation of an earlier (dead) body in our resurrection should match exactly the case of Christ's resurrection. Under (b) above I have drawn attention to two items (his role as Saviour and Son of God) which set his resurrection apart from ours. Difficulties in accounting for some bodily continuity in our resurrection do not as such affect the case of Jesus' resurrection from the dead.

(d) Lastly, the New Testament frankly recognizes that the fact of the empty tomb had to be interpreted through the appearances of the living Christ. Otherwise it remains an ambiguous fact, open to the obvious explanation that grave-robbers had been at work (John 20:2).

However, in one place at least it is implied that the empty tomb could trigger off faith for someone perfectly disposed to believe. The beloved disciple, who had both suffered through the crucifixion with Jesus and was bound to him by a special bond of love, found in the empty tomb and the grave cloths a sign of the resurrection: 'He saw and believed' (John 20:8). Those who love can recognize the divine truth in signs which remain ambiguous for others. Love predisposes some people to see the presence of the living Lord in situations which are nothing but obscure puzzles for others.

If the real reasons which lead some to eliminate the empty tomb concern theological rather than historical issues, I hope this brief treatment has gone at least some distance towards interpreting and justifying the ultimate significance of Jesus' empty tomb.

A POSTSCRIPT

To adapt 1 Corinthians 1:18, we can say that 'the word of Jesus' resurrection is folly to those who are perishing, but to us who are being saved it is the power of God'. The attempts to reduce or explain away the

Easter event began almost at the beginning of Christianity and have continued ever since. 1 Corinthians 15 shows how an empty, shallow 'spiritualizing' set in early. Any certainty about the precise errors of the Corinthian Christians may elude us. But Paul's polemic in that chapter seems directed against some reductive tendencies in presenting Jesus' resurrection from the dead.

In this chapter I might have discussed in detail the hypothesis of those who connect Good Friday and Easter Sunday with pagan myths of dying and rising gods. In such a hypothesis the Easter story would be no more than a projection of the human need to cope with the changing seasons and the common challenges of life. Nowadays, however, this particular reductive approach has become far less popular. Christians never claimed Jesus' resurrection to be something which happens over and over again. It was always understood to be a once-and-for-all event coming after the public execution – not of some mythical hero or agricultural deity, but of a thoroughly historical person from Nazareth in Galilee.

This chapter could also have branched out to include topics I treated either briefly or at length in my *The Easter Jesus* and/or *What are they saying about the Resurrection?* For instance, how should we interpret the 'Descent into Hell'? Is it a way of saying that Jesus was *fully in the realm of death* before receiving the fullness of life – a kind of counterpoint to his risen exaltation? Is it rather (or as well) a way of expressing Jesus' *relationship to all mortal human beings*, even those who had died before him? In his death he truly entered into solidarity with all the dead, and then through his resurrection created a new solidarity beyond death with all men and women.

But the chapter has aimed to lay the ground-work for what follows. What did and does the Christian belief in Jesus' resurrection say about his function as Saviour of the world and his personal identity as Son of God? In other words, the systematic clarification of what the first Christians claimed to have happened to the crucified Jesus leads forward to examining the redemptive and revelatory implications of his resurrection.

NOTES

1 See my *EJ*, pp. 31, 101–107.
2 I recognize that the question of the sources for Acts is still far from being really settled. For example, Acts 2:36 is perhaps only a *different* rather than an *early* way of referring to Jesus' messianic Lordship. In that case Luke would be 'tolerantly' including a variant confession (of a later decade) rather than faithfully reporting an old formula which goes back to the thirties. For further details and an extensive bibliography see U. Becker and others, 'Proclamation', *DNTT* 3, pp. 44–68, esp. pp. 62–68.
3 One might, however, argue that Paul preserves the *earliest* formulations, which simply announced that Jesus 'was put to death' or 'died'. It was Luke's interest in history which led him to clarify the traditional expressions by adding the detail that Jesus'

execution took the form of crucifixion.

4 On 1 Cor 15:3–8, see *EJ*, pp. 3–17.

5 See R. Bultmann, *Kerygma and Myth*, ed. H. W. Bartsch (ET: New York, 1961), pp. 38–43.

6 See K. Dahn, 'See, Vision, Eye', *DNTT* 3, pp. 511–518.

7 J. Macquarrie, *The Scope of Demythologizing* (London, 1960), p. 86.

8 L. Evely, *The Gospels Without Myth* (ET: New York, 1971), p. 165. Contrast the position of Küng (*OBC*, p. 379) and Rahner (*Foundations*, p. 277), who both agree that the Easter experiences of the first witnesses were unique, 'reserved to a definite phase in salvation history' (Rahner), and as experiences which were 'strictly *sui generis*' (Rahner) were not (and cannot be) enjoyed by later Christians.

QUESTIONS FOR DISCUSSION

(1) What are the main difficulties against accepting Jesus' resurrection which you find in your country and culture? Yet are there any special features in your environment which could support your preaching and believing in his resurrection?

(2) Do the catechisms used in your diocese and country respect sufficiently the centrality of Jesus' resurrection?

(3) What does his resurrection indicate about questions of social justice and human rights?

(4) Compare and contrast the apostles' experiences of the risen Christ and visions of him received by Teresa of Avila and other mystics.

(5) How can you make sense of the risen body? What insights and analogies help you to say something about the nature of resurrection existence? In 'I have a dream' Martin Luther King exclaimed, 'Free at last, free at last; thank God Almighty, we are free at last'. Can these words be applied to our risen life after death?

(6) What are your favourite paintings and sculptures of the risen Christ? What appeals to you in the works you have selected?

ADDITIONAL READING

Besides the works already mentioned in this chapter, the following items could be helpful:

R. E. Brown, 'The Resurrection of Jesus', *JBC* 2, pp. 791–795.

R. E. Brown, *The Virginal Conception and Bodily Resurrection of Jesus* (London and New York, 1973), pp. 69–129.

L. Coenen and C. Brown, 'Resurrection', *DNTT*, pp. 250–309.

J. D. G. Dunn, *Jesus and the Spirit* (London and Philadelphia, 1975), pp. 95–134.

R. H. Fuller, *The Formation of the Resurrection Narratives* (Philadelphia, 1980). With R. E. Brown (see above), perhaps the best exegetical study of the Easter texts in Paul and the Gospels.

J. P. Galvin, 'The Resurrection of Jesus in Catholic Systematics', *Heythrop Journal* 20 (1979), pp. 123–145.

W. Kasper, *Jesus the Christ* (ET: London and New York, 1976), pp. 124–160.

X. Léon-Dufour, *Resurrection and the Message of Easter* (ET: London, 1974). A fine account of the New Testament witness to the resurrection. The book moves beyond 'mere' exegesis to issues of interpretation.

W. P. Loewe, 'The Appearances of the Risen Lord: Faith, Fact and Objectivity', *Horizons* 6 (1979), pp. 177–192.

F. J. Moloney, 'Resurrection and Accepted Exegetical Opinion', *Australasian Catholic Record* 58 (1981), pp. 191–202.

C. F. D. Moule (ed.), *The Significance of the Message of the Resurrection for Faith in Jesus Christ* (London, 1968). A detailed evaluation of Willi Marxsen's interpretation of the resurrection.

A. Oepke, 'anistēmi', *TDNT* 1, pp. 368–372.

A. Oepke, 'egeirō', *ibid.* 2, pp. 333–339.

W. Pannenberg, *JGM*, pp. 53–114.

J. Radermakers and P. Grelot, 'Resurrection', *DBT*, pp. 494–499.

K. Rahner, *Foundations*, pp. 266–278. Rahner shows how and why human beings are open to hear the Easter message.

K. Rahner and others, 'Resurrection', *SM* 5, pp. 323–342 (= *EncTh*, pp. 1430–1453).

J. A. T. Robinson, 'Resurrection in the NT', *IDB* 3, pp. 43–53.

E. W. Saunders, 'Resurrection in the NT', *IDB* supplementary vol., pp. 739–741.

P. Selby, *Look for the Living* (London, 1976). Selby shows that accepting Jesus' resurrection necessarily involves the believer in the life and (liberating) practice of the Christian community.

J. Sobrino, *Christology*, pp. 236–272.

B. Vawter, *This Man Jesus* (New York: Image Book ed., 1975), pp. 35–55.

H. Wansbrough, *Risen from the Dead* (Slough, 1978). An accurate and readable account of the New Testament witness to Christ's resurrection.

R. C. Ware, 'The Resurrection of Jesus', *Heythrop Journal* 16 (1975), pp. 22–35, 174–194. A classic survey of modern approaches to Jesus' resurrection.

5
Jesus the world's Redeemer

What good would life have been to us,
  had Christ not come as our Redeemer?

THE EASTER PROCLAMATION

I have been waiting all my life for someone like you. I knew that
someone like you would come and forgive me.

FEDOR DOSTOEVSKY

I have lived these last few years with the conviction that unearned
suffering is redemptive.

MARTIN LUTHER KING

In its 1980 statement, 'Select Questions on Christology', the International
Theological Commission declared: 'The person of Jesus Christ cannot be
separated from the deed of redemption. The benefits of salvation are
inseparable from the divinity of Jesus Christ' (IV. A. 1). Yet which issue
should be taken up first? The *person* of Jesus Christ as divine Son of God? Or
his *deed* of redemption as the Saviour of the world who brought the benefits
of salvation for all and once for all? If not separable, the issues are at least
distinguishable and can be treated in sequence.

The liturgy of the Church encourages me to begin with redemption.
Admittedly the Nicene Creed first acknowledges *who* Jesus Christ is ('the
only Son of God, eternally begotten of the Father' etc.) before confessing
that 'for us men and for our salvation he came down from heaven'.
However, the liturgy generally highlights the saving work of Christ more
than professions of faith in his person. It is Soteriological rather than
Christological. What the Prefaces of the Latin rite say about him readily
illustrates this preference:

> By rejecting the devil's temptations
> he has taught us
> to rid ourselves of the hidden corruption of evil (First Sunday of Lent).

Though he was sinless, he suffered willingly for sinners.
Though innocent, he accepted death to save the guilty (Passion
Sunday).

Through his cross and resurrection
he freed us from sin and death (Ordinary Sundays I).

We find a similar Soteriological stress in the eucharistic acclamations. For
instance, the fourth acclamation reads:

Lord, by your cross and resurrection
you have set us free.
You are the Saviour of the world.

This acclamation does not end by declaring 'You are the Son of God, you are
true God and true man', At the Veneration of the Cross on Good Friday the
priest sings three times 'This is the wood of the cross, on which hung the
Saviour of the world'. The people reply 'Come, let us worship'. Obviously
the response of *worship* implies the divine identity of Christ's person. But the
emphasis is on salvation. The celebrant does *not* sing 'This is the wood of
the cross, on which hung the Son of God'. We find the same concern for the
theme of redemption in a refrain used during the Stations of the Cross: 'We
adore thee, O Christ, and we bless thee, because by thy holy cross thou hast
redeemed the world'.

In her liturgical and devotional life, the worshipping and praying Church
dwells on Christ's redemptive benefits (which, of course, derive from his
identity and status as Son of God). Quite naturally those utterly Soteriological prayers from Luke's Gospel, the *Benedictus* and the *Magnificat*, find
their daily place in the Morning and Evening Prayer of the Divine Office.

The Christian scriptures, like the liturgy, give somewhat more attention
to the saving benefits brought by Jesus Christ than they do to the question
of his personal identity. This preference shows up in the normal priority
which words concerned with saving activity enjoy over words concerned
with revelation (*Fundamental*, pp. 56–59). In general the New Testament has
less to say about the disclosure of Jesus Christ as Son of God than it has to say
about the redemption he effected through his life, death and resurrection.

Thus both the scriptures and the liturgy encourage me to examine first
what Jesus did (and does) as Saviour of the world and then in the next chapter
look at *who* he is as Son of God. Historically matters took that course. By
experiencing what he did, his first followers came to know in faith who he
was. By calling him 'Jesus Christ' or 'the Saviour who had been anointed',
they also suggested that they *first* knew him for what he had done for them.

A further preliminary point. At the end of Chapter 1, I pointed out how
right from the beginning of the Church her liturgy has witnessed to Christ's
death and resurrection as the central mystery which focuses the experience of
faith. One must admit that some early Greek Fathers virtually equated the

incarnation as such with the redemption. Their conviction is enshrined in the credal statement 'for our salvation he came down from heaven' and in a daily prayer said during the Preparation of the Gifts for the Eucharist:

> By the mystery of this water and wine may we come to share in the divinity of Christ, who humbled himself to share in our humanity.

But these reminders of the incarnation are contextualized through what follows in the Eucharist: the words of institution and the memorial acclamation. The dynamic of the incarnation pointed forward to what fully and finally redeemed and saved us, the events of Good Friday and Easter Sunday.

The liturgy also witnesses to the *unity* of Christ's death and resurrection as two events which made up an *integral whole*, the one Paschal mystery which effected and continues to effect human salvation. Thus the prayer after Communion on Good Friday begins:

> Almighty and eternal God,
> you have restored us to life
> by the triumphant death and resurrection of Christ.

The eucharistic acclamations all hold together the crucifixion and resurrection. It is likewise with the prayer of absolution in the Rite of Penance:

> God, the Father of mercies,
> *through the death and resurrection of his Son*
> has reconciled the world to himself
> and sent the Holy Spirit among us for the
> forgiveness of sins [italics mine].

Granted that Jesus acted as the Saviour of the world in that one mystery of his dying and rising, how have Christians experienced, interpreted and expressed that salvation?

THE HUMAN CONDITION

When we begin to talk about redemption, the data from Christian origins, history and experience may come across as so complex that they threaten to frustrate any attempt at understanding. So much diverse material turns up at once in response to the two basic questions: What is it about the human condition which calls for salvation? How should we describe and present the salvation effected by Christ?

What we need here is some workable typology. Of course, as such, pure or ideal types do not exist in our world. They are intellectual constructs. Nevertheless, typology can be useful here, inasmuch as it will help us both to classify the data from scripture, tradition and experience and to elaborate some kind of understanding. In fact a threefold typology will organize ways in which Christians have experienced and expressed our human condition and the redemption God brought us in Christ.

How then have believers presented the mystery of evil, suffering and sin which makes human beings candidates for salvation? And how can we classify and elucidate further the interpretations which have been given of redemption? My approach will reverse the order embodied in the title of Pope John Paul II's 1979 encyclical, *Redemptor Hominis*, by outlining first a threefold typology of '*homo*' and then sketching a corresponding threefold typology of the '*Redemptor*'.

Basic and pervasive needs of human existence were met by the historical intervention of Christ. He was the ultimate reply to *the* issue of human history: that universal expectation of salvation so poignantly expressed by the words of the two disciples in Luke's Emmaus story: 'We had hoped that he was the one to redeem Israel' (24:21). As we shall see, the benefits brought by his dying and rising aimed to satisfy the human hunger for life, meaning and love.

(1) *Oppressed*.   One persistent reason given by Christians (and others) to explain why redemption is an issue can be called 'oppression from without'. Thus sin, death and various evil forces have often been experienced and represented as outside powers which come to enslave and destroy human beings.

In Luke's Gospel, Zechariah prophesies at the circumcision of his son John that through God's tender mercy light would be given to 'those who sit in darkness and the shadow of death' (1:79). A little further on in that Gospel, Jesus begins his ministry by quoting the words of Isaiah: 'He has sent me to proclaim release to the captives . . . to set at liberty those who are oppressed' (4:18). In Mark, Jesus describes his conflict with diabolic forces as an over-powering act of burglary: 'No one can enter a strong man's house and plunder his goods, unless he first binds the strong man; then indeed he may plunder his house' (3:27). Healing the sick means liberating them from Satan's power (Luke 13:16). The implication of all such passages is clear. There are evil forces holding human beings in bondage.

St Paul does not speak of a direct conflict between Jesus and Satan. He thinks rather in terms of 'vaguer' forces. Sin invades the world and through sin death comes to afflict all human beings (Rom 5:12). Sin and death dominate them and hold them enslaved (Rom 5:14, 17, 21; 6:6ff.). The letter to the Colossians speaks of 'principalities and powers' (2:15) which had to be disarmed before Christ's followers could be free. In Galatians, Paul reminds his troublesome community of their former state when they were 'slaves to the elemental spirits of the universe' (4:3; see 4:9). He warns them against lapsing into a new bondage to the Law and the fruitless effort to win salvation simply through one's own spiritual performance. The Jewish law was given by God but has become intolerably oppressive, a 'curse' from which believers need to be delivered (Gal 3:13).

After the apostolic age Christian teaching, liturgy, theology, spirituality and art continued to portray human beings as needing to be saved from various kinds of oppression. Right down to the Second Vatican Council (*Gaudium et Spes*, 4ff.), the Puebla document (87–92) and John Paul II (*Redemptor Hominis*, 15f.), men and women have been seen as threatened and destroyed by forces beyond their control or at least beyond the control of suffering individuals.

Nowadays we remain as much menaced by *death, sin, law* and *demonic forces*, albeit these oppressive evils may wear somewhat new masks. Modern advertising presents men and women as if they were overwhelmingly young, healthy and beautiful. But anxiety can flare up whenever human beings allow themselves to recall that old age, sickness, decay and death wait for them just a few decades ahead. Does life end in annihilation? All too many people find themselves powerless before drugs, sexual drives, greed for possessions and other forces. They can be or become victims of various compulsions and obsessions. Caught in activity which is both self-destructive and destructive of others, they echo Paul's cry, 'Wretched man that I am! Who will deliver me?' (Rom 7:24).

The laws of profit and material success hold groups, nations and whole continents in bondage. It is bad enough when greed for wealth enslaves individuals and makes them inhuman towards themselves and others. But it is much worse to see the laws of economics and scientific technology keeping whole populations deprived of their proper human rights and living under fresh forms of slavery.

Demonic forces abound in the contemporary world where 'the principalities and powers' have not disappeared, but merely bear new faces as the personification of the power structures which dominate our corporate lives. Bondage to the irrational forces of nature has widely been replaced by a bondage to evil forces on a national and international scale: uncontrollable greed, exploitation, institutionalized injustice, the arms race, revenge attacks and violence of all kinds. Anxiety and impotence in the face of evil forces 'out there' have not disappeared; they have simply relocated.

Repeatedly the Old Testament identifies idolatry as the root sin, *the* evil from which God's people had to be freed (Exod 20:2ff.). They often bowed down before other gods and served them. In the New Testament the book of Revelation unmasks the powers of evil which seek to enslave people to the worship of idols (2:14, 20; 9:20; 13:4 etc.). In such twentieth-century forms as National Security, Communism and the Gross National Product, demonic idols continue to exercise their evil power. In place of figures of silver and gold, human beings have produced and worshipped idolatrous systems and goals. In turn these false gods have seized power over millions of men and women to make them slaves of these 'works of human hands'. Oppressive bondage rather than true freedom always results when men and women sinfully turn from God to their own inventions (*aversio a Deo, conversio ad creaturam*).

(2) *Contaminated.* Long before the Christian era the psalmists and others witnessed to the impure state of sinful human beings. The Israelites prayed for deliverance from their stained condition: 'Wash me from my guilt, cleanse me from my sin' (Ps 51:2). The prophet Isaiah expressed this primordial feeling of defilement before his unclean lips were cleansed (6:5, 7). This sense of human contamination which needs to be expiated turns up repeatedly in the Old Testament, it finds a place in the practices and writings of various world religions, and it is endorsed by the New Testament. Quite naturally baptism gets understood in these terms: 'You were *washed*, you were sanctified, you were justified in the name of the Lord Jesus Christ and in the Spirit of our God' (1 Cor 6:11). The Letter to the Ephesians compares the whole community of the redeemed to a bride who was ceremonially cleansed and purified for her husband: 'Christ loved the Church and gave himself up for her, that he might sanctify her, having cleansed her by the washing of water with the word' (5:25f.).

The sense that sin and evil soil and stain both individuals and even entire nations seems, in one way or another, a universal conviction.[1] Moral disorder is recognized as some kind of 'dirt' which requires purification. It can make one unfit to stand in the divine presence and share in worship. Some highly secularized societies may tend to suppress conscious guilt, but they reveal their desire for cleansing in an extreme concern for public hygiene. In general, studies in anthropology and the history of religions illustrate how widely human beings believe themselves to need cleansing from the contamination of sin and guilt.

(3) *Wounded within.* A third persistent way of expressing the human condition looks to the inner wounds, sickness and hard-heartedness that call for the healing touch of divine love. Thus Ezekiel assures the people that God will not only cleanse them but also will put within them a new heart and a new spirit:

> I will sprinkle clean water upon you, and you shall be clean from all your uncleannesses, and from all your idols I will cleanse you. A new heart I will give you, and a new spirit I will put within you; and I will take out of your flesh the heart of stone and give you a heart of flesh (Ez 36:25f.).

The conviction that there is something deeply wrong *within* human beings shows up over and over again in the New Testament. Jesus comes as the divine physician to cure sinners of their sickness (Mark 2:17). Through sin people become 'heartless' (Rom 1:31), closed in on themselves and incapable of real love. Jesus sees how evil emerges from a wicked heart: 'From within, out of the heart of man, come evil thoughts, fornication, theft, murder, adultery, coveting, wickedness, deceit, licentiousness, envy, slander, pride, foolishness. All these evil things come from within' (Mark 7:21–23). In his classic letter to the Romans Paul expresses this interior problem as sin 'dwelling within me' (7:17, 20). At the heart of unredeemed human beings sin dwells rather than the Holy Spirit of God (5:5; 8:9ff.).

Behavioural psychologists, of course, have maintained that there are no wicked hearts and no bad people. There are only bad environments. If we correctly manipulate the environments, we can fix their behaviour. But human and Christian experience supports the teaching of Ezekiel, Jesus and Paul. Cold indifference towards the sufferings of others, rampant greed and fear, failure to forgive, and institutionalized hatred all point to something wrong within, some woundedness and basic selfishness at the heart of human beings.

(4) *Reflections on the typology.* This threefold typology, which illustrates why the human condition calls for redemption, moves from external oppression through 'surface' contamination to interior evil. Things on the outside, the surface or the inside conspire to make men and women candidates for salvation.

(a) The typology can be dignified by being decked out in Latin. We could speak of *homo servilis* (or perhaps *homo oppressus*), *homo contaminatus*, and *homo egocentratus* (or, to use Augustine's phrase, *homo incurvatus in se*).

Evil – specifically, the moral evil of sin – generates a destructive slavery for onself and for others, a pattern of contamination, and an empty selfishness within. This is the enslaved, defiled and unloving state into which the prodigal son falls when he leaves home and goes into the 'far country' (Luke 15:13).

(b) In his *The Crucified God* (ET: London, 1974) and other writings, Jürgen Moltmann has developed a theme which is relevant here: the history of suffering. His Catholic contemporary, Johann Baptist Metz, has a similar (but by no means identical) approach in *Faith in History and Society* (ET: London, 1980). In *Christ* (ET: London, 1980), Edward Schillebeeckx presents grace and salvation as the divine answer to the human mystery of suffering. The threefold typology sketched above can be related to the common theme of Moltmann, Metz and Schillebeeckx as follows. Human history is *a history of suffering* (*Leidensgeschichte*) which can be distinguished (but not separated) in three ways as the history of that oppression, guilt, and selfishness under which and from which men and women suffer.

(c) Another notion which satisfactorily links the three types is that of *fear.* Human beings instinctively shun the deadliness which results from oppression, the senselessness of being contaminated by guilt, and the empty isolation brought by selfish hardheartedness. They look for someone who can save them in these three ways. We would not be hopelessly wrong about salvation if we named Jesus the Deliverer from Fear, the One who sets people free from these three primordial anxieties. I shall come back to this point later in the chapter.

(d)   Before leaving behind this account of the human condition, I should hasten to add an important qualification. The fact that men and women are oppressed, contaminated and inwardly wounded should not be exaggerated to the point of alleging a complete unfreedom, total corruption and utter egocentrism. The Council of Trent rightly set its face against those Reformers who alleged that sin had totally 'depraved' human beings (*DS*, 1521 and 1555). Evil could spoil and damage but never totally destroy that divine image in men and women.

> God created man in his own image, in the image of God he created him; male and female he created them . . . God saw everything that he had made, and behold, it was very good (Gen 1:27, 31).

What was free, pure and good in the divine creation could never be completely wiped out. The Second Vatican Council recognized that sin has 'diminished' human beings but not destroyed them (*GS*, 13).

What is at stake here is the relationship between creation and redemption. It would be false to 'prove' the human need for redemption by *either* denying what had already been effected through creation, *or* claiming that sin had utterly wrecked the created works of God. Rather the forces of oppression, contamination and selfishness, although they offered and continue to offer resistance to the development and spiritual progress inherent in God's overall design, nevertheless, did not reduce redemption to a subsequent rescue operation as if the initial scheme of creation had simply failed. Redemption was not a totally new start.

(e)   My sketch of the human condition implies the Christian conviction that only the divine initiative can deliver us. The oppression, the contamination and the inner wounds of evil and sin will not go away of themselves. Left to our own resources, we cannot set ourselves free, cleanse our guilt or give ourselves new hearts. There is no self-redemption.

Here I want to distinguish between *the need* for redemption (or, more accurately, for the Redeemer) and *the felt need* for redemption. Like the Israelites in Egypt, slaves may become so used to their condition that they are reluctant to be liberated. Sick people may cherish their illnesses, neither expecting nor even hoping to be cured. I can still remember the person with a severe spiritual problem who told me: 'I don't like the way I am, but I don't want to change or be changed'. This chapter, however, is concerned as such with the human need for redemption and the way Christ has met that need. At the same time one must recognize just how many individuals and groups may either feel little need for salvation, or refuse to avail themselves of the benefits of redemption, or else – and this is much sadder – believe themselves to be so bad that they are beyond redemption.

(e)   Finally, a word about *original sin*. The Easter Proclamation (*Exsultet*), the most classical statement on redemption during the whole liturgical year, represents redemption as God's response to original sin: 'O happy fault, o necessary sin of Adam, which gained for us so great a Redeemer'. What was and is this 'sin of Adam' which made us candidates for salvation? How should it be interpreted in the light of the Scriptures (Gen 3; Rom 5), the teaching of the Council of Trent (*DS*, 1510–16), the liturgy and the reflections of modern theologians?

Essentially, as the Easter Proclamation indicates with dramatic clarity, original sin points to a basic *solidarity* in sin and salvation shared by 'us' human beings. From the beginning we have let ourselves become enslaved by sin and consequently we require radical redemption through Jesus Christ. Over and over again the *Exsultet* speaks in the first person plural ('we', 'us', 'our'). The whole community of sinful human beings needed to be saved by 'the Lamb of God, who takes away the sin of the world' (John 1:29).

Specifically, original sin recalls the fact that we are all born into a (partly) *bad environment*. We inherit standards and patterns of behaviour which come from sin and push us towards sin. Rather than simply mediating freedom, holiness and love, the community provides newcomers with a situation which is at least somewhat oppressive, contaminated and hardhearted.

Besides involving a sinful situation, original sin also entails a certain inward 'alienation' from God. Because of the present state of the human race, people are born affected by universal sin and deprived of the benefits of grace which they might otherwise have had. On the one hand, this situation and state of deprivation in which individuals find themselves is not due to their personal fault. On the other hand, through their own sins they will proceed to ratify what they have inherited.

As in the *Exsultet*, the 'sin of Adam' serves to sum up that common sinfulness which calls for a universal Saviour. That same Easter Proclamation piles up terms and images which show how that 'happy fault' brings with it the three elements of *oppression, contamination* and *inner brokenness*. Like the Israelites, 'our fathers', we need to be delivered from slavery. Through Christ believers experience themselves as 'washed clean of sin and freed from all defilement'. They know also that there is 'hatred to be cast out' and 'pride to be humbled', so that 'this holy night' can bring us peace. The *Exsultet* confesses our human solidarity in sin and need, but it confesses even more our solidarity in the benefits coming from 'the risen Saviour'.[2]

'SO GREAT A REDEEMER'

Building on their Jewish background, Christians have experienced and expressed the redemption effected by Christ in three basic ways: as liberation, expiation and transforming love. Each of these models of redemption can be misused or wrongly absolutized as if this or that model were the only legitimate way of interpreting redemption. Each of these models must face certain objections. But all of them have something valuable to say and complement each other in elucidating the redemptive benefits which come from Christ. The models correspond to the threefold typology for describing the evil which afflicts the human condition.

By chance the names of the three writers associated most with the three models all begin with the letter 'A'. The title of his classic *Christus Victor* (London, 1931) indicates how Gustav Aulén (1879–1977) interpreted redemption as a victory over or redemption from evil powers. St Anselm of Canterbury in his *Cur Deus Homo* (completed 1098) was the first Christian to devote a treatise explicitly to the atonement. His theory of satisfaction, which won a wide following during the Middle Ages, the Reformation period and later, was one way of developing the model of expiation of guilt or reparation for sin. Finally, Peter Abelard understood redemption in terms of the supreme example of love which Jesus gave in obedient suffering and death.

(1) *Liberation.* The sense that a victorious God delivers us from evil reaches well back into Jewish history. The Easter Vigil includes that classic song in which the Israelites praised God for their deliverance from Egypt:

> I will sing to the Lord, glorious his triumph!
> Horse and rider he has thrown into the sea! . . .
> The Lord is a warrior! The Lord is his name.
> The chariots of Pharaoh he hurled into the sea . . .
> Your right hand, Lord, glorious in its power,
> Your right hand, Lord, has shattered the enemy (Exod 15:1, 3f., 6).

The memory of the Exodus, *the* great act of deliverance which created the Jewish people, made it practically inevitable that from the outset Christians would reach for the language of liberation and victory to describe the benefits brought by redemption. Christ's death and resurrection meant a triumph over sin, death and the demonic powers which menace, enslave and terrify human beings. From Paul's vision of Christ 'reigning until he has put all his enemies under his feet' (1 Cor 15:25) to John's 'Fear not, I have overcome the world' (16:33; see 12:31), and from Paul's gospel of liberation from the curse of the Law (Galatians) to the conflict and victory imagery of

Revelation, we find the New Testament pressing this language into service to express the nature of redemption.

The conflict with evil inaugurated during Jesus' ministry (Luke 11:14–23 parr.) reached its climax with the events of Good Friday and Easter Sunday. That conflict led to his death. But the New Testament writers are not content to interpret the crucifixion as a mere miscarriage of justice or a human tragedy. For them the crucifixion and the subsequent resurrection meant that 'death is swallowed up in victory':

> The sting of death is sin, and the power of sin is the law. But thanks be to God, who gives us the victory through our Lord Jesus Christ (1 Cor 15:54, 56f.).

In the language of Revelation 'the Lamb who was slain' has brought a universal deliverance from evil (5:6ff.). This book designates Christ twenty-eight times as the Lamb. But the Lamb has shown himself to be the conqueror (Rev 3:21; 5:5; 6:2; 19:11 etc.).

It is certainly paradoxical to identify the slain Lamb as the victor over the world's evil. St Paul defends the same paradox. It seems absurd but it is true that powerful deliverance came in and through the appalling vulnerability of the cross; 'He was crucified in weakness, but lives by the power of God' (2 Cor 13:4). Jesus' victory meant *changing* suffering and death into instruments of redemption, not taking them away (see also John 12:24).

Writers who fashion Christ-figures for their dramas or novels at times catch hold of this paradox. The central person in Bernard Pomerance's play *The Elephant Man*, John Merrick, is terribly deformed and utterly hideous. His nightmare appearance produces horror and disgust in those who see him. Dr Frederick Treves rescues this helpless person, but is then touched and changed by him. Merrick's body is grotesque and indecent, but his unbroken spirit shines through his powerlessness and redeems others.

From early on, the Christian tradition picked up the biblical language about deliverance coming through conflict with evil. I think here of the hymns with which Venantius Fortunatus (c. 530–c. 610) celebrated the coming of the relics of Christ's cross to Poitiers (*Vexilla regis prodeunt*, *Fulget crucis mysterium* and *Pange, lingua, gloriosi proelium certaminis*), as well as of the *Victimae Paschali*. This magnificent Sequence shows 'death and life' fighting 'an extraordinary conflict' (*mors et vita duello conflixere mirando*). In the Anglo-Saxon religious poem *The Dream of the Rood* and other medieval works, Christ appears as the heroic warrior whose endurance wins the victory, despite the seeming defeat of the crucifixion. The Easter Vigil preserves this traditional language in the Easter Proclamation and elsewhere:

> This is the night when Jesus Christ
> broke the chains of death
> and rose triumphant from the grave.

To express redemption as deliverance from the multi-faceted oppression of evil is thoroughly in accord with the Scriptures and Christian liturgy. But does this language still work?

(a)   A few years back it was conventional to criticize this first model of redemption *for being mythological* and hence unconvincing to that splendid creation of Bultmann and some other theologians, 'modern man'. The stunning success of such films as *Star Wars* and *The Empire Strikes Back* shows how well images of cosmic struggles and victories continue to communicate. C. S. Lewis and his friends never doubted the powerful impact of that language on perfectly modern men and women. On the contemporary scene, accounts of redemption in terms of conflict with and victory over 'the powers and principalities' and the demonic forces of death remain alive and well. To prove that one needs only to check current hymns, the proceedings of the 1980 World Conference on Mission and Evangelism, and any representative sample of writings in liberation theology.

(b)   A more telling objection finds the language of victory *unrealistic*. Faced with the massive nature of evil in our world, how can believers proclaim 'Christ conquers, Christ reigns'? When we recall all the injustice, violence, cruelty and senseless suffering which millions of human beings endure, how can we justify calling Christ 'the conqueror of sin and death' (Preface of the Ascension I)? Honesty would suggest picking out and defending that telling remark at the end of 1 John: 'The whole world is in the power of the evil one' (5:19).

Here it is important to hit some kind of balance between the fullness of redemption which is obviously *not yet* here and the liberation *already* achieved. The New Testament is properly realistic. On the one hand, it speaks in the past tense of Christ's conclusive victory over the forces of evil (Col 2:15; Eph 1:20ff.; 1 Pet 3:22; John 16:33; 1 John 3:8). On the other hand, it recognizes that evil powers here and now can still operate even against Christ's followers (2 Thess 2:3–10; 1 Cor 5:5; 2 Cor 2:11; Gal 4:9; 1 Pet 5:8f.). The full working out of Christ's liberating redemption has yet to take place (1 Cor 15:22ff.). There are victories of grace already present (Gal 3:28; Col 3:11). But it is also true to say that we still wait for redemption and are only saved in hope (Rom 8:23–25).

Theologically *Star Wars* was correct. That film ended with the powers of evil defeated but not annihilated. Their deadly force flared up again in *The Empire Strikes Back*.

(c)   There is a facile view that our first model of redemption turns believers into *mere spectators*. We watch and applaud as Christ wins the victory for us, but remain uninvolved ourselves.

This objection is superficial. It misses the New Testament's clear teaching. The recipients must become agents. The beneficiaries of Christ's redemptive liberation are called to take up their spiritual weapons and share in the ongoing struggle against the powers of evil (1 Thess 5:8; 2 Cor 6:7; 10:4; Rom 13:12; Eph 6:10ff.). The freedom received through Christ's victory must not be forfeited (1 Cor 7:29ff.; Gal 5:1). The case of believers also verifies the paradoxical principle of divine power in human weakness (2 Cor 12:9f.) and life through death. In Galatians St Paul moves from the once-and-for-all, historical event of Calvary, when Christ 'gave himself [the aorist tense in Greek] for our sins to deliver us from the present evil age' (1:4) to note the impact of the cross on the lives of Christians. In their case the passion still goes on. The apostle declares: 'I have been crucified [perfect] with Christ' (2:20; see 6:14). Hence he can also say: 'I bear [present] on my body the marks of Jesus' (6:17). To believe, be baptized (Rom 6:3) and suffer in the ministry is for Paul to identify with Jesus in his dying. Such sufferings amount to a continuing experience of death.

Yet to share thus in the crucifixion is to share in *that* unique death which resulted in the victory of resurrection. The consequence of dying with Christ is a state of life *in* him (Gal 2:19f.). Identifying with the crucified Christ means suffering evil, finding it transformed into good, and experiencing even now something of his life through death. The apostle speaks of himself as

> always carrying in the body the death of Jesus, so that the life of Jesus may also be manifested in our bodies. For while we live we are always being given up to death for Jesus' sake, so that the life of Jesus may be manifested in our mortal flesh (2 Cor 4:10f.).

The Easter liturgy expresses the same conviction: those who are delivered through Christ's victory over evil must themselves become participants in the struggle. The Sequence *Victimae Paschali* may speak in the past tense: 'Death with life contended: combat strangely ended'. But for the followers of Jesus, death remains a potent force. The combat goes on. The alternative reading which precedes the Sequence calls on Christians to celebrate the Easter festival by driving out 'malice and evil' (1 Cor 5:6–8).

(2) Redemption as expiation. The second model of redemption takes up the theme of expiation from guilt, purification from the contamination of sin, or reparation for (and of) a disturbed moral order. Nowadays this interpretation of Christ's redeeming 'work' is sometimes played down, if not openly rejected. For instance, the preparatory papers for the 1980 World Conference on Mission and Evangelism had a great deal to say about redemption as liberation but next to nothing about expiation.[3] Jürgen Moltmann's *The Crucified God* barely touched the theme (p. 183).

Admittedly there are serious problems: for instance, the high risk of constructing a theory of expiation simply in *our* terms. The prodigal son intended to make expiation for his sins. He had decided on his penance and prepared his speech: 'Father, I have sinned against heaven and before you; I am no longer worthy to be called your son; *treat me as one of your hired servants*' (Luke 15:18f.). When he met his father, however, he could not finish his speech and ask to be treated as a hired servant. The father interpreted the situation differently, cut short his son's speech and brought him home for a feast of joy (Luke 15:22–24). Later in this chapter I wish to return to the parable of the prodigal son. But it is good to keep the story in mind right from the outset, given the temptation to construct a theory of reparation merely in terms of what *we* think to be fair.

(a) Essentially this second model comes to this. Through his death and resurrection Christ acted as both priest and victim *to offer a sacrifice* (John 1:29, 36; Heb 4:14 – 10:39), which both *expiated* sins (Rom 3:24f.) and brought *a new covenant* relationship between God and human beings (Mark 14:24 par.; 1 Cor 11:25 par.). Jesus did all this *representatively* – or, as the Pauline letters so often echo from the primitive Christian tradition, he did it 'for us' (Rom 5:6; 8:31ff.; 1 Cor 8:11; Gal 1:4; Eph 5:2; 1 Thess 5:10 etc.). There are four points to explain and relate to each other.

The Old Testament records a range of functions for *sacrificial* acts. They could expiate sins, bring communion with God, or simply serve to worship, praise and thank God for the divine blessings. Old Testament sacrifices were not, or were not meant to be, means of manipulating, bribing or persuading God to do (or refrain from doing) certain things. Primarily they were understood to be divinely authorized institutions through which saving grace could be received. Secondarily they were rituals through which the people pledged themselves to live and die in obedience to God. This may sound paradoxical. But even in the Old Testament *the primary direction* of authentic sacrifice seems clear: from God to human beings rather than from human beings to God.

As we saw in Chapter 3, the early Christians saw the sacrificial implications of the Passover setting for the crucifixion and resurrection: 'Christ, our paschal lamb, has been sacrificed' (1 Cor 5:7). They also connected his death with Yom Kippur, the great Jewish day for the expiation of sins. God appointed Jesus (Heb 5:1–10) as 'a merciful and faithful high priest . . . to make expiation for the sins of the people' (Heb 2:17f.), to 'offer for all time a single sacrifice for sins' (Heb 10:12), and become 'the mediator of a new covenant' (Heb 9:15).

How much treatment do *the four key terms* (sacrifice, expiation, covenant and representation) deserve? The short answer is, of course, a book each. But I suspect that one needs to battle it out more for expiation and representation. The institution of marriage keeps happily alive the notion of a binding contract or *covenant* between those lovingly committed to each other. In ordinary language *sacrifice* maintains its position in expressing devoted self-surrender and the offering of something precious. This means that there is or should be little difficulty in appreciating the force of texts like Ephesians 5:2 ('Christ loved us and gave himself up for us, a fragrant offering and sacrifice to God'), or the question about God in Romans 8:32: 'He who did not spare his own Son, but gave him up for us all, will he not also give us all things with him?'

(b)   With easy assurance St Paul expresses his belief that the crucifixion made amends for human sin: 'Christ died for the ungodly' (Rom 5:6). But how could his undeserved suffering *expiate the guilt of sinful humanity* and so cleanse a contaminated world? How could such a physical evil (death by crucifixion) provide a remedy for the moral evil of sin? This execution would seem to be an enormous injustice which adds to human guilt rather than an event capable of setting right a disrupted moral order. A diagram can serve to illustrate the issues:

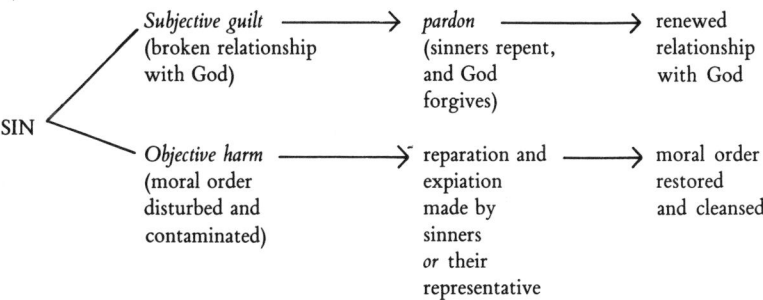

Once sin has been truly committed and subjective guilt incurred, surely we should not look for anything more than that sinners should repent and be forgiven? An autonomous moral law cannot forgive them. But a personal agent (God) can. Once sinners go beyond mere regret to genuine repentance, we need not demand anything further from them. God's mercy will be there to renew their life of grace. The steps outlined on the *top* line of the diagram seem both required and sufficient.

However, in spite of the obvious priority of the steps outlined on the *top* line, those outlined on the *bottom* line still make sense and maintain their place. The subjective guilt of sinners remains personal and non-transferable. But through his expiatory suffering Jesus stepped in to make reparation and cleanse the contamination of objective guilt. In that sense he atoned for human sin and renewed a disrupted moral order. Representatively he made expiation, but he was not representatively punished.

Of course, the atonement made by Jesus in no way exempts sinners from the need to repent, accept divine forgiveness and enter a new relationship with God. In my diagram the top line remains primary. Reparation has at best a subordinate place. Further, the innocent Jesus unilaterally offered reparation for others: 'While we were yet sinners, Christ died for us' (Rom 5:8). But sinful men and women need to ratify this deed by accepting with gratitude the fact that he representatively made amends on their behalf. I shall come back to this point shortly.

As we saw in Chapter 3, the belief that the suffering destiny of one person could representatively atone for the sins of others was alive not only in pre-Christian Judaism but also in Greco-Roman religious thought. Suffering endured on behalf of others could cleanse and renew the moral order. This conviction turns up in Paul's letters, the Gospels, the Letter to the Hebrews and later books of the New Testament. According to the Letter to Titus, for instance, 'Christ . . . gave himself for us to redeem us from all iniquity and to purify for himself a people of his own who are zealous for good deeds' (2:13f.). The belief that Jesus died for our sins goes right back to those early kerygmatic formulations which Paul quotes. 'I delivered to you', he assures his Corinthian converts, 'what I also received, that Christ died for our sins' (1 Cor 15:3). But was this inherited doctrine of atonement no more than a superseded structure which the first Christians took time to dismantle – a deviation which continued to offer emotional resistance to the good news brought by Jesus Christ? At this point I want to discuss some standard *objections* to the theme of expiation.

(c)   Among the major difficulties with the doctrine of expiation has been the sense that (i) it appears *to set limits to the divine mercy*. Can it be reconciled with that lovingly generous forgiveness classically expressed by the story of the prodigal son?

It would be misguided to make a point-for-point application of every detail in that parable. But there are certain aspects of the story which seem relevant to the theme of expiatory suffering. What if the prodigal had calculated the rate at which his friends and money were running out, and avoided hunger and humiliation by going home earlier? The father's merciful love would presumably have expressed itself in the same way, but the parable would leave us feeling uncomfortable. It would lack the element of suffering which is secondary but integral. In the actual story the boy accepts as his due the afflictions which come to him as a consequence of his wrong-doing. This suffering brings him to repentance and helps to purify him from guilt. When he returns home, his self-appointed penance ('treat me as one of your hired servants') is swept aside. The forgiving love of the father calls for a feast of joy. Is it too much to think here of the boy's pain in facing such selfless and overwhelming love? There is pain, as well as joy, in being so loved. The human instinct is often to prefer being treated strictly in accordance with our deserts. In the musical *Man of La Mancha* it rings very true when a prostitute (Aldonza/Dulcinea) reacts to the way Don Quixote idolizes and loves her in an utterly unselfish way. 'Tenderness', she says, 'I cannot bear.' Finally, am I pushing matters too far in drawing attention to the hostility of the elder son (Luke 15:25–32)? To be sure, he speaks only with his father. But he refuses to go inside and refers in a cold, insolent way to his younger brother as 'this son of yours' (15:30). When the prodigal comes home, he has to cope not only with the love of his father but also with the resentful hostility of his elder brother.

To sum up. The prodigal son is forgiven and begins a fresh life of enhanced love in his father's home. At the same time there are *also* in his story elements which indicate how he himself makes amends for his sins through some purifying suffering.

Four chapters later in Luke's Gospel there occurs an episode which can help us grasp the same point. A rich superintendent of taxes named Zacchaeus had been spiritually lost but was saved when Jesus came to his home (19:1–10). The central point of the story is expressed in Jesus' words: 'Today salvation has come to this house, since he also is a son of Abraham. For the Son of man came to seek and save the lost.' In terms of my diagram this is my top line. But the lower line is also represented in that Zacchaeus proposed to repay four times over anyone whom he had cheated. Jesus did not reject this offer of reparation on the grounds that receiving the divine mercy was enough.

Why is it that the divine mercy does not rule out the role of expiation, but allows the moral order to be cleansed by sinners themselves, or rather by Jesus acting representatively on their behalf? To deny any such expiation appears to portray God as granting a cheap forgiveness which would scarcely differ from condoning evil. In that case God would seem to lack fidelity towards the created universe and its moral order which sin defiles. On the one hand, the cross and resurrection reveal the divine mercy 'in its fullness'. 'Believing in the crucified Son' means

> believing that love is present in the world and that this love is more powerful than any kind of evil in which individuals, humanity, or the world are involved. Believing in this love means *believing in mercy*. For mercy is an indispensable dimension of love; it is as it were love's second name and, at the same time, the specific manner in which love is revealed and effected vis-à-vis the reality of evil that is in the world (John Paul II, *Dives in Misericordia*, 7).

On the other hand, this 'mystery of mercy, supremely revealed in Jesus Christ' also entails 'reparation for evil' (*ibid.*, 14).

(ii) In his *Cur Deus Homo* St Anselm of Canterbury developed the classical version of this second model of redemption. His theory of '*satisfaction*' aimed to describe and explain how Christ's death restored the divine 'honour' which sin offends. After centuries of great popularity Anselm's approach has fallen on hard times. It has become conventional to dismiss his theory of redemption as legalistic and centred on the divine honour rather than the divine love.

However, John McIntyre, Gispert Greshake and Walter Kasper have come out in defence of Anselm's theology of satisfaction. His version of redemption appreciates God's fidelity to creation and the moral order. Understood within the feudal context, talk of the divine 'honour' implies rather than excludes love. For Anselm, true 'honour' guarantees peace, order and justice.

Personally I prefer to avoid the language of 'honour' and 'satisfaction'. Nowadays it seems a little too open to misunderstanding. Historically speaking, however, we should respect Anselm's intentions. Kasper sums up well the case for the defence (*Jesus the Christ*, pp. 219ff.).

(iii) The two objections so far discussed come from those who think that in a Christian context talk of expiation (or satisfaction) goes too far. But there are also those who believe that what I have been saying does not go far enough. They would alter this second model of redemption and make it come out in a 'fiercer' form. God the Father treated his Son as a sinner, judging and punishing him in our place as a substitute for guilty humanity. Through his suffering and death Christ propitiated an angry God, turned away the divine wrath and won us redemption. What should we say about this *penal substitution theory*?

First of all, one should be quick to point out that Anselm rejected this interpretation. After him punitive elements turned up in the accounts of redemption offered by Alexander of Hales (*c.* 1186–1245), St Thomas Aquinas and other medieval theologians. This development reached a peak with John Calvin (1509–64). In his view Jesus became the personal object of divine reprobation. Through his passion he suffered an abandonment by God that corresponded to the lot of those condemned to hell. This suffering as a penal substitute turned away God's anger and won the divine favour for the human race.

Catholics had no difficulties with such an interpretation of the redemption. Thus Bishop Bossuet (1627–1704), one of the great preachers of all time, described the passion as follows:

> The man, Jesus Christ, has been thrown under the multiple and redoubled blows of divine vengeance. . . . As it vented itself, so his [God's] anger diminished; he struck his innocent Son as he wrestled with the wrath of God . . . When an avenging God waged war upon his Son, the mystery of our peace was accomplished.

Bossuet credited the Virgin Mary with sentiments on Calvary that corresponded to his theology: 'She dreams not of asking the Eternal Father to lessen her anguish by one single throb, when she beholds him pouring out the full vials of his wrath on the head of his Only-begotten' (see my *Calvary Christ*, pp. 94f.).

Such language of anger, punishment and propitiation has flourished down to our own day. Some theologians, preachers and hymn-writers continue to represent the suffering Christ as being punished in substitution for sinful men and women. Even Karl Barth (1886–1968), one of the greatest theologians of this century, endorsed this view. Jesus Christ, the man-for-others, entered the heart of their alienation from God, took the place of those judged by divine justice, and became himself the object of God's anger. On Calvary Jesus carried human sin and culpability, for which he was judged, condemned and punished by death. 'He stands', Barth wrote, 'before the Father at Golgotha burdened with all the actual sin and guilt of man and of each individual man, and is treated in accordance with the deserts of man as the transgressor of the divine command' (CD II/2, p. 758).

I regret to say that elements of the Calvin–Bossuet–Barth tradition surface in Moltmann's The Crucified God. That book interprets Jesus' cry of abandonment (Mark 15:34) as revealing Jesus' 'rejection' by his Father, becoming 'the accursed of God', being divided from his Father by 'the utmost degree of enmity' and suffering 'the torment of hell'. On the Catholic side Hans Urs von Balthasar uses similar language in a number of publications. In Love Alone (New York, 1969), for example, he declares that 'hell is . . . a reality that Christ knew fully in his dereliction' (pp. 76f.). Easter meant raising 'the already stinking body of the sinner from the grave' (ibid., p. 120). One could not fail to detect the influence of von Balthasar in Section IV. C ('The Eschatological Redeemer') of the Theological Commission's 1980 statement. That section spoke of Christ's 'expiatory substitution' (italics mine), his 'will to take on himself as a proxy . . . the sin of the human kind'. 'Substitution', while not meaning that Christ was 'punished or condemned in our stead', nevertheless stresses 'the fact that Christ truly takes on the condition of sinners'. That section of the document assures us:

> No matter how great be the sinner's estrangement from God, it is not as deep as the sense of distance which the Son experiences vis-à-vis the Father in the kenotic emptying of himself (Phil 2:7) and in the anguish of 'abandonment' (Matt 27:46).[4]

Let me introduce one last example to illustrate how the penal substitution view of redemption still lingers on in various guises. In Romans 3:25a St Paul writes of Christ becoming 'the means of expiating sin (hilastērion)' through his bloody death. The New International Version (London, 1979) translates the passage as follows: 'God presented him as a sacrifice of atonement'. But then a footnote adds an alternative translation for hilastērion: 'as the one who would turn aside his wrath, taking away sin' (twelve words for the one Greek term!). Apparently that footnote would have us think of the suffering Christ as a substitute propitiating an angry Father.

Should we be willing in this way to push beyond the language of expiation and reparation? Can we agree that Christ was not merely representatively expiating human guilt by accepting suffering but was a substitute whose punishment appeased the divine anger?

On the positive side it is clear that such an approach to redemption takes human culpability seriously. Sin could cause God to strike down even his own Son, the substitute for his guilty brothers and sisters. Nothing less than Calvary could appease the divine anger at human sin. By way of contrast, some contemporary views of the redemption can let the vicious face of evil slip out of the picture – particularly those views which content themselves *simply* with the example of faith and love given by Jesus. In that case his life, suffering and death become merely exemplary events which challenge us to generosity. But one could never accuse penal substitution theologies of failing to take seriously the contamination brought by sin and human malice.

These versions of redemption, however, fail on two scores: *their monstrous view of God* and *their misinterpretation of the New Testament*. It seems atrocious to picture God the Father acting with extreme cruelty towards his Son and treating him as a sinner even though he is utterly innocent. Yet Calvin, Bossuet and their latter-day followers can tolerate such an image of God as an angry punisher requiring propitiation. This image has nothing in common with the parable of the prodigal son. In that story the father does not need to change from anger to gracious love. He is not waiting to be appeased but waiting for the return of his son. When that happens, he runs to fling his arms around the boy and kiss him.

Certain human causes lurk behind the image of God as an angry punisher. A punishing God has helped to justify and protect authority in families, society and religion. This is not necessarily to allege that parents, rulers and religious leaders have consciously fostered such an image of God as a prop for their position. The image resulted naturally enough from the way they (and those under them) experienced and interpreted human authority. Fear of God has been mobilized to support human subjection. Furthermore, at a personal level the notion of a punishing God corresponds somewhat to self-destructive tendencies within human beings. Drives to self-punishment, the anxiety to propitiate forces within oneself and crippling worries about possible evil consequences of one's actions – all of these elements can coalesce to project a God made in their image and likeness.

To turn to the New Testament. The passion and crucifixion may not be construed as punishment from God. When hostility arose from various groups, Jesus never interpreted that as indicating divine displeasure or the desire to punish him. On the contrary, we saw in Chapter 3 how he associated himself with the fate of persecuted prophets. In their case and his, suffering and death in no way implied condemnation by God. Such persecution was due to the hardness of heart of those to whom they were sent.

Supporters of penal substitution theologies are quick to point out a detail of the agony in the garden, that 'cup' which Jesus prayed to be taken from him (Mark 14:36 parr.). Undoubtedly in the Old Testament a 'cup' can not only be 'the cup of salvation', but also can symbolize divine anger and punishment. Likewise in the Book of Revelation the guilty must drink the cup of God's anger (14:10; 16:19; 18:6). However, the 'cup' in Gethsemane stands for that suffering and death for others which Jesus *freely accepted* (see Mark 14:23 parr.). His followers could also be invited to accept freely similar suffering and martyrdom. That would be to share in the cup which Jesus himself drank (Mark 10:38f. par.). In the description of his arrest given by the Fourth Gospel, Jesus' rebuke to Peter coheres with what Mark reports: 'Shall I not drink the cup which the Father has given me?' (18:11). Jesus does not ask 'Shall I not drink the cup which the Father has *imposed* on me and with which the Father is *punishing* me?' Rather, here, as in Mark, he freely accepts the violent death he is to undergo.

As John's Gospel has slipped in at this point, it offers the chance of noting something about judgement. More than the other Gospels, John uses juridical language and imagery. *Krisis* (judgement) occurs eleven times in John and *krinein* (to judge, condemn) turns up nineteen times. Yet never does this Gospel suggest that God passed judgement on Jesus in his passion or at any other time. Early on, John states the motive of the incarnation: 'God sent his Son into the world, not to condemn the world, but that the world might be saved through him' (3:17). Our text does not read: 'God sent his Son into the world, to condemn him as a sinner'. A little later, the Gospel speaks of *krisis* in this way: 'The Father judges no one, but has given all judgement to the Son' (5:22). Several chapters on, the statement gets modified when Jesus says: 'If I do judge, my judgement is true, for it is not I alone that judge, but I and he who sent me' (8:16; see 8:50). We do not need to explore very far the juridical terminology of John's Gospel to appreciate that it offers no support for the theory that for the sake of human redemption the Father judged, condemned and punished the Son. The language of judgement is there, but is used in a totally different way.

Just above, I recalled Revelation and its theme of *the cup of divine anger* being drunk by the wicked. That same book also refers to God's anger in other places (11:18; 15:7; 16:1ff.). Can those who support a penal substitution theology of redemption find some foothold here? The divine anger forms a part of their theory.

The Old Testament certainly does not credit God with giving vent to outbursts of irrational, spiteful rage as pagan deities often do. Yet it speaks of God's anger and other emotions in vivid, anthropomorphic terms. From Amos on, the classical prophets testify to a divine anger which has been aroused because Yahweh's people have forgotten and despised his faithful love towards them. The divine anger is another name for that wounded love which tries to win human beings back from their sins.

The New Testament generally portrays the divine anger in less vivid terms. Paul simply speaks of 'the wrath of God' being 'revealed from heaven against all ungodliness and wickedness of men who by their wickedness suppress the truth' (Rom 1:18). Sin means 'storing up wrath' for oneself 'on the day of wrath when God's righteous judgement will be revealed' (Rom 2:5). The Synoptic Gospels, however, report anger among Jesus' most striking emotions. He showed sorrowful anger at some Pharisees who were against healing on the Sabbath (Mark 3:5), he angrily threatened demons (Mark 1:25; 9:25 parr.), and manifested indignation at the terrible disease of leprosy (Mark 1:41).

In the New Testament the divine anger characteristically expresses two things: that incompatibility between God and sin which the coming judgement will reveal, and Jesus' feelings when confronted with evil forces which hold human beings in bondage. In other words, at times God's anger is associated with the inauguration of Jesus' redemptive work during his ministry, and especially with future judgement (see Luke 3:7 par.; John 3:36). But *no one in the New Testament links the divine anger with the suffering and death of Jesus*. We should emphasize this point. Paul, the evangelists and other New Testament writers both maintain the theme of divine anger and proclaim the crucifixion of Jesus. But none of them ever uses the notion of divine anger to explain Calvary.

To round off this critique of the penal substitution interpretation of redemption, I wish to look briefly at three texts from St Paul which the supporters of that interpretation repeatedly appeal to: Galatians 3:13, 2 Corinthians 5:21 and Romans 8:3. None of these passages provides the required backing.

The verse from Galatians reads: 'Christ redeemed us from the curse of the law, having become a curse for us – for it is written, "Cursed be everyone who hangs on a tree" '. In dying like a legally condemned criminal and being exposed dead on a gibbet (Deut 21:22f.), Jesus delivered us – paradoxically – from the curse entailed by the regime of the law (and the vain attempt to be justified through keeping that law). The text of Deuteronomy runs as follows:

> And if a man has committed a crime punishable by death and is put to death and you hang him on a tree, his body shall not remain all night upon the tree, but you shall bury him the same day, for *a hanged man is accursed by God*.

When he quotes Deuteronomy, Paul carefully removes the words 'by God'. It was *not* God but those human beings administering the law who treated Jesus as a criminal worthy of death.[5]

The final verse from 2 Corinthians 5 states: 'For our sake he [God] made him [Christ] to be sin who knew no sin, so that in him we might become the righteousness of God'. We need to unpack the first half of Paul's dense text and can do so in several ways:

- 'Christ came in a humanity like that of sinners, except for his being innocent of sin';
- 'Christ came as a victim for sin and an offering for sinners, even through he was innocent of sin';
- 'In spite of being innocent of sin, Christ submitted to the regime of the law which was the regime of sin'.

The first interpretation highlights that solidarity with sinners and their sinful world implied by the incarnation. The second refers to the expiatory value of Jesus' suffering. The third interpretation sees him suffering evil results from the law and sin. (This interpretation is less likely, inasmuch as 2 Corinthians nowhere mentions the law.) We might express the point of the different interpretations as follows. Jesus suffered *with* sinners, as a victim *for* sin (sinners), and as a victim *of* (law and) sin (sinners). It takes strong dogmatic pre-conceptions to make the passage mean: 'God treated the sinless Christ as a sinner. That is to say, God piled the full weight of human sin upon the innocent Christ, condemned him as a sinner, and punished him with death.'

Lastly, Romans 8:3 fails to support punishment and propitiation accounts of the redemption: 'God has done what the law, weakened by the flesh, could not do: sending his own Son in the likeness of sinful flesh and [a] for sin, [b] he condemned sin in the flesh'. The two phrases (a) and (b) call for brief comment. The New English Bible proposes alternative paraphrases of the cryptic 'for sin': 'as a sacrifice for sin', or 'to deal with sin and take away sin'. As for (b), defenders of the penal substitution view insist on taking it to imply 'God in his anger passed judgement against a *sinner* (his Son, who personally bore all human guilt thanks to the nature he had assumed), and condemned him to death'.

Paul in fact maintains that the divine judgement was passed *against sin*, not against Christ. Besides, could we ever explain how the subjective culpability for personal sins was transferred from those who actually committed them to another person, the innocent Christ? It seems absurd to hold that God could literally transfer personal guilt to someone who has not subjectively sinned and therefore is not personally sinful. Paul does not defend such nonsense. We can unpack his text as follows:

> God sent his own Son to deal with sin by undergoing the sign and consequence of sin, death. The Son died innocent of sin, but 'in a form like that of our own sinful nature' (NEB). Through that death God condemned and triumphed over sin by making the means of sin (the flesh) the means of victory.

At the end of this chapter I want to elucidate somewhat some reasons for believing that the redemption which Christ brought about had an absolute (once for all) and universal (for all) character and value. We need to ask: Why should the saving benefits of his suffering, death and resurrection affect everyone, so that he can truly be called 'the Saviour of the world' (John 4:42)? Here I plan to outline the way Christ's solidarity with others takes the form of his *being a representative rather than a substitute*. These notions have already come up. What is the difference?

Substitution does not necessarily require any conscious, free and mutual arrangement between the parties concerned. Only mere 'location' may be involved. One piece can be taken from a chess board and another set in its place. One footballer may be injured in an accident on his way to a match and another player is called in.

> On the field the substitute takes the place of the injured man, who may be unconscious and hence without knowledge that someone is acting as his substitute. In wartime another prisoner may be shot in place of the one who has escaped. There should be no need to pile up further examples to illustrate the point. In the case of substitution between persons, the parties concerned may neither know nor be willing that substitution is taking place. There is less intentionality and more passivity apparent in the way we use the language of 'substitution' (*What are they saying about Jesus?*, p. 45).

Furthermore, in all the examples I can imagine, substitutes do something for us (playing in a match etc.), and then we are excluded from doing it ourselves in any way. The game is over, for example, before we enter the scene.

Representation, however, can come about only through the conscious acceptance by free moral agents on both sides. Someone represents me at a meeting or acts as my legal representative, only when we have agreed that this should be so and that the representation should take place within defined limits. By mutual consent the representative assumes responsibility for a limited period and for limited objectives.

In the case of our redemption, 'while we were yet sinners Christ died for us' (Rom 5:8). He acted on our behalf, and to our advantage atoned for our sins *before* we agreed to this. However, individuals must hear this story of redemption and freely, if subsequently, accept what was representatively done for all.

Here again, redemption entails participation. Expiation is no mere transaction between Father and Son which remains extrinsic to us. We are called to act out what we receive. Christ's Sacrifice (upper case) does not make our sacrifices (lower case) unnecessary. It makes them possible. It is an event into which we should also ourselves be drawn.

It is no surprise that St Paul and other New Testament authors use *sacrificial terminology* to describe the lives of Christians. Thus the apostle encourages the Romans: 'I appeal to you therefore . . . to present your bodies as a living sacrifice, holy and acceptable to God, which is your spiritual worship' (12:1). From prison Paul writes to the community in Philippi: 'Even if I am to be poured as a libation upon the sacrificial offering of your faith, I am glad and rejoice with you all' (2:17). He speaks of the gifts they sent him as 'a fragrant offering, a sacrifice acceptable and pleasing to God' (4:18). A final example. The Letter to the Hebrews also interprets Christian existence as one of sacrifice:

> Through him [sc. Jesus] then let us continually offer up a sacrifice of praise to God, that is, the fruit of lips that acknowledge his name. Do not neglect to do good and to share what you have, for such sacrifices are pleasing to God (13:15f.).

When from his prison cell Paul refers to himself as being 'poured as a libation' (Phil 2:17), this recalls the *suffering* entailed in our being joined to Christ's expiatory sacrifice. The apostle prays

> that I may know him and the power of his resurrection, and *may share his sufferings, becoming like him in his death*, that if possible I may attain the resurrection from the dead (Phil 3:10f.).

This solidarity with Christ's passion means, among other things, a certain sharing in its expiatory function: 'I rejoice in my sufferings for your sake, and in my flesh I complete what is lacking in Christ's afflictions for the sake of his body, that is, the church' (Col 1:24; see Eph 3:13). Apostles and Christians in general can suffer *for* others. When they accept suffering as an extension of Christ's passion, they can properly believe that this helps to purify and renew a contaminated world. Thus in his first recorded message four days after he was shot, Pope John Paul II declared: 'United with Christ, who is priest and victim, I offer my sufferings for the Church and the world'.

(3) *Transforming love.* The third model of redemption centres on the power of Christ's love to heal and transform human hearts. His death and resurrection work through the love which they reveal.

In the first model Christ is the *victorious* lamb of the Book of Revelation. The second sees him as the lamb of sacrifice 'who takes away the sin of the world'. For the third model of redemption he is no longer a lamb but 'the good shepherd' who 'lays down his life for the sheep' (John 10:11). He dies in order 'to gather into one the children of God who are scattered' (John 11:52). His love goes through 'to the end' (John 13:1). In his final discourse the Johannine Jesus expresses this theme in a classical way: 'Greater love has no man than this, that a man lay down his life for his friends' (15:13).

First John indicates that the initiative of the divine love (model three) expiates sin (model two) and brings life (model one) to believers.

In this the love of God was made manifest among us, that God sent his only Son into the world, so that we might live through him. In this is love, not that we loved God but that he loved us and sent his Son to be the expiation for our sins (4:9f.).

St Paul appreciates the way Christ accepted death not only for those who were already his friends but also for those who were still God's enemies.

While we were still weak, at the right time Christ died for the ungodly. Why, one will hardly die for a righteous man – though perhaps for a good man one will dare even to die. But God shows his love for us in that *while we were yet sinners* Christ died for us . . . If *while we were enemies* we were reconciled to God by the death of his Son, much more, now that we are reconciled, shall we be saved by his life (Rom 5:6-8, 10).

In a word, Christ died to touch and change the hearts of enemies. Even if our representatives crucified him, we are still loved by him and his Father.

This third model allows us to spot the deep difference between the true Redeemer and false redeemers. In parodies of divine redemption they may show themselves to be victorious liberators (model one) or even expiate contamination by repairing old wrongs (model two). But it takes the true Redeemer to give and offer himself totally by accepting death through love. The fate of Jesus reveals the loving self-sacrifice of the best, not the victorious survival of the fittest.

(a)   Does this third model of redemption say anything special? After all human history in its entirety can be interpreted as the history of God's love at work. The divine compassion always bears with the infidelity of men and women and lovingly calls them back from their sin (Mic 6:3f.; Isa 54:7-10).

However, the divine love revealed itself progressively and was at work with different degrees of intensity and engagement. The absolute and unique high-point came with Jesus Christ: 'God so loved the world that he gave his only Son' (John 3:16). This supreme initiative from God aimed at bringing about *a new and final covenant* – a change of hearts and a permanent relationship of love both vertically (with our God) and horizontally (with one another).

(b)   At the same time can we really maintain here a unique role for Jesus? The classical formulation of redemption through love ('Greater love has no man than this') simply speaks of 'a man laying down his life for his friends'. This sounds like *a general principle* that, given the appropriate circumstances, any loving and generous person might put into practice. In these terms the self-sacrificing heroism of Jesus might differ in degree but not in kind from that of any genuine martyrs of present and former times.

What then made the example of Jesus' suffering love uniquely different and powerful? Ultimately it was a matter of his *human innocence* and *divine identity*. Unlike other martyrs he died utterly guiltless and totally sinless. Unlike any other martyrs his identity was such that we can join the Roman centurion in confessing 'Truly this man was the Son of God' (Mark 15:39). The following chapter will develop the themes of Jesus' divine identity and human innocence.

(c) Frequently it has been argued that even the most startling example of love can prove effective only if it is known. What of those who lived before Jesus or who lived after him but have never heard of him and his self-sacrificing love? Love must be communicated to touch and transform human hearts.

Even in merely human affairs, however, this objection may not be taken too far. Any life and death full of generous love can spread infectiously to affect people who may never identify the source of this influence. In the case of Jesus we meet 'the Love that moves the sun and the other stars' (Dante, *The Divine Comedy*). The power of his love works universally and retro-actively even for those who remain unaware that he died (or would die) for them.

A key passage in Paul's Corinthian correspondence bears on the point at issue:

> The love of Christ controls us, because we are convinced that one has died for all; therefore all have died. And he died for all, that those who live might live no longer for themselves but for him who for their sake died and was raised (2 Cor 5:14f.).

As usual, I have quoted here the Revised Standard Version. The control exercised by 'the love of Christ' depends on our being convinced that he has died for all. Presumably in this translation the genitive is understood objectively: our love for or towards Christ. This psychological interpret-ation comes through even more clearly in the New English Bible translation: 'The love of Christ leaves us no choice, when once we have reached the conclusion . . .'. The fact that we have reached such a conclusion (*krinantas*) rules out any choice (*sunechei*) in the matter. Knowing that Jesus died for all causes us to love him.

The New American Bible, however, allows for an explanation which matches the strength of Paul's theology: 'The love of Christ impels us who have reached the conviction . . .'. In this case the genitive appears to be taken subjectively: *Christ's own love towards us*, expressed in his death for all, exercises its force on us and brings us to acknowledge what that event of love entailed. His love for us causes us to have a new faith conviction ('one has died for all; therefore all have died') and a new way of life ('no longer for themselves but for him'). In short, Christ's initiative of love makes our response possible.

(d) By any reckoning the idea of redemption as transforming love is very close to that of *reconciliation*. Paul's letters contain two key passages on reconciliation (Rom 5:10f.; 2 Cor 5:18-20). In both contexts God's reconciling activity is invoked in close association with the divine love (Rom

5:5, 8; 2 Cor 5:14). It was love which impelled God to seek reconciliation with us sinners.

In our psychological age one point should be insisted on strongly. In the first instance we need to be and in fact are reconciled with God. Then we can be reconciled with ourselves. (Here I am speaking of a logical, not necessarily a temporal, priority.) Hence I feel uneasy with Schillebeeckx's formulation: 'Deliverance, redemption, consists in so being reconciled to one's past that confidence in the future is again made possible' (*Jesus*, p. 672). The *primary* point of the prodigal son is not so much that the boy 'accepts himself', but that he is accepted by his compassionate father. St Paul does not say that 'God through Christ reconciled us to ourselves', but that 'God through Christ reconciled us to himself' (2 Cor 5:18).

(e) Those who know themselves to be transformed through the Redeemer's love are called to act accordingly (1 Cor 13). All three models of redemption include that theme: *the beneficiaries must become participants*. In terms of the third model, those who receive love from God should pass it on: 'If God so loved us, we also ought to love one another' (1 John 4:11). In their 'Message to the Peoples of Latin America' the bishops at Puebla invited their audience 'to be self-sacrificing constructors of the civilization of love' (n. 8).

If truly practised, such love will bring people to real suffering and even to death. A North American writer, Paul Goodman, once said that the only way for a Christian to live is to risk love and hope for resurrection. A friend of mine, Peter Steele, commented: 'He assumed, rightly, that love will pin us to a cross and that crucifixion has only one outcome'.

(f) Earlier in this chapter I remarked that the three classical models for expressing Christ's redemption (victorious liberation, expiation and transforming love) complement each other. Nevertheless, one can also admit *a certain priority of the third model*. As the old adage puts it, 'love conquers all' (*amor vincit omnia*). Love overcomes all the forces which menace and enslave human beings. Love wants to live and give life – opening up for others the freedom to live (model one). As 1 John 4:10 indicates, love also cleanses and purifies: 'God . . . loved us and sent his Son to be the expiation for our sins' (model two). Finally, love transforms selfish hearts and brings a new unity (model three). Love is the final and deepest meaning of redemption and, indeed, of all reality.

CLOSING CONSIDERATIONS

To interpret and express the redemption which Jesus brought to the human condition, I have expounded the three traditional models to speak of a deliverance from the power of evil and sin, an atonement for sin's contamination, and loving reconciliation from sin's isolation. Without attempting to document matters exhaustively, I have noted how the scriptures and liturgical texts provide a basis for each model. Even one book alone, the Gospel of John, offers a biblical starting-point for all three models. We could debate whether sacrificial imagery is incidental in John or central and determinative. Nevertheless, texts relating to that and the other models are all to be found in the Fourth Gospel: 'Be of good cheer, I have overcome the world' (16:33); 'Behold, the Lamb of God, who takes away the sin of the world' (1:29); 'Jesus . . . having loved his own who were in the world, he loved them to the end' (13:1).

Christian hymns, poetry, theology, spirituality and art also witness to these three ways of expressing redemption. In those fields I know no better summary than the sonnet 'Easter' by Edmund Spenser (1552–99):

> Most glorious Lord of life, that on this day
> > Didst make thy triumph over death and sin;
> > And having harrowed hell didst bring away
> > Captivity thence captive, us to win:
> This joyous day, dear Lord, with joy begin,
> > And grant that we for whom thou didst die
> > Being with thy dear blood clean washed from sin,
> > May live forever in felicity.
> And that thy love we weighing worthily,
> > May likewise love thee for the same again;
> > And for thy sake that all like dear didst buy,
> > With love may one another entertain.
> So let us love, dear love, like as we ought.
> Love is the lesson which the Lord us taught.

(1) *The mystery of faith.* The first encyclical by John Paul II, *Redemptor Hominis*, frequently refers to 'the mystery of redemption'. This can serve as a useful reminder that we can never hope to describe fully, let alone explain comprehensively, what Jesus has done for the salvation of the world. The three models of redemption all have something to say about the nature of redemption, but none exhaustively accounts for that mystery. We can put them together and speak of a victorious, purifying and reconciling love effectively manifested in Jesus' life, death and resurrection. But even then our theology fails to match and catch the mysterious depth of the paschal mystery which brought our salvation. At best we can only hope for partial insights.

I have been talking of the *nature* of redemption. As regards the *fact* of redemption, human history and experience never offer irresistible and overwhelmingly clear evidence that redemption has occurred. Certainly there are hints and signs of its presence – when we share the sacramental life of the Church, when seemingly incurable, hopeless situations in our personal lives and social relationships are set right, or when we witness unbreakable hope in the face of the loss and absurdity of death. Nevertheless, Christ's redemptive activity is both limited in its present impact and not yet unambiguously revealed. We are left struggling with the question: Has his liberating, atoning and loving power truly touched our lives and made a real difference? Has the redemption he effected on Good Friday and Easter Sunday genuinely overcome the powers of evil, atoned for sins and transformed human hearts? Likewise those who strive with Christ to combat evil forces, purify guilt and reach out to others in love may sometimes or even often wonder whether anything is achieved. But we are here proclaiming and living 'the mystery of faith'. So far we enjoy only glimpses and signs of Christ's redemptive power and presence.

(2) *The blood of Jesus.* One way of recapitulating the three models of redemption turns up in the letter to the Colossians: 'God was pleased . . . through him [Christ] to reconcile to himself all things, whether on earth or in heaven, making peace *by the blood of his cross*' (1:19f.). At once I must admit that some recent translations of the New Testament and theological writings seem reluctant to mention the blood of Jesus. *Good News for Modern Man*, the New Testament in *Today's English Version*, repeatedly refuses to translate exactly references to Jesus' blood and often introduces a vaguer term, death. That version renders Colossians 1:20 as follows:

> Through the Son, then, God decided to bring the whole universe back to himself. God made peace through his Son's death on the cross, and so brought back to himself all both on earth and in heaven.

Earlier I appealed to a key Pauline passage about the nature of redemption which speaks of Jesus expiating sins *through his blood* (Rom 3:25). The *New English Bible* modifies Paul's concreteness and calls Jesus 'the means of expiating sin by his sacrificial death'.

When contemporary theological works deal with the suffering and death of Jesus, they regularly fail to discuss how he made peace *through the shedding of his blood upon the cross*. An easy way of verifying this sweeping judgement is to review the chapter (or sections) devoted to Jesus' death in the Christologies of Kasper, Küng, Moltmann, Pannenberg, Schillebeeckx, Schoonenberg and others. Let me cite two examples. In the relevant chapter of his *Jesus the Man and the Myth*, James Mackey has one passing reference to the spilling of Jesus' blood (p. 74). Jon Sobrino in his *Christology at the Crossroads* also does no more than merely touch the theme (p. 189).

I wonder whether Bible translators and theologians are losing something of great significance for redemption when they play down or even ignore the blood of Jesus shed for us on Good Friday. We have here a theme which runs through the New Testament. At the Last Supper Jesus takes the cup and says

'This is my blood of the new covenant, which is poured out for many' (Mark 14:24 parr.). St Paul teaches that we are 'justified' by the blood of Christ who 'died for us' (Rom 5:8f.). 1 Peter assures its readers that they have been 'ransomed' by 'the precious blood of Christ' (1:18f.). The Letter to the Hebrews expounds the priestly service of Christ whose blood purifies us 'to serve the living God' (9:12, 14; see 13:12). The Book of Revelation pushes language to its limits when it 'explains' that the heavenly multitude 'have washed their robes and made them white in the blood of the Lamb' (7:14).

What did it originally mean and what might it mean today to believe and proclaim that Jesus effected 'our peace and reconciliation' with God through 'the blood of his cross'? How is his blood associated with the three models of redemption developed earlier?

(a) Before examining the symbolism of blood in the New Testament, we should organize the ways in which the Israelites already thought about and used blood in their relationship with God.

The Israelites remembered how before leaving Egypt they smeared their doorposts with the blood of a lamb (Exod 12:7, 13, 22f.). The sign delivered them from the destruction which afflicted the homes of the Egyptians. The blood of the paschal lamb saved the Israelites from losing their first-born.

Besides proving a sign which brought *deliverance from death*, blood was closely associated with *life*. The Israelites understood life to be 'in the blood' (Lev 17:11ff.; see Deut 12:23). Since life was sacred, they regarded blood also as sacred. Yahweh was the God of life. Hence blood, the seat of life, belonged to God alone. In the ancient Near East and Middle East the Israelites appear to have differed from all their neighbours *in linking blood with life and hence with what was sacred and divine*. In the *Journal of Biblical Literature* (1969, 1973) Dennis McCarthy has shown how this was a uniquely Hebrew notion – at least in the symbolism dealing with sacrifice.

In its own way modern science has more than vindicated the Old Testament conviction that life, the divine and sacred gift *par excellence*, is 'in the blood'. Oxygen, nutrients, hormones and other items essential for life are carried by our blood. Its complex structure enables us to endure wide variations of temperature and changes of diet. Every day around the world massive transfusions of blood save lives that are slipping away. Medical discoveries and practice have dramatically associated the miracle of life with the miracle of blood.

Besides expressing deliverance and life, blood was believed to cleanse the stains of human sin. On the Day of Atonement the high priest sprinkled blood as part of a ritual recalling God's willingness to purify the Israelites from their sins. Yahweh wished to remove human guilt, destroy sin and effect reconciliation with his people. The ceremony of sprinkling blood on the 'mercy seat' symbolized the divine desire to wipe away the contamination of sin (Lev 16).

Today, of course, we may not appreciate the practice of slaughtering bulls and goats to release and use their blood. But we should still be able to recognize the religious logic of the Israelites. Insofar as it was the element in which life resided, blood enjoyed a peculiarly divine and sacred character. Hence it appropriately served and stood for the purification of sin and the restoration of loving relations between Yahweh and his people.

Finally, blood sealed the covenant at Sinai (Exod 24:3–8). Even today some cultures and sub-cultures maintain this symbolism. Rituals involving blood bind together formerly hostile groups and bring new relationships of peace, friendship and love. In the desert the Israelites solemnly accepted Yahweh's offer of a special relationship with them and used blood to represent this loving union with their God. The sacrificial blood was shared by the people and their God (represented by the altar).

These then are three perspectives on blood recorded in the Old Testament: as (a) a sign of deliverance and life, (b) a ritual means of expiating human guilt, and (c) a way of sealing and expressing a new relationship of friendship. Even in the advanced industrial culture of the late twentieth century this triple typology persists at least dimly.

When a society lacks life, we call it anaemic. Parents show alarm when their children suffer cuts. There is a danger that blood will be lost and dangerous infection will set in. The blood-stained seat of a car can speak very powerfully of a precious life being terminated by terrorists. Blood donors literally give new life to others. The point does not need to be laboured. Both positive and negative associations of ideas link blood with deliverance from death to life.

I have wondered what produced the extraordinary impact of those photographs from the assassination of Archbishop Oscar Romero. He lay there at the altar, his vestments red with his life's blood. Admittedly we have become sadly used to the fact that noble people may dedicate themselves in heroic service only to be murdered and soon forgotten. So much bloodshed seems irrelevant for the purifying and healing of a contaminated world. But did some of us instinctively hope that the martyrdom of Oscar Romero would by way of exception truly make a difference? Even now, can the death of this priest and victim still in some way work to cleanse and atone for the sins of his society?

Lastly, the call to give one's life for others has been introduced in a thousand evil causes. But no misuse can rob Jesus' words of their truth: 'Greater love has no man than this, that a man lay down his life for his friends' (John 15:13). Whether in fiction or in real life, there can be no more powerful way of symbolizing and enacting a relationship of love than by shedding one's blood for others. True love always makes people vulnerable.

Sometimes it literally turns them into targets for killers.

(b) It takes no great imaginative leap to see how the triple typology outlined above was supremely realized in the case of Jesus' bloody crucifixion. As 'our paschal lamb' (1 Cor 5:7) he freely accepted death to deliver us from the power of sin and bring us life and freedom. To eat the flesh of the Son of Man and drink his blood is to receive eternal life (John 6:53–56). Second, 1 John witnesses to 'the blood of Jesus' which 'cleanses us from all sin' (1:7). Finally, the shedding of his blood effected a new covenant of love between God and the whole human race (Mark 14:24 parr.). This death expressed the divine love towards us (Rom 8:31–39), and aimed at bringing a loving reconciliation between God and all people (Rom 5:10f.).

St Paul's classic passage in Romans 3:25 (about Jesus becoming 'through his blood' the 'means of expiating sin for all who believe') serves to summarize redemption. Three perspectives lie behind the apostle's words. This blood delivered us from death and bondage like the blood smeared on the doorways of the Israelites at the time of their *liberation* from Egypt (model one). Jesus died on the new Day of Atonement, which was not simply valid for a year (Lev 16) or even for half a century (Lev 25). His act of *expiation* touched all men and women for all time (model two). Then his blood sealed a relationship which went beyond the covenant made with the Israelites at Sinai. A new and definitive covenant of *love* was established with all people (model three).

(3) *The Trinity.* Early on in this chapter I spoke of Christ's redemptive activity aiming to satisfy the human hunger for *life*, *meaning* and *love*. These three headings lead into an analysis of the human condition which relates to the account offered at the beginning of this chapter. Men and women spend their time avoiding three things and seeking three things.

First, they want to escape death in all its forms. Death is not only oppressively there at the end of their biological story, but it also invades their lives in all the many deaths through which they suffer loss of people, places, opportunities and personal powers. Everyone wishes to avoid death (understood in that complete sense) and live life to the full (however differently individuals interpret what such a full life entails). Second, men and women look for meaning in what they do and constantly flee from absurdity. Where situations appear meaningful, even awful difficulties can be cheerfully faced. But if a sense of hollow meaninglessness dogs people, they can find existence to be intolerable. Finally, human beings are like a sponge with an unlimited desire and capacity to be affirmed and loved. They instinctively avoid hatred and indifference and long to receive appreciation and love.

Granted that this threefold account of human existence matches our experience, we can see how this radical quest for life, meaning and love is in fact a quest for the Father, Son and Holy Spirit. Our threefold need opens us up to the redemptive benefits coming to us from the triune God. In the Father we find 'the God of the living' (Mark 12:27), the ultimate source of all life, that 'living and true God' who delivers us from the bondage of idols which bring only death (1 Thess 1:9). Christ himself comes as the wisdom of God, the one who gives purpose and meaning to existence. Here one might easily adapt the prologue to John's Gospel and make it read: 'In the beginning was the Meaning and the Meaning was with God, and the Meaning was God. . . . And the Meaning became flesh and dwelt among us. . . . And from his wisdom we have all received.' Last, the Holy Spirit is the divine love poured into human hearts (Rom 5:5) – both to show how deeply God loves and affirms humanity and to enable a loving response to take place. In brief, the human search for life, meaning and love can be properly identified as a profound quest for the Father, Son and Spirit.

This threefold orientation towards a full life, a clear meaning for existence and an affirming love is ultimately a hunger for the triune God and the fullness of salvation. It does not seem unreasonable to associate this radical orientation with the three models of redemption. The quest for life matches the liberation from all those forces of evil which set us in 'darkness and the shadow of death'. Second, as the one who brings meaning and truth, Christ deals with the absurd contamination and meaninglessness of guilt. Third, the transforming love communicated through the Holy Spirit changes the selfish hearts of human beings and brings them out of their empty isolation.

In short, interpreting redemption as a deliverance from the three primordial anxieties of our human existence to receive life, meaning and love sets together *salvation* and *revelation*. There is a threefold shape to the salvation which came to us through the paschal mystery, just as it took the events of Good Friday and Easter Sunday to reveal to us the triune God. From the Middle Ages into the Renaissance paintings and sculptures of 'the Mercy Seat' portrayed the Father holding the dead body of the Son – their faces joined by the Holy Spirit represented under the form of a dove. As I remarked in Chapter 3, these works express the belief that through the crucifixion and resurrection the revelation of the triune God reached its climax. The disclosure of the mystery of the Trinity went hand in hand with a salvation whose threefold aspect allowed Christians to develop the three classical models of redemption.

(4) *The Saviour of the world.*   The death and resurrection of Christ were not just inspiring events which brought life, meaning and love to some people. They were events which changed the world, so that Hebrews could speak of his 'tasting' death 'for everyone' (2:9) and 1 John could confess: 'He is the expiation for our sins and the sins of the whole world' (2:2). Back in Chapter 2 I noted the universal dimension of the mission to which the

earthly Jesus dedicated himself. Chapter 3 not only recalled the fact that the early Christians interpreted Jesus' crucifixion as a sacrificial death which atoned representatively for the sins of *all*, but also argued that in some way this conviction went back to claims which Jesus had made about his coming death. How can we elucidate theologically the belief that his crucifixion and resurrection brought redemption once and for all and for all? What was it about these events which made them burst through the normal limits of history to enjoy a universal saving influence over the entire story of human beings and their world? Ultimately two lines of argument are available to us, depending on whether we favour an eschatological or an incarnational mind-set. The first answer takes shape around time and history, the second around the being of Christ.

(a)   The *eschatological* answer finds the ultimate and universal significance of the events of Good Friday and Easter Sunday in their essential link with *the end of all history*. What happened to and through Jesus was nothing less than the beginning of that *eschaton* (1 Cor 15:20; Col 1:18). The general resurrection and final end of all history will be nothing less than the ultimate consequence of what was entailed in the crucified Jesus being raised to new life. As it was the beginning of the end of all history, what Jesus went through took on universal value.

(b)   The One who died and rose was in his being the incarnate Son of God. From this perspective we can also appreciate the universal impact of Jesus' crucifixion and resurrection. In a unique way the God of all the world was involved in those events. If it was Jesus' humanity that made his dying and rising possible, it was his divinity that gave that dying and rising a cosmic value.

NOTES

1   P. Ricoeur, 'Defilement', *The Symbolism of Evil* (ET: London and New York, 1967), pp. 25–46.

2   Curiously enough, there has been very little *theological* reflection on the *Exsultet*. Forthcoming publication(s) by Christopher Willcock should help to fill this gap.

3   The conference itself agreed that it did not want to highlight 'the salvific atonement on the cross' (*Your Kingdom Come. Report on the World Conference on Mission and Evangelism* [Geneva, 1980], p. xi).

4   This is a latter-day example of a cherished theme in Christian rhetoric. But in Philippians Paul is *not* employing early Christian hymnic language to speak of a deeply experienced 'sense of distance'. The cry of abandonment in Matthew's account of the passion is a quotation from a psalm, which does *not* allow us to compare Jesus' interior state with the sinner's feeling of estrangement from God.

5   Deuteronomy refers to the practice of hanging on a tree the corpse of a criminal *who had already been executed*. Yet before Paul in at least one place the Qumran scrolls already apply the text of Deuteronomy to the fate of someone *crucified*. Paul himself wants to stress the fact that the death on the cross meant Jesus' total rejection by those who administered the Jewish religion.

QUESTIONS FOR DISCUSSION

(1) In the quotation which follows from the 1980 statement of the International Theological Commission (III. B. 4), how many of the points represent real difficulties in your environment? Has this chapter met any of these difficulties? What needs to be added by way of response?

> Today many voice . . . difficulties with regard to the soteriological aspects of the christological dogmas.
>
> They recoil from any notion of salvation which would inject heteronomy into existence as project.
>
> They take exception to what they regard as the purely individualistic character of Christian salvation.
>
> The promise of a blessedness to come seems to them a utopia which distracts people away from their genuine obligations which, in their view, are all confined to this world.
>
> They want to know what it is that mankind had to be redeemed from, and to whom the ransom had to be paid.
>
> They grow indignant at the contention that God could have exacted the blood of an innocent person, a notion in which they sense a streak of sadism.
>
> They argue against what is known as 'vicarious satisfaction' (that is, through a mediator) by saying that this mode of satisfaction is ethically impossible. If it is true that every conscience is autonomous, they argue, no conscience can be freed by another.
>
> Finally, some of our contemporaries lament the fact that they cannot find in the life of the Church and the faithful the lived expression of the mystery of liberation which is proclaimed.

(2) How do people in your country and culture experience and interpret the evil from which they desire to be saved?

(3) In the Eucharistic prayers and your other liturgical texts, what model of redemption appears most frequently?

(4) What does Jesus' death and resurrection promise now for those who fear that there can be 'nothing new under the sun'? For those who feel themselves to be locked into a seemingly senseless cycle of birth, poverty and death?

(5) What would you say to those who experience God as an oppressor, who see the choice as 'God or freedom', and believe that they need to be saved *from God*? How could you show that apart from God we will never find real freedom but only a new slavery?

(6) In the quotation (from the International Theological Commission) with which this chapter began, are 'redemption' and 'salvation' used synonymously? Do you wish to use these terms interchangeably? Is it the same to call Jesus 'Saviour' and 'Redeemer'?

(7) As regards the relationship between creation and redemption, would you agree that redemption enhances and perfects creation in that it brings more freedom (and life), renewed purity (and meaning), and greater love?

(8) If we relate the three models of redemption with the sacramental life of the church, are there grounds for associating the first with baptism, the second with the sacrament of reconciliation, and the third with the reception of the Eucharist?

ADDITIONAL READING

Besides the works already indicated in this chapter, the following items could be helpful:

'Atonement', *ODCC*, pp. 104f.

D. M. Baillie, *God was in Christ* (London, 1948), pp. 157–202.

K. Barth, *CD* IV, *The Doctrine of Reconciliation*.

F. Büchsel, '*Agorazō, exagorazō*', *TDNT* 1, pp. 124–128.

F. Büchsel, '*Katallassō*', *ibid*. 1, pp. 254–259.

F. Büchsel, '*Lutron*' etc., *ibid*. 4, pp. 340–356.

R. J. Daly, *The Origins of the Christian Doctrine of Sacrifice* (Philadelphia, 1978).

F. W. Dillistone, *The Christian Understanding of the Atonement* (Grand Rapids, 1974).

J. A. Fitzmyer, 'Pauline Theology', *JBC* 2, pp. 800–827, especially pp. 814–826.

W. Günther and W. Bauder, 'Sin', *DNTT* 3, pp. 573–587.

P. Hefner, 'The Cultural Significance of Jesus' Death as Sacrifice', *Journal of Religion* 60 (1980), pp. 411–439.

J. Herrmann and F. Büchsel, '*Hileōs, hilaskomai*' etc., *TDNT* 3, pp. 300–323.

J. Jensen, 'Redemption (in the Bible)', *NCE* 12, pp. 136–144.

John Paul II, *Dives in Misericordia* (Vatican, 1980).

H. Küng, *OBC*, pp. 419–436.

F. Laubach and others, 'Blood, Sprinkle, Strangled', *DNTT* 1, pp. 220–226.

H. -G. Link and others, 'Reconciliation' etc., *DNTT* 3, pp. 145–176.

S. Lyonnet and L. Sabourin, *Sin, Redemption and Sacrifice* (Rome, 1970).

J. Macquarrie, *Principles of Christian Theology* (rev. ed.: London, 1977), pp. 311–327.

D. J. McCarthy, 'Blood', *IDB* supplementary vol., pp. 114–117.

J. Milgrom, 'Atonement' and 'Atonement, Day of', *IDB* supplementary vol., pp. 78–83.

C. F. D. Moule, 'The Scope of the Death of Christ', *The Origin of Christology* (Cambridge, 1977), pp. 107–126.

J. K. Mozley, *The Doctrine of Atonement* (London, 1915).

W. Mundle and others, 'Redemption' etc., *DNTT* 3, pp. 177–223.

W. Pannenberg, *JGM*, pp. 245–280.

E. L. Peterman, 'Redemption (Theology of)', *NCE* 12, pp. 144–160.

K. Rahner, *Foundations*, pp. 282–285, 288, 292f.

K. Rahner and others, 'Salvation', *SM* 5, pp. 405–438 (= *EncTh*, pp. 1499–1530).

J. Reumann, 'Reconciliation', *IDB* supplementary vol., pp. 728f.

J. Rivière, *The Doctrine of the Atonement* (ET: St Louis, 1909).

F. Thiele and C. Brown, 'Sacrifice' etc., *DNTT* 3, pp. 415–438.

P. Tillich, *Systematic Theology*, III: *Existence and the Christ* (Chicago, 1957).

H. E. W. Turner, *The Patristic Doctrine of Redemption* (London, 1952).

B. Vawter, *This Man Jesus* (New York: Image Book ed., 1975), pp. 77–89.

H. -R. Weber, *The Cross* (ET: Grand Rapids, 1978).

F. M. Young, *Sacrifice and the Death of Christ* (London, 1975).

See also various articles in *DBT*: 'Expiation', 'Hardness of Heart', 'Reconciliation', 'Redemption', 'Sin', etc.; and in *IDB*: 'Atonement', 'Expiation', 'Propitiation', 'Reconciliation', 'Redeem', etc.

6
The Son of God

God, grace and Jesus are all one.

WALTER HILTON

Your life is hid with Christ in
God.

COLOSSIANS 3:3

Both the biblical and the liturgical texts of Christians take up salvation as a more primary category than revelation. To put this in terms of Jesus Christ: these written witnesses to faith attend first to what he did and does for us, and only then to who he is revealed as being. This movement from Saviour to Son of God forms a natural order of knowledge and matches the development of the early Christians. They came to know who Jesus was through what he did. His value and significance were grounded in his being. I chose to follow that order in reflecting on his redemptive work before coming to his personal identity.

In the year A.D. 112 a Roman governor, Pliny the Younger, reported to the Emperor Trajan that when Christians met, they 'recited a hymn to Christ as [their] God' (*Letters* X, 96). Half a century or more before that date, the letters of St Paul indicated how at the origins of Christianity the risen and exalted Jesus was already worshipped as existing in power and dignity at the divine level. In Chapter 1 I recalled some *pre*-Pauline formulations which illustrate that their experience of the crucified and risen Jesus had driven the first generation of Christians to assert his divine status. They believed him to be more than one who had simply conveyed to them God's ultimate promises and demands. The union of activity between Jesus and God implied a union of being.

The kind of evidence I pointed to in Chapter 1 leads to the conclusion that early Christians believed Jesus to be personally identified with God. Some passages in the New Testament apply the term 'God' to Jesus (John 1:1, 18; 20:28; Heb 1:8–9). Other passages probably also do the same (Rom 9:5; Tit

2:13; 2 Pet 1:1; 1 John 5:20). John distinguishes the type of sonship that Jesus communicates to those who believe in him and become *tekna* (1:12) from Jesus' own divine Sonship which remains unique to him as *huios* (1:14). Paul likewise attributes adoptive sonship to Christians (Gal 4:5; Rom 8:15), but speaks of Jesus as God's 'own Son' (Rom 8:32).

Modern attempts to deny that *first-century Christians* acknowledged the risen Jesus' divine status will go the way earlier such attempts have already gone. The New Testament evidence all too clearly tells against that reductionist case. What is a much more difficult and crucial matter concerns *present* belief in Jesus' divinity. For us today, does historical evidence (from the first and later centuries) count for (or against) his divinity? *By itself* could such evidence suggest or even demand the acceptance of a more than merely human Jesus? But supposing we agree that *merely* historical research and judgements – if such do exist – *by themselves* could never lead to the conclusion (of faith and theology) that Jesus is divine, what social and personal factors might help to bring one to that conclusion? What factors could properly lead one beyond merely admiring and loving Jesus to worshipping him as Son of God?

In this book I do not plan to deal directly with the formation of faith in Jesus' divinity. Chapter V of *Fundamental Theology* (together with its excursus on historical knowledge and faith) should convey the kind of answer I would want to offer. The purpose of this chapter is rather to describe and clarify orthodox Christian belief about humanity and divinity existing together in the one person of Jesus Christ. If I succeed somewhat in clarifying the nature and meaning of this central belief, to that extent I shall be making it appear more credible. The appreciation of the possible meaning(s) of any proposition like 'Jesus is both truly human and truly divine' inevitably makes assent to its truth easier.

Where should we begin this endeavour to clarify the mystery of Jesus Christ's personal identity? If the prologue to John were to focus our reflections, several basic questions would emerge at once. We deal with One who existed before his being in the world ('in the beginning was the Word'). This pre-existence raises the issue of the relationship between eternity and time. Then how are we to think of One who was related to and identified with God from the beginning ('the Word was with God and the Word was God')? Further, how are we to express that union of Spirit and matter brought by the incarnation ('the Word became flesh')?

In no way, however, did wrestling with the mystery of the Saviour's identity stop even after that majestic statement with which John's prologue crowns the Christological thought of the first century. Apropos of Jesus' redemptive work, official Church doctrines were to add little to the teachings of the New Testament. But, as we saw in Chapter 1, the early centuries of Christianity gave shape to their belief about Christ's person in a series of creeds and solemn conciliar statements. The climax was the classic text of the Council of Chalcedon (A.D. 451). Its definition of the one person in two natures became the enduring model for answering *who* (= the person) Christ was (and is), *what* (= the natures) he was, and *how* (= the union between person and natures) he was what he was.

THE DEFINITION OF CHALCEDON

Nowadays some fearful Christians see the definition of Chalcedon as a theological safety-net, something to fall back on if things should go seriously wrong. It would be better to follow Karl Rahner and appreciate that this definition and other such classic formulas 'derive their life from the fact that they are not end but beginning, not goal but means, truths which open the way to the – ever greater – Truth' (*ThInv* 1, p. 149). Let us look at the text of Chalcedon which exemplifies splendidly the validity of Rahner's thesis. Proper reception and interpretation will help us to move forward in our faithful exploration of the mystery of Christ.

> Therefore, following the holy Fathers,
> we all with one accord *teach* men to acknowledge
> ONE AND THE SAME Son, our Lord Jesus Christ
> at once complete in divinity and complete in humanity,
> truly God and truly man, consisting also of a rational soul and body;
> of one substance (*homoousion*) with the Father as regards his divinity,
> and at the same time of one substance with us as regards his humanity;
> like us in all respects, apart from sin;
> as regards his divinity, begotten of the Father before the ages,
> but yet as regards his humanity begotten, for us and *for our salvation*,
> of Mary, the Virgin, the God-bearer;
> ONE AND THE SAME Christ, Son, Lord, only-begotten,
>
> recognized in two natures (*physeis*),
> without confusion, without change, without division, without separation;
> the distinction of natures being in no way annulled by the union,
> but rather the characteristics of each nature being preserved
> and coming together to form one person (*prosōpon*) and subsistence (*hypostasis*),
> not as parted or separated into two persons,
> but ONE AND THE SAME Son and only-begotten God the Word, Lord Jesus
>   Christ;
> even as the prophets from earliest times spoke of him,
> and our Lord Jesus Christ himself taught us,
> and the creed of the Fathers has handed down to us (*DS* 301f.).

(1) *Some limitations.* I have used italics and capitalization, as well as introducing a break between the two parts of the definition, to bring out its major features. To begin with, certain limitations show up. First, the text is a piece of teaching ('we all with one accord teach'), and is not as such a creed

to be used in Christian worship. It records the teaching, not the praying, Church of the past.

Second, the definition barely touches the earthly life and history of Jesus. It recalls his birth ('begotten of Mary, the Virgin'), refers to his ministry ('our Lord Jesus Christ himself taught us'), and has nothing to say about the crucifixion and resurrection. Everything that Chalcedon affirms could still be valid if Jesus had been miraculously snatched away from this world and never died on Calvary. At best his death is only hinted at in phrases like 'truly man' and 'like us in all respects, apart from sin'. Chalcedon does not spell out the distinction between the earthly and glorified state of Jesus, let alone fill in the details of his historical life.

The New Testament, however, strongly attests the fact that through the resurrection Jesus became and was known to be the divine Lord of 'the living and the dead' (Rom 14:9; Matt 28:18). The resurrection of the crucified Jesus not only illuminated his personal relationship with God, but also marked his passage from one state to another. He who 'was descended from David according to the flesh' was 'designated Son of God in power by his resurrection from the dead' (Rom 1:3f.; see Phil 2:5-11; 1 Tim 3:16; 1 Pet 3:18). This *two-stage* Christology (the earthly Jesus and the risen Christ) finds *some* equivalent in the *two-natures* Christology ('complete in humanity' and 'complete in divinity'). But the historical passage of Jesus through life and crucifixion to resurrection is missing.

Third, Chalcedon acknowledges Jesus' divine and human characteristics in a variety of ways ('complete in divinity and complete in humanity, truly God and truly man' and so forth) *before* it introduces its own special contribution ('recognized in two natures, without confusion' and so on). In other words, the Council notes the way in which earlier Christian tradition had already elaborated diverse expressions for the being human and the being divine in Christ. Presumably later Church teachers and writers would produce further ways of speaking about him. Nowhere does Chalcedon impose its 'two-natures' terminology as the *only* language to be used henceforth by all Christians of all times.

Fourth, although the definition does affirm that Jesus was 'begotten, for us and for our salvation', Piet Schoonenberg rightly observes that Chalcedon tends to represent

> Christ to us merely as an object of knowledge. Such a view detaches Christology from soteriology. This objection holds for many Christological treatises which, as formal elaborations of the *unio hypostatica*, are completely distinct from soteriology (*The Christ* [ET: London, 1972], p. 63).

In fairness to Chalcedon, however, we should not forget that concerns about redemption lay behind its teaching on Christ's divine and human nature. Any tampering with either component was understood to undermine the experienced reality of his saving work. If he were not truly divine, he would not have liberated us to participate, as far as we can, in God's life. If he were not truly human, he would not have taken hold of and saved human life in all its fullness.

(2) *Chalcedon's scope.* We can reasonably express the essential message of Chalcedon as follows: 'The human is so united with the divine in Christ, that the *one* Christ can be confessed to be both truly God and truly man'. At the beginning, in the middle and at the end of its definition, the Council insists on the oneness of Jesus Christ ('one and the same Son'). It does not really describe, let alone explain, *how* this unity of the divine–human relationship works.

This unity functions within a double reality (the 'two natures'), but in such a way that one component does not prevail at the expense of the other. Although the two natures 'come together to form one person and subsistence', nevertheless, 'the distinction of natures' is 'in no way annulled by the union' and 'the characteristics of each nature' are 'preserved'. In the original (Greek) text four adverbs nestle at the heart of the definition to reject errors and safeguard 'the characteristics of each nature': 'without confusion, without change, without division, without separation'. 'Without confusion' and 'without change' are aimed against any 'Monophysite' view which would understand the union of the two natures to alter a real humanity or even to amalgamate the humanity into the divinity. 'Without division' and 'without separation' exclude Nestorian tendencies to partition Christ into two beings (the Logos and the man Jesus) co-existing side by side.

TRULY HUMAN

In the light of Chalcedon I want next to reflect on what it means to accept Jesus as being truly human. At least from the Middle Ages down to modern times many Christians were so anxious to safeguard the divine side of Christ that they made the human side incredible. He was often represented during his earthly life not as being genuinely human but as the Son of God wandering around in human disguise. The 1980 document of the International Theological Commission was certainly not overstating matters when it declared: 'The untold riches of Jesus' humanity need to be brought to light more effectively than was done by the Christologies of the past'. It saw 'a return to the earthly Jesus' to be 'beneficial and indispensable today in the field of dogmatic theology'. As 'Jesus' brotherhood and solidarity with us by no means detract from his divinity', any opposition 'between the humanity and divinity of Jesus' could only be a 'pseudo-opposition' (I. B. 2. 6).

(1) *Fully human.* We can put this in the terms of Chalcedon. The being of one substance or consubstantiality with the Father must not be considered separately from the consubstantiality with us. The consubstantiality with the Father did not alienate Jesus from us, nor did the consubstantiality with us alienate him from the Father. The being truly and fully divine did not destroy the being truly and fully human, and vice versa. 'Proximity' to divinity did not mean the diminution, let alone the destruction, of Jesus' genuine humanity. Rather, that situation enhanced and fulfilled his human nature. He was, in the words of Chalcedon, 'complete in humanity'. Leo the Great, the Pope who stood behind the Council, in his 'Tome' described Christ as being *'totus in nostris'* – as we might say, 'completely part of our human world' (*DS*, 293).

(2) *Our sense of humanity.* Once we move further into the material, we need to admit that our experiences of humanity and the human condition will colour and contribute to what we say about Jesus as 'truly man'. Our notions of what is human have been determined religiously, culturally, politically and economically by our lives in Scotland or Singapore, Nigeria or California. We belong to our particular environments, and that inevitably, if not totally, shapes the way we understand human life.

Despite all the intercultural differences, however, the conviction is widely shared today that both for society at large and for individuals in particular, being human is an open, dynamic process. It would be wrong to allege that the mind-set of the Church leaders at Chalcedon was simply one of eternal truths and fixed situations. After all, their fifth-century scene was rapidly crumbling and changing under the impact of the barbarian invasions. For a thousand years no foreign armies had breached the walls of Rome. Then Alaric the Goth sacked the city in 410 and Genseric the Vandal would do so in 455. Nevertheless, there is still some truth in contrasting their classical world-view of static essences with our contemporary concept of changing, evolving existence.

Hence one term in the Letter to the Hebrews seems more congenial in our times. Chalcedon describes Jesus Christ simply as 'complete' or 'perfect' in his humanity. Hebrews several times speaks of him as 'being made perfect' (2:10; 5:9; 7:28). This letter's high sense of his divinity (1:8f.) in no way means drawing the line against a humanity in process. In the case of Jesus and indeed of all other human beings it could be better to speak of 'becoming human' rather than of 'being human'.

(3) *Jesus illuminates humanity.* Above I pointed out that our experience of the human condition (in its growth, freedom, limitations, masculine and feminine traits, cultural differences and the rest) will affect the way we interpret Jesus' being 'truly man'. But things also run in the opposite

direction. The actual human existence of Jesus and the destiny to which his historical life, death and resurrection led challenge and change our schemes for understanding and interpreting the human condition. By actualizing human possibilities as he did, he put our humanity in a new light and defined what it is to be a true human being. Later in this chapter I plan to examine issues which concern Jesus' human mind and will: his knowledge of God and his sinlessness. For the moment I only wish to state the principle that his humanity is not to be appreciated merely in terms of what we 'already' knew or believed to be the 'best' or 'highest' possibilities for an authentically human life. His death by crucifixion in powerless disgrace breaks down our 'natural' notion about the right manner of ending a 'great' human life.

(4) *Uniquely human.* Was there something unique in Jesus' way of being (truly) human? This question can be put in terms of possibilities. Could he have had an unparalleled participation in God's life without there having been anything at all unique in his way of being human, acting as a man and expressing his humanity? In principle we would not expect that the divinity would have remained totally hidden 'behind' the humanity, or that God would have been revealed in and through Jesus, *despite* Jesus' humanity.

The record of the ministry shows that such an expectation is not false. The evidence gathered in Chapter 2 demonstrates that through his human words and deeds Jesus announced final salvation with a unique authority and compassion which can only be called divine. He knew himself to have an absolute role in revealing God's will and conveying God's mercy to sinful men and women. It was because of *what* (= the divine nature) he (= the person of the Son of God) *also* was that Jesus could speak with divine authority and compassion. Since this person spanned and unified two natures, he shared in the 'natural' authority and compassion of God. The human history of Jesus could reveal and offer to us the loving but demanding presence of God. The earthly Jesus was the human way of being God and acting as God. He was the human face of God (2 Cor 4:6), *the* historical symbol expressing God to us and for us.

(5) *The divine presence.* The New Testament itself suggests several models for relating Jesus' being human to his being divine. The Letter to Titus takes up *theophany* language to speak of 'the goodness and loving kindness of God' having 'appeared' in Jesus' life, death and resurrection (3:4; see 2:11). The hymn in Philippians goes in the opposite direction to hint rather at the element of hiddenness.

> Christ Jesus, . . . though he was in the form of God, did not count equality with God a thing to be grasped, but *emptied himself*, taking the form of a slave, being born in the likeness of men. And being found in human form he humbled himself and became obedient unto death, even death on a cross (2:5-8).

John's Gospel provides what became the dominant model of *incarnation*: 'the Word became flesh and dwelt among us' (1:14). Lastly, 2 Corinthians has served as a biblical warrant for the model of *presence*: 'God was in Christ reconciling the world to himself' (5:19).

Each of these models contained possibilities of deviation and led some to tamper with the full humanity or full divinity of Christ. For instance, the theophany model risked lapsing into Docetism, the heresy which held that the Son of God merely appeared to be a human being. Each of these models can be developed to clarify a little how humanity and divinity 'came together' in the one person of Jesus Christ without prejudice to his being truly and fully human. Here I want to look briefly at the model of presence.

Like ourselves, God can act in different ways at different times. God can be present to particular people in particular situations with greater or lesser degrees of engagement. Here and there, events in history – and, specifically, in that special history of revelation and salvation recorded in the Bible – send forth signals and signs of special divine activity through which we can conclude to a special divine presence. Variations on the visible, created scene manifest some unusual action, intention and presence of the Creator.

Some religious thinkers leave no room for special divine intervention in the world. They deny any particular involvements of God. There are only naturally occurring situations in the created world and its general history. Every now and then, prophets and others emerge who in fresh and powerful ways appreciate God's universal activity and presence. But in such situations the only difference is the presence of a more perceptive observer, not some special revealing and saving activity on the part of God.

David Hume classically expressed this point of view: 'It is impossible for us to know the attributes or actions of such an [Almighty] Being, otherwise than from the experience which we have of his productions, in the *usual* course of nature' (italics mine).[1] This addresses the question of what *we* can know about God. We can reasonably translate Hume's remarks into what God can do and disclose to us: 'It is impossible for such an Almighty Being to disclose his attributes or actions, otherwise than through his productions, in the *usual* course of events'. In short, Hume and all his latter-day followers exclude on principle unusual activities of God which could manifest special divine presences and intentions. That is to undercut the possibility of some special involvement of God not only in Jesus' life, but also in high moments and great figures of Israel's history.

In the case of Jesus, however, Christians acknowledge not just an unusual divine activity and presence, such as we meet in the lives of the Old Testament prophets, but a personal engagement of God which is qualitatively different and more intense. In and through *this* human life – which culminated in the crucifixion and resurrection – God was uniquely active and present, so that for all time the man from Nazareth was to be *the* focal point of God's encounter with us. In a particular human being, God entered history, became historical and became known as fully and personally present through *this* example of humanity. Thus the human life and history of Jesus could serve as the supreme medium of God's presence, self-revelation and self-communicating love.

TRULY DIVINE

When Chalcedon repeated the terminology of Nicaea and taught that Jesus Christ was 'of one substance with the Father', it made no real attempt to describe, let alone define, God's 'substance' or 'nature'. The 'begotten of the Father before the ages' implies a contrast between the divine existence which is eternal and our human existence which begins in time. (Pre-existence simply as such – that is to say, some kind of existence before one's human birth – would not necessarily be a divine attribute. But *eternal* pre-existence is.) In general, the Council clearly believed that whatever attributes constituted the divine reality and were assigned to the Father must also be assigned to the Son. But it left open the question of how these attributes were to be conceived and expressed. In fact, ways of thinking and talking about God have differed considerably: from ancient Palestine to medieval Europe, from nineteenth-century Bengal to twentieth-century New York. The variety of concepts and language is impressive. Can we sort out some ways of speaking of Christ's divinity?

(1) *What is God?*   Human understanding of God is linked to the collective self-understanding of cultures. God does not change but cultures do. Let me inject some examples. (a) Imperial Rome encouraged a cosmological, monarchic view of divinity. God was *the* principle of order, who lived 'above' chaos, possessing and dominating all. This scheme of things represented God as a static substance beyond the dynamic, changing processes of history. (b) The liberal individualism of modern democracy finds its God 'within' – either within one's own conscience or within the sphere of interpersonal relations and 'I–Thou' encounters. The divine 'Other' belongs to the private sphere. (c) Victimized groups and peoples look for a God of change and liberation, who through suffering will deliver them for future freedom and justice. Their God is not so much 'above' or 'within', but 'before' them. This understanding of divinity corresponds to two central symbols in the book of Revelation: The Lamb who was slain, and the new Jerusalem in which 'death shall be no more, neither shall there be mourning nor crying nor pain any more' (21:4).

In all three cases, however, God is taken to be of definitive significance for all human beings. God is to have a determinative effect in settling the ultimate purpose of life for everybody. This is so because notions of the divinity take shape around a sense of totality. From the outset to the end, God is the *all*-determining reality,[2] and that ultimate reality is personal and loving. Hence God supplies the final and most profound meaning of everything and for everything.

Therefore, by acknowledging Jesus Christ as the One who determines the totality of things, we are in effect confessing him to be divine. As the centre of creation and redemption he is there from the outset to the end as the ultimate, all-determining reality. By rising from the dead, he initiates the definitive end of all things. In him we find our conclusive salvation and final good. To call Christ the Lord of our lives and our world is to recognize in him the ultimate and most profound meaning of reality as a whole – in short, One who can properly be named as 'truly God'. A Christmas prayer puts this point with luminous simplicity: 'Jesus is Lord. Jesus is King. Jesus is *our everything*.'

(2) *Beyond humanity.* Karl Rahner and Teilhard de Chardin have developed ways of reflecting on Christ's being both human and divine within the larger context of God's relationship with the whole of creation. In Teilhard's evolutionary scheme the emergence of Jesus Christ stands for the supreme unfolding of the possibilities latent in the material world. After the breakthrough from matter to plant and animal life came the leap to human life. Can we interpret Christ as the breakthrough to the divine dimension – as it were, the ultimate divine face of matter?

Teilhard's approach shows to better advantage if complemented by Rahner's concern to safeguard both sides of the process. On the one hand, the incarnation is the absolute culmination of humanity's openness to the infinite God who exists beyond the limits of the created universe. Whether they become consciously aware of their innate orientation or not, all human beings are dynamically open to God. Christ embodied that openness to God in a uniquely profound way, thus realizing something which is potentially true of any man or woman. On the other hand, however, the incarnation is also the culmination of the highest communication of God. The God who reaches out to us in an endless variety of ordinary and extraordinary ways does so in the highest possible way in Jesus Christ. This divine self-giving could take no more generous form than the incarnation itself.

(3) *Divinity in relationship.* Finally, the liturgy decidedly encourages us to depict Christ's divinity in relational terms (as 'Son of God' etc.), rather than in terms of his sharing in the one divine nature or substance. That is to say, Jesus Christ is divine through his relationship to the Father in the Holy Spirit.

In the past, Christological studies often made little mention of the Father and the Holy Spirit. The test question assumed the form: 'Was Jesus Christ

God?' It would have been truer to full Christian faith to have put the question as follows: 'Was Christ the Son of God?'

The Church's liturgy has remained faithfully Trinitarian in its manner of expressing Christ's divinity. So many prayers end:

> Glory be to the Father and to the Son and to the Holy Spirit.
> As it was in the beginning, is now, and ever shall be, world without end. Amen.
>
> We make our prayer through our Lord Jesus Christ, your Son,
> who lives and reigns with you and the Holy Spirit,
> God, for ever and ever. Amen.

The liturgy proclaims and confesses our God by praying 'through Christ in the Spirit to the Father'. Theology can only benefit by reviving its capacity to speak of Christ's divinity in such relational terms.

ONE PERSON

The Council of Chalcedon named the 'one person and subsistence' as the principle of unity between Christ's two natures. *That which* acted revealed a duality (the divine and human natures), but *he who* acted was one (the one person of the 'one and the same Son and only-begotten God the Word'). Back in Chapter 1 I recalled how the doctrine of 'one person' came out of several centuries of controversy and expressed the resolution to safeguard the unity of Christ as an acting subject. Yet here as elsewhere, Chalcedon proved to be more a beginning than an end. The notion of 'person' was to undergo a long development which would seriously affect what we might mean when we speak of Christ's person. I plan to sketch that story and then return to Christ.

(1) *What is a person?* Above all through his *Confessions* (397–398), St Augustine had presented personhood in terms of psychological experience and consciousness, an approach which was to recur in modern times. But it was Boethius (*c.* 480–*c.* 524) who fashioned the classical definition: 'The person is the individual substance of a rational nature' (*De duabus naturis*, 3). This account highlighted individuality and rationality. It had nothing to say about the freedom, history and inter-relatedness of persons. Medieval theology maintained Boethius' definition, modifying it by adding the characteristic of incommunicability. Richard of St Victor (d. 1173) spoke of 'the incommunicable existence of an intelligent nature' (*De Trinitate*, IV, 22, 24). As before, rationality remained dominant among the characteristics of a person.

I do not want to dramatize out of all proportion the changes which modern times have brought. But we ignore at our peril new or partially new elements in contemporary accounts of personhood. René Descartes

(1596–1650) helped to add self-consciousness. We can give Immanuel Kant (1724–1804) particular credit for the will and its freedom becoming a standard part of the modern answer to the question 'What is a person?' Struggles for human rights, various existentialist movements, the emergence of psychology and other human sciences, and further forces have all made their contributions. A person is not a thing to be disposed of at will but has an absolute dignity. Persons are relational beings who grow and develop their self-identity in an interpersonal milieu.

Nowadays a working account should include at least the following items:

(a) Persons are distinct and individual beings,
(b) who enjoy rationality and freedom,
(c) exist and act in relationship with other persons,
(d) experience their self-identity in such a relational existence,
(e) and have an inalienable dignity.

Several comments are needed here. First, we could draw together (a) and (b) to express as follows an updated version of Boethius' classical definition: 'A person is an independent centre of consciousness capable of rational choices'. That would cover cases like unborn children who have not yet exercised the power of rational self-determination in conscious experiences. At the same time, however, being a (human) person is something to be actualized, developed and completed in and through a personal life and history. Personhood is something which at every level is discovered and shaped through experiences of oneself and others.

Second, there are those like Schillebeeckx who make much of (c) and (d) and insist that being a person entails interpersonality. An irreducible consciousness and freedom are secondary elements. Primarily persons are relational beings who go out of themselves to others and then return to themselves in conscious freedom. There are theological advantages in putting matters this way. For if we part company with Schillebeeckx and primarily present persons as independent centres of consciousness capable of rational choices who exist or subsist in and for themselves and *only then* relate to others, what of the Trinity of divine persons? An independent centre of consciousness and freedom does *not* make them persons, as the Father, Son and Holy Spirit share in one and the same (intelligent and free) divine nature. It is rather in their relational existence that they have their self-identity. In the case of human beings also it may be better to follow Schillebeeckx and interpret personhood *primarily* in terms of relational existence (*Jesus*, pp. 662ff.). In that case items (c) and (d) would take priority over (b).

Third, ordinary speech – even the 'ordinary' speech of the Church – often draws few distinctions when it moves from one term to another: nature, person, personality and man. A 'good-natured woman' can equally well be described as having a 'pleasant personality'. What real difference is there between saying 'his experiences have made a great man of him' and saying 'his experiences have made a great person of him'? Pope John XXIII's encyclical *Pacem in Terris* (1963) at times uses 'the dignity of the human person' and 'the nature of man' interchangeably.[3] *Gaudium et Spes* slips from 'the human person' to 'man' as if they were simply synonymous (nn. 59, 63). It maintains that the 'full cultural development of man' will not happen without 'a deeply thought-out evaluation of the meaning of culture and knowledge for the human person' (n. 61; translation corrected). Outside the context of Christology, official Church documents can resemble ordinary speech in its fluid and flexible uses of 'nature', 'person' and 'man'.

(2) *The person of Jesus Christ.*   An attentive reading of the Definition of Chalcedon shows that it did not literally describe Christ as a 'divine person'. It spoke of the one *hypostasis* uniting the two natures, but did not in so many words declare this to be the pre-existent divine person of the Logos. (It was left to the Second Council of Constantinople to uphold and interpret the unity of subject in Christ by identifying the principle of union as the pre-existing Logos.) Nevertheless, Chalcedon got very close to identifying the one *hypostasis* when it moved straight from affirming the oneness of person to talk of 'one and the same Son and *only-begotten God the Word*, Lord Jesus Christ'.

Such then is the doctrine of the 'hypostatic union'. A fully human existence was 'enhypostatized' in the Word. Christ was not a human person, but a divine person who assumed a complete human nature without assuming human personhood. The divine person of the Logos identified with a full humanity to the point of 'personalizing' that particular example of human nature. To use Thomas Aquinas' account: the person of the Son of God became a person of human nature.[4]

Jesus Christ was (and is) then a man, a human being and a human individual, *but not* a human person. But can this deprive him of something which belongs to full humanness? Does it do justice to his human individuality? Can he be 'complete in humanity' and 'truly man' without being a human person? There is a danger here of moving beyond legitimate reflection to wrong-headed attempts to describe and explain clearly what is a divine mystery. Yet something can be said. The hypostatic union means that the human reality of Jesus belongs to the Son of God in a personal and absolute way, but not that this humanity is in any way diminished through the absence of human personhood. Full humanity is not necessarily identified with or dependent upon the presence of human personhood. Human characteristics and 'perfections' come at the level of nature and of a given individual's qualities as a human being. At that level personhood as such contributes nothing.

What role then does personhood play? The answer comes if personhood is understood to be and to be manifested relationally. The Son of God has his personal being in relation to the Father. We shall shortly reflect on the primordial self-consciousness of Jesus as an 'I' in relation to the 'Thou' who is the Father. The Gospels never give a hint of a dialogue between divine and human components in Jesus – let us say, between Jesus and the Word. In Gethsemane Jesus does not cry out 'To the Word I must be true'. Still less does he say 'To my own divinity I must be true'. He simply prays 'Abba, Father, . . . remove this cup from me; yet not what I will, but what thou wilt' (Mark 14:36).

Let me put matters in terms of the working account of personhood offered above. Jesus Christ was (and is) (a) a distinct and individual being, who (c) existed and acted in relationship with others and (d) experienced his self-identity in such a relational existence – above all, in and through his unique relationship to the One he called 'Abba'. As *divine* person he had no independent centre of consciousness and freedom, but participated with the Father and the Spirit in one intellect and will. Yet through his humanity (b) Jesus Christ enjoyed his own rationality and freedom. Lastly, his existence as Son of God (e) gave his person an absolutely sovereign dignity.

(3) *One subject.* The Second Council of Constantinople (553) anathematized anyone who 'does not confess that our Lord Jesus Christ who was crucified in the flesh is true God, . . . the Lord of glory and one of the Holy Trinity' (*DS*, 432). In a word, orthodox Christian faith holds that the Son of God died.

What we meet here is the doctrine of *communicatio idiomatum* or 'interchange of properties' – a logical consequence of maintaining the union of the divine and human natures in the one person of Jesus Christ. The attributes of one nature may be predicated of the person even when the person is being named with reference to the other nature: for example, 'the Son of God died', or 'the Son of Mary created the world'. Despite the duality of natures, there is only one subject of attribution – the divine person of the Son of God who can act through his divine nature as well as through his human nature. This allowed Leo I in his 'Tome' to say that 'God was born' (*DS*, 293).

JESUS' HUMAN KNOWLEDGE

We come now to an issue which did not surface at Chalcedon. The Council insisted on the one person of Jesus Christ, but did not consider the truth and implications of his being the subject of a double consciousness and freedom. To believe that he lived as one who was 'completely human', however, was to imply that Jesus had human knowledge and a distinct centre of human consciousness.

How extensive was Jesus' *human* knowledge of the divine reality? Was he conscious of his divine identity? Or did he wander around as Son of God without a really clear idea of who he was? How far did his consciousness of his mission go? Did he know clearly and comprehensively that his life, death and resurrection would have a final saving power for all men and women of all times? In brief, did the earthly Jesus know himself to be Son of God and Saviour of the world?

(1) *Some approaches.* Some Church Fathers, fearing that there would have been something sinful if Jesus had suffered from limited knowledge or ignorance, argued that he only appeared to be ignorant when he asked 'Who touched my garments?' (Mark 5:30). On these and similar occasions Jesus really knew. He merely feigned ignorance as a pedagogical device to help us.

Medieval theology followed suit in maximizing the scope of Jesus' knowledge. It developed a threefold scheme: *scientia visionis, scientia infusa* and *scientia experientiae.* Through the *scientia visionis* he already enjoyed a direct, face-to-face, beatific vision of the divine reality and in that vision of God he also knew all created realities. Through the *scientia infusa* he had the kind of infused knowledge which the Scholastic theologians attributed to the angels. Thirdly, Jesus also learned things in the normal human way during the course of his life (the *scientia experientiae* or experimental knowledge). Behind this maximal view of the extent and nature of his knowledge was what we might call the (Greek) Principle of Perfection. The Scholastic theologians believed that the utterly full perfection of a man demanded the presence of every possible kind of knowledge. As a perfect man, Jesus must have been all-wise and all-knowing. Hence from the first instant of his conception Jesus must have known all things (including his divine identity and mission) through the beatific vision and infused ideas.[5]

Karl Rahner and some other contemporary theologians no longer attribute 'infused' knowledge to the historical Jesus and, while recognizing Jesus' direct knowledge both of his Father and of his own divine identity, they interpret it as a pre-reflective, primordial consciousness rather than a beatific vision. There is no reason to believe that such a direct contact with the divine reality need always be beatific. In any case, if the earthly Jesus did enjoy a vision which was beatific, that would have required a constant miracle to stop the vision having its proper effect. Otherwise such a vision would have excluded genuine human experiences like fear and suffering.

Back in Chapters 2 and 3 I marshalled some scriptural and theological reasons which led to two conclusions: Jesus had a primordial awareness of his personal identity and mission, but there were real limitations in his knowledge. Before pursuing matters in further detail, however, it could be worth recalling the difficulties inherent in exploring the knowledge and inner experience of any human being – particularly one who lived nearly two thousand years ago and who, unlike a St Augustine, left no personal writings. And then which of us is wise enough or holy enough to speak with great assurance about the knowledge and mind of Jesus?

Further, nobody should be expected to answer 'Yes' to the question 'Did Jesus know himself to be the Son of God and Saviour of the world?', *unless* the questioner is willing to recognize the complex nature of human knowledge. Such knowledge forms a many-layered structure, whether we deal with knowing things, knowing other persons or knowing ourselves. Knowing that some tropical fruit is edible because we have identified it in a tourist guide differs from knowing this after we have eaten a piece of the fruit. Through experience we can know some people intuitively and instinctively, without ever having made full acts of understanding and judgement about them. It may be only the tip of the iceberg that shows up clearly in the total structure of what we call our 'knowledge' of them. Further, consciousness of oneself – unlike other forms of knowledge – is not a matter of knowing a separate object. It takes place without reflective, conceptual knowledge. Fully explicit self-consciousness is the result of a history of self-exploration. It takes years for people to come to themselves and learn to know who they are. Anyone's awareness of his or her own personal identity at the age of six will differ greatly from that awareness at the age of thirteen or thirty. What has it been like for Prince Charles at different stages since his infancy to 'know' that he stands first in succession to the British throne? In short, a large range of possibilities opens up when we ask if somebody 'knows' something.

To come back then to the question: 'What did Jesus know about himself and his mission?' One can answer in terms like this. He knew that he stood in a unique relationship to the Father and that as Son he had a mission of salvation for others. These were not discoveries to be made, but primordial facts of his consciousness. His basic awareness of his Sonship did not mean observing the presence of God, as if Jesus were facing an object 'out there'. It was rather a self-consciousness and self-presence in which he was intuitively aware of his divine identity.

(2) *Jesus' knowledge of his identity.* In principle we can justify the position just expressed – along the lines developed by Rahner in his 'Dogmatic Reflections on the Knowledge and Self-Consciousness of Christ' (*ThInv* 5, pp. 193–215). Being and knowledge reciprocally affect each other. The higher a being, the more it is conscious of itself and lucidly open to itself. In the case of Jesus' humanity we meet a reality which – through its assumption by the Word – had the very highest degree of being possible for a created reality. Hence we would expect that in his human consciousness Jesus would have enjoyed at least some basic awareness of that radical determination of his being which was the hypostatic union.

At the same time, to be human is to be limited in knowledge and to grow in knowledge (including knowledge of self). One naturally supposes that Jesus' basic awareness of his own identity would also develop and gradually be spelled out in a fuller conceptualized way. In the name of our belief in Jesus' full humanity we would expect that like everything else his self-knowledge and sense of his own identity would 'grow' (Luke 2:40).

Chapter 2 of this book gathered data from the Synoptic Gospels which suggested that the earthly Jesus had a consciousness of the God whom he called 'Father dear' which set him apart from others. The evidence points to his having been 'in the know' about the divine truth and will. Even if the data do not help us to say much about the details of Jesus' inner life, he obviously experienced and knew the divine reality in a specially clear and intimate way.

The Synoptic Gospels also include data which imply some limits to Jesus' knowledge of the divine reality. They report his practice of prayer as a vital part of his life. Apart from the fact that he constantly prayed, little comes through about the actual experience of Jesus in prayer. However, we are provided with a little information about both his consolation (Matt 11:25f. par.) and his struggles in prayer (the agony in the garden and cry of abandonment on the cross). All of this supports the conclusion that the divine reality was not fully and comprehensively present to the mind of Jesus. To be sure, we are trespassing here on an extremely sensitive area, the quality of Jesus' experience in prayer. But if he simply saw the divine reality in all its entire scope and beauty, real struggles in prayer would be ruled out. So too would genuine obedience. To be obedient one needs to know something (so as to identify the will of God). But the comprehensive, face-to-face knowledge of the beatific vision would rule out freedom and the possibility of an obedient response. Whatever else was happening in Gethsemane and on the cross, we can be sure that Jesus was not merely pretending to struggle through prayer to maintain his obedience. He was praying as someone on his earthly pilgrimage who did yet have the full and final vision of God but who was called to walk obediently in faith.

(3) Jesus' knowledge of his mission. Chapter 2 mustered the evidence for maintaining that in his ministry Jesus was aware of his uniquely important role in establishing the right final relationship between God and human beings. Chapter 3 argued that Jesus went willingly to his death and, at least to some extent, knew and intended that death to bring God's salvation to others. The fourth Eucharistic prayer is soundly based when it addresses the Father as follows: 'In fulfilment of your will he gave himself up to death'.

A proper concern to defend Jesus' basic awareness of his work for human salvation should not, however, lead us into slipping over certain limitations and probable changes in his knowledge of his mission and destiny. He was remembered to have admitted his ignorance about the timing of the end: 'Of that day or that hour no one knows, not even the angels in heaven, *nor the Son*, but only the Father' (Mark 13:32 par.). Then it *seems* that Jesus shifted from an awareness that his mission was to proclaim God's kingdom to an awareness that his death would bring about the kingdom. He who had acted as a servant *of others* came to recognize that he was called to be the suffering servant *for others*.

There are problems to be faced by this thesis about a shift of consciousness in Jesus' sense of his destiny. For the most part the order and context of what Jesus said and did have been lost (see Chapter 2). It is very difficult to establish any real chronological framework over and above such statements as: he was baptized at the beginning of his ministry; his ministry in Galilee came before his arrest and crucifixion in Jerusalem. Some would risk the following reconstruction of events: after a spectacular success at the start Jesus found his message rejected by many, especially in Galilee; he made a final effort and offer to his public by sending out the disciples on a mission; but realizing that he was called to be a victim whose death and vindication were to bring salvation, he gave himself to training the core-group of the twelve, and went up to Jerusalem for his final Passover and fatal confrontation with the authorities there.

Nevertheless, the thesis about a shift in Jesus' perspective on his mission does not call for such a detailed reconstruction of the order of events. For that thesis it would be enough to agree that Jesus *first* preached repentance and the good news of the divine kingdom (Mark 1:15 parr.) and *at some later point* – without our necessarily identifying the time of this change – came to accept his victim-role (*Calvary Christ*, pp. 26–34). Against this one might maintain that from the outset Jesus clearly knew that he was to bring salvation through his violent death. He carried this 'suffering secret' around with him, but broke the news about it only late in his ministry. Obviously one cannot rule out absolutely this 'suffering secret' hypothesis. In theory, Jesus could have kept this grim secret to himself until shortly before the end. However, as Schillebeeckx reasonably argues, such a procedure would have injected an element of play-acting into Jesus' initial proclamation of the kingdom:

> There would have been an element of play-acting about his commitment to his message of *metanoia* and the rule of God, if he had thought and known from the very start that salvation would come only in consequence of his death (*Jesus*, p. 306).

Apropos of this shift-of-perspective hypothesis, the 1980 statement from the International Theological Commission appears to acknowledge just that kind of change on the part of the earthly Jesus. The document speaks of his 'fundamental attitude' of 'existence-for-others' being given 'more vitality and concreteness' as events unfolded and questions emerged for Jesus.

Among the questions which came to confront him were these:

> Would the Father want to establish his reign, if Jesus should meet with failure, death, nay, with the cruel death of martyrdom? Would the Father, in the end, ensure the saving efficacy of what Jesus would have suffered by 'dying for others'?

Jesus 'gathered affirmative answers to these questions', and hence went to death confidently reasserting at the Last Supper 'the promise and presence of the eschatological salvation' (IV. B). Thus the statement seems to allow for some shift or at least clarification in Jesus' mind about the specific shape of his vocation and destiny. His fundamental attitude of self-giving led him from an awareness that through his preaching, actions and personal presence he was establishing God's final salvation to a subsequent acceptance of his victim-role. The Jesus who began by proclaiming the final reign of God ended by obediently agreeing to be the victim whose death and vindication would bring salvation.

Shortly I will examine the issue of the earthly Jesus' faith. Agreed that he had a primordial awareness of his self-identity and basic mission and that both in his articulation of these primary facts and in 'other' areas of his human knowledge he was limited, grew and changed, what does this say about the possibility of recognizing Jesus as a man of faith? Can we not only believe *in* him, but also believe *like* him? But before launching into that discussion, I want to wedge in a few more observations on Jesus' knowledge and consciousness.

(4) *Scripture, demons and the future.*   In the course of his ministry Jesus drew on the scriptures, expelled demons and spoke of the future. In these areas did he manifest special, superior knowledge which enabled him to correct contemporary ideas and communicate information that was otherwise inaccessible? Or did he at times reflect the imperfect and even mistaken ideas of his culture?

Here and there the record of Jesus' preaching shows up the limits in first-century knowledge of the scriptures. Jesus cited Psalm 110 in an argument which supposed that King David himself composed that psalm (Mark 12:36 parr.). Contemporary Old Testament scholarship considers it most unlikely that David authored that psalm. Then Jesus' appeal to Jonah apparently implied that the story of this comic parody of a prophet was historical (Luke 11:29–32 par.). In fact the book of Jonah is properly understood as an extended parable. It is beyond question that Jesus showed a profound and sensitive knowledge of the Jewish scriptures, but his genuine humanity made him share the limited notions of his time. In the two cases indicated the mistakes do not concern any central religious message but such secondary matters as authorship and literary genre.

Except for one or two indications (Luke 13:1–4; John 9:2–3), Jesus apparently shared the popular view of his culture (and many other cultures) that sin and demons caused sickness and disasters (see Luke 13:16). Or at any rate our sources do not recall that Jesus went out of his way to correct that inadequate view.

It has been Jesus' vision of the future which has occasioned the most troubled debates. (a) Did he (wrongly) expect the parousia or end of history to occur imminently (the 'consistent' eschatology of Schweitzer)? (b) Did he announce that the 'end' had already happened (the 'realized' eschatology of Bultmann and C. H. Dodd)? (c) Or did he proclaim a future end but not expect it all to happen either during his ministry or immediately after his death and resurrection (the 'mediating' eschatologies of many scholars)? In that case Jesus differentiated between the parousia and his own resurrection. If hypothesis (c) is correct and Jesus believed or knew that after his suffering, death and resurrection some interval was to elapse before the parousia, did he expect the end to come during the lifetime of his audience (Mark 9:1), or was a delayed end to be preceded by various signs (the persecution of his followers, disasters for the Jewish people, their capital city and Temple, etc.)?

Clearly this is a very broad topic which calls for a detailed analysis of many texts. According to Mark 9:1 Jesus said: 'There are some standing here who will not taste death before they see that the kingdom of God has come with power'. If we take this to be an authentic logion going back to the historical Jesus, did he refer to the parousia or to something else (the powerful coming of the divine kingdom to be brought by his death and resurrection)? Did Mark (or his sources in the early community) mistakenly interpret this saying as pointing to a parousia which would occur in the lifetime of the first Christian generation? Another text which undoubtedly touches the discussion is Mark 13:32: 'Of that day or that hour no one knows, not even the angels in heaven, nor the Son, but only the Father'. We seem to be on firmer ground here. This is the only place in Mark's Gospel where Jesus refers to himself absolutely as 'the Son', and yet the verse goes against the early Christian tendency to glorify Jesus by frankly admitting his ignorance.

Rather than attempt to argue matters out piecemeal, here I can only make several general points. (a) Whether (in Mark 13 parr.) he was speaking of the impending destruction of Jerusalem (which did actually happen) or of the parousia (which has not yet happened) or both, Jesus spoke like a prophet in heavily symbolic language. It is wrong to turn such prophetic visions into precise predictions which can be expected to enjoy a precise fulfilment. Prophetic knowledge is limited knowledge which offers a symbolic vision of the future, not an exact forecast of events. (b) We should take Jesus at his word (Mark 13:32). He did not know just when the parousia was to occur. In any case, knowing the timing of the end hardly seems essential to his mission. Besides, limited knowledge here and elsewhere belongs to his genuine humanity. So far from being any kind of embarrassment, it is precisely what believers should expect.

(5) *The human consciousness and the divine self.* Was the divine 'I', 'ego' or conscious thinking subject who was/is the eternal Son of God *humanly* conscious of himself – that is to say, conscious of himself *through* the human mind of the man Jesus? Did the Son of God take cognizance of himself through a human centre of consciousness? Is such a human consciousness able to 'seize' a divine Self?

Some theologians, noting the disproportion of a human activity before an 'object' which is a divine person, have concluded that there were two 'egos' in Christ: a divine 'I' and a human 'I'. For them Christ's human ego permitted and expressed the observable coherence of his earthly experiences. But this human, empirical ego did not directly express the one, ultimate, ontological subject, his divine ego. Nevertheless, although there was only one such ontological subject in Christ, there were two egos. The 'I' of Jesus' statements was a human 'I'. This theory represents a plausible conclusion from one aspect of Chalcedon's teaching. The Council maintained a clear distinction between Christ's two natures. That should bolster the resolution to preserve a clear distinction between his two consciousnesses. His real human consciousness (which he had individually as a man) was neither replaced by nor interfered with by his divine consciousness (which as Logos he shared/shares with the Father and the Spirit). Since consciousness is on the side of nature and not of person, Chalcedon's doctrine supports this kind of distinction between Christ's human and divine consciousness.

But a proper regard for one side of the Chalcedonian stance (no 'confusion' between the two natures) should not go to the other extreme of a certain 'psychological' Nestorianism. The supposition of two egos in Christ, even if it is granted that only the divine 'I' is the ultimate subject, certainly smacks of a Nestorian-style separation of two selves in Christ.

What we meet in Jesus Christ is one (divine) person acting under the conditions of human consciousness, human feelings and the rest. Through the incarnation the eternal Son became humanly conscious of himself in his relationship to his Father. He now perceived his divine 'I' or Self in a human way. Thus in this unique case a human consciousness was able to 'seize' a divine Self, albeit in a human way.

THE FAITH OF JESUS

In the light of my conclusions about the scope and nature of Jesus' human knowledge, can I also establish something about his human faith? To begin with, one must recognize that, even though the noun 'faith' (*pistis*) and the

verb 'to believe' (*pisteuein*) are among the commonest words used by the
New Testament – and used with different nuances – no author ever comes
out into the open to describe Jesus as the subject of faith. At times the
Synoptic Gospels report Jesus as speaking about faith so vividly and with
such conviction (Mark 4:40 par.; 9:23; 11:23; Matt 17:20 par.) that he
appears to talk out of his own experience.

At the heart of a call to faith, the Letter to the Hebrews lists heroes and
heroines of faith – Abel on through Abraham and Sarah to Moses and later
(11:1ff.). The climax of this 'cloud of witnesses' comes with Jesus, 'the
pioneer and perfecter of faith' (12:2). Even though the Greek text does *not*
include the possessive adjective, translations regularly qualify the faith in
question as 'our' faith. Thus Jesus ceases to be *the* example of faith but
becomes the one who initiates and perfects *our* faith, the person on whom
our faith 'depends from start to finish' (New English Bible). The verse in
question provides a classic test for translators and their willingness to add to
the Greek text for the sake of an interpretation which they believe to be
correct. If, however, we understand Hebrews to refer to Jesus' own faith,
this would cohere with other themes in the letter: his learning obedience
(5:8), his being made perfect through suffering (2:10), his fidelity (3:1–2),
and his prayer when threatened with pain and death (5:7). Nevertheless, one
must admit that not even Hebrews 12:2 unequivocally ascribes faith to
Jesus.

Perhaps the Christians of New Testament times would have found it
confusing to talk of believing both *in* Jesus Christ and *like* Jesus Christ.
Moreover, the verb 'to believe' is often employed as a technical term for the
appropriate response to the proclamation of Jesus' past death and
resurrection (Rom 10:8ff.). And, of course, the faith of the earthly Jesus
could not and did not take the shape of responding in faith to such a
proclamation.

Where, however, the New Testament does prove clear and unambiguous
is in attributing to Jesus attitudes which can be appropriately summarized as
faith. Even if faith is a total orientation of one's life, it expresses itself in
three distinguishable but not separable moments (*Fundamental*, pp.
130–160): (a) *confession* or judgements about the way things are, (b)
commitment or obedient decisions about courses of action, and (c) *confidence*
or trust for the future. Do we and how do we find these three elements
expressed by Jesus?

As regards confession or 'believing that' (*fides quae*), we have seen how
Jesus' essential judgements about his personal identity and mission were
matters of knowledge, not of faith. He could not *believe* that he was Son of
God and Saviour. He could and did grow in his understanding and interpretation of what his identity and mission entailed. But he was 'in the know'
about these basics and they could not become the object of his faith. Was

there anything left that could make up the confessional content of Jesus' faith? The short answer is: the history of revelation and salvation recorded and expressed by the Jewish scriptures, traditions and prayer-life. That story which unfolded from Abraham, through Moses, to the Babylonian exile and beyond, provided adequate content for the faith of Jesus. There is no reason to hold that he enjoyed special knowledge about that past. He took it on faith, absorbed it with fidelity and proclaimed his confession in word and deed.

It may be worth noting here that in the Pauline theology of faith (around which the analysis in terms of confession, commitment and confidence is built) the *content* of the confession is not absolutely decisive. Paul named Abraham as a paradigm of faith (Rom 4), even though the confessional content of Abraham's faith obviously could not include a profession of future events, above all Christ's saving death and resurrection. If on that score it was not anachronistic to speak of Abraham's faith, there should be no difficulty in allowing for a substantial difference between the content of the earthly Jesus' faith and that of later Christian believers. Because of where he came in the history of God's people, Abraham's confession of faith was limited. In the case of Jesus, other reasons set limits to his possible confession of faith (namely, his primordial awareness of his identity and mission). But the principle seems the same: certain limitations in the content of what can be confessed through faith do not preclude calling someone a believer.

As regards the second dimension of faith, the Gospels repeatedly witness to Jesus' obedient commitment to his Father's will. In Gethsemane he struggled through prayer to maintain his fidelity. It was not a matter of obeying himself, as if the man Jesus were obeying the divine Logos. The man Jesus was the divine Logos, the Son of God become flesh and now under human conditions relating to the Father through a total dedication and radical obedience which entailed 'death, even death on a cross' (Phil 2:8).

Third, Chapter 3 of this book noted that unconditional confidence in the Father which Jesus showed in the face of death. Despite his rejection and the human failure of his mission, Jesus trusted that he would be vindicated and that his death would bring salvation to the world. Hebrews highlights this third dimension of faith: 'Now faith is the assurance of things hoped for, the conviction of things not seen' (11:1). In other words, faith enables us to hope for the invisible things of the future which we do not yet see. At the end, even though he lacked full and clear knowledge about the future course of events, Jesus entrusted his cause to his Father. Even if the dying Jesus never literally said, 'Father, into thy hands I commit my spirit' (Luke 23:46), those words beautifully sum up the unshakeable trust he showed when celebrating the Last Supper.

There are other ways in which I might have justified the attribution of faith to Jesus. For instance, would we attribute a credible humanity to him, if we denied that he had faith or needed to have faith? An earthly Jesus who lived by the light of some unique knowledge and did not walk in the relative obscurity of faith would be very remote from the conditions of human and Christian life as we experience them. The call to imitate Jesus Christ goes back to the beginning of Christian literature (1 Thess 1:6; see 1 Cor 11:1). But what would we make of such a call if in fact Jesus lived his earthly life by vision and not by faith?

Certainly our response to Jesus is not simply confined to imitating his faith. Even during his earthly life he did not merely show us his example of faith. He also showed us the compassionate face of his Father. The historical Jesus was not only the model for believers, but also as the final and absolute Revealer of God's grace and will, he had begun his work as Saviour. In short, narrow alternatives are out of place here. Believing *like* Jesus in no way excludes believing *in* him as divine Revealer and Saviour.

THE SINLESSNESS OF JESUS

The discussion of Jesus' faith naturally leads to an issue which bears above all on the quality of his commitment. Was he in fact so dedicated to the divine will that he was free from all sin (= sinlessness *de facto*)? Was he even incapable of sin (= sinlessness *de iure*)? In that case was Jesus truly free? And how should we understand and interpret his freedom?

It might have been better to have dropped the word 'sinlessness'. Admittedly it is the traditional term used in this context, but it suggests all too readily some negative quality through which an individual is free from sin. What we are concerned with is the consistency and strength of Jesus' *freedom for others*: for the service of his Father and of sinful human beings.

Too often we slip into putting the issue of freedom as a choice between good and evil. In that case, of course, God would not be free. An infinitely good Being cannot choose to do either good *or evil*. We describe freedom more successfully in terms of emancipation from external control. Being free from 'foreign' control, one is self-possessed, self-determining and able to act with creative freedom.

The Gospels present Jesus as one who is totally oriented towards his Father and unconditionally obedient to the divine will. In that dedicated mission in the service of God's kingdom, he does not appear to be controlled by some inner compulsion or outer force but to be self-determining vis-à-vis his Father and other human beings. In Gethsemane he sees his freedom in an I–Thou relationship with his Father and a call to do the divine will, cost what it may. We can express matters this way. The relation of the man Jesus to the Father is that of the pre-existent Logos. Transposed into human conditions that relation becomes one of total, sinless obedience.

Are we justified in going further to hold that it was (psychologically and ontologically) *impossible* for Jesus to have sinned? Much depends here on how we present such sinlessness *de iure*. We could and should maintain that in view of his divine personhood and mission as absolute Saviour of the world, Jesus was guided and totally preserved from sin through the Holy Spirit. If, however, we allege that it was Jesus' own subjective dispositions rather than the role of divine providence which made it simply impossible for him to sin, we seem to be casting doubt on his genuine human freedom. If in himself he was so totally taken up by his mission in the service of the kingdom that *under no circumstances whatsoever could he ever have done otherwise* than follow the divine will, are we still maintaining that true freedom which belongs to a full humanity operating under the conditions of this life?

Besides, the Gospels and the Letter to the Hebrews remember Jesus as having been tempted – in fact Hebrews describes him as 'one who *in every respect* has been tempted as we are' (4:15). It would be puzzling, to say the least, to acknowledge that as part of his human life Jesus was not immune from temptation but at the same time to allege that his human will in and of itself could never do anything but follow the divine will. In other words, a real openness to temptation seems incompatible with a (subjective) *de iure* sinlessness.

By and large the New Testament is content to profess Jesus' radical obedience (Phil 2:8; Heb 5:8 etc.). The Second Vatican Council also preferred to speak of his utter obedience (see, for example, *Lumen Gentium*, nn. 36, 37, 42). John's Gospel in one place moves beyond such language to that of sinlessness, when Jesus asks his critics: 'Which of you convicts me of sin?' (8:46). Luke stresses Pilate's testimony to Jesus' innocence (23:4, 14–16, 22). But the point here is to protest the civil and political innocence of Jesus before the law of the Roman Empire – not his private, moral innocence before God.

Several New Testament authors clearly take up Jesus' sinlessness in the context of their beliefs on sacrifice. As a *victim* he was spotless (2 Cor 5:21; Heb 9:14; 1 Pet 1:19; 2:22–24; 1 John 3:3–5; and also perhaps 1 John 1:7 – 2:2). Jesus did not die because of his own guilt. Since he was innocent his death could expiate representatively the sins of others. In similar terms Hebrews also draws attention to the sinlessness of Jesus as our high *priest* (4:15; 7:26–28).

All in all, the scriptural witness to Jesus' utter innocence and obedience is clear. When it solemnly maintained his sinlessness (*DS*, 556), the Third Council of Constantinople (A.D. 680) expressed a Christian conviction which has been in unruffled possession since the beginning of Christianity.

Finally, to clarify matters further it could help to contrast two questions: *Why* must the earthly Jesus have been sinless? *How* in fact was he sinless? Ultimately we can only answer the 'why' by recalling his divine identity.

An infinitely good divine Person cannot sin. The 'how' is concerned with the 'mechanism' which prevented his human will from sinning. There it seems appropriate to hold simply a *de facto* sinlessness rather than go further and allege that the nature of his human will was such that it was *de iure* sinless. As I indicated, such a position on the 'mechanism' of Jesus' sinlessness appears to be incompatible with the true freedom of a genuine humanity operating under the conditions of this life.

THE VIRGINAL CONCEPTION

Before concluding this chapter on the Son of God, I would be outrageously at fault if I were to add nothing about his human origins as son of Mary. On the basis of Matthew and Luke's infancy narratives, the Christian tradition and ordinary Church teaching has always held that Jesus had no human father but was conceived by Mary through the power of the Holy Spirit. This belief in the virginal conception is at least implied by the Apostles' Creed: 'He was conceived by the power of the Holy Spirit and born of the Virgin Mary'.[6]

Over the last century the virginal conception of Jesus has been challenged on a number of grounds. (a) Some rule it out as part of their overall questioning or rejection of any miraculous intervention by God. (b) Others maintain that certain early Christians were under pressure to invent the story of the virginal conception: Jewish critics claimed that Jesus was illegitimate, which led members of the early Church to assert that he was virginally conceived.[7] Or did pagan stories about male gods impregnating human women to produce extraordinary children influence Christians (who already believed in Jesus' divinity) to construct the legend of his virginal conception?

Chapter 2 has already discussed (a) and attempted to clarify the status of the miraculous in Christian faith. As regards (b), Raymond Brown argues that 'we simply do not know whether the Jewish charge of illegitimacy, which appears clearly in the second century, had a source independent of the infancy narrative tradition' (*Birth of the Messiah*, p. 542). In other words, this charge of illegitimacy may have arisen only *after* the composition of the Gospels of Matthew and Luke and perhaps as a reaction to their narratives of the virginal conception. In that case the story of the virginal conception would not have been a Christian reaction to a charge of illegitimacy which was *already* in circulation. Brown likewise shows how the alleged parallels to Jesus' virginal conception to be found in pagan legends are by no means close: 'they are not really similar to the non-sexual virginal conception that is at the core of the infancy narratives' (*Virginal Conception*, p. 62).

(c) Another challenge to the virginal conception has come from those who, albeit in different ways, think that Christians have misinterpreted the

intentions of Matthew and Luke in their infancy narratives. Through the
device of the virginal conception they really did not want to communicate
some historical truth about the miraculous way Jesus was conceived, but
merely aimed to express their faith in his unique status and role as Son of God
and Messiah. Schillebeeckx, for example, adopts that kind of argument. He
maintains that the tradition about the virginal conception preserved by
Matthew and Luke did not intend 'to impart any empirically apprehensible
truth or secret information about the family history, but a truth of
revelation'. This tradition offered 'a theological reflection, not a supply of
new informative data' (*Jesus*, pp. 554f.). Here Schillebeeckx allows only for
the alternative: *either* some 'informative data' which would have constituted
an 'empirically apprehensible truth', *or* 'a truth of revelation' to serve
'theological reflection'. But must it have been a matter of an either/or?
Could not the tradition preserved by the two evangelists have intended to
embody *both* informative data (about the virginal conception) *and* some truth
of revelation (about Jesus' divine filiation)?

However, rather than indulge an enormous parenthesis to describe and
assess all the major counter-positions, let me outline some relevant pieces of
data which can lead on to an informed position.

(1)   In the hierarchy of Christian truths the virginal conception does not
rate 'at the top'. On any showing the personal identity and mission of Jesus
as Son of God and Saviour of the world are more important than how he was
conceived and the fact that he had no human father.

(2)   St Paul, the author of Hebrews and John acknowledge the divine
status of Christ, as was noted in Chapter 1 and at the beginning of this
chapter. John clearly credits the person of Jesus Christ with eternal pre-
existence. And yet none of these authors refers to his virginal conception.
They confidently profess his divinity and pre-existence without introducing
anything about his being virginally conceived through the power of the
Holy Spirit.

Moreover, the early kerygma cited by Paul and other New Testament
authors (see Chapter 4) did not include in its summary of the Christian
message the proclamation that Jesus 'was conceived by the Holy Spirit and
born of the Virgin Mary'. That 'article' became a credal formulation only in
post-New Testament times.

(3)   Since medieval times Catholic theology has been clear that the
divinity of Jesus Christ would not have been affected if he had been Joseph's
son. In theory he could have been the product of normal human marriage
and intercourse, without ceasing to be Son of God. Divine and human
generation are on different levels and not mutually exclusive.

(4)   Apropos of the infancy narratives in the first two chapters of
Matthew and Luke, the evidence does not indicate how the traditions they
drew on – and, specifically, that of the virginal conception (which they tell

in different ways) – originated, were transmitted and reached them. One might guess that the tradition of the virginal conception originated in the testimony of Mary, Joseph and perhaps others. Even so, we have no way of tracing the way that tradition was preserved and reached the evangelists.

(5) It is as well to remind ourselves that in the infancy narratives we deal with material that is strikingly different from the material which Matthew and Luke share with Mark (and John): the events that followed the baptism of Jesus. Chapter 2 of this book set out various reasons which justify us in holding the Synoptic Gospels' accounts of *the ministry* to be substantially reliable. But the infancy narratives take us back thirty years or more. It is not simply a problem of a longer chronological gap between the events and their written record. So far from being the opening chapters of official biographies, the infancy narratives are symbol-laden stories of Jesus' human origin which draw heavily on Old Testament language and motifs to express dramatically the mystery of his person and destiny. Certainly Matthew, Luke and their sources reported and wanted to report some factual data. But if we insist on identifying as historical everything in those infancy narratives, we may well be misinterpreting material which the evangelists intended to be taken rather in terms of theological significance.

(6) That said, I believe Raymond Brown correctly holds that 'both Matthew and Luke regarded the virginal conception as historical', even if 'the modern intensity about historicity was not theirs' (*Birth of the Messiah*, p. 517). The two evangelists refer to the conception of Jesus from different standpoints – Matthew from that of Joseph, Luke from that of Mary. But both concur that the conception came about without human intercourse and through the power of the Holy Spirit.

(7) I strongly suspect that it has been *difficulties at the level of meaning* which have led many people to doubt or reject *the fact* of the virginal conception. In early Christianity the Apocryphal Gospels developed biological aspects of Jesus' conception and birth, so that their readers increasingly lost sight of the deep religious significance of those events. In modern times many people believe that it would have derogated from Jesus' full humanity not to have been conceived in the normal way. Or else they reject the virginal conception, because they react against the (generally implicit) view that Jesus had to be virginally conceived, since sexual intercourse is impure.

Brown echoes the language of the Constitution on Divine Revelation from the Second Vatican Council (*DV*, n.11) when he asks: 'Should one rank the biological manner of Jesus' conception as a truth God wanted to put into the Sacred Writings for the sake of our salvation?' (*Birth of the Messiah*, p. 528, fn. 28). If truth has to be meaningful, what religious meaning(s) does the biological manner of Jesus' conception convey and contribute to the process of our salvation? Ultimately the event of the

virginal conception yields meaning apropos of two items': *Jesus' divinity* and
the role of the Holy Spirit.

(8)   Traditionally the major value of his virginal conception has been to
symbolize and express Jesus Christ's divine origin. The fact that he was born
of a woman pointed to his humanity. The fact that he was born of a virgin
pointed to his divinity. This understanding should be fitted into the wider
and developing pattern provided by the New Testament.

Christians began by recognizing the personal identity and saving function
of Jesus as Son of God in his resurrection from the dead (Rom 1:4). When
Mark composed his Gospel he included 'a baptism Christology': at the
beginning of his ministry Jesus is declared by God to be 'my beloved Son'
(1:11). Matthew and Luke moved matters further back to add a 'conception
Christology': the unique divine intervention in the conception of Jesus
revealed that there was never a moment in his history when Jesus was not
Son of God. Finally, other New Testament authors went even further back
to add a 'pre-existence Christology' (John 1:1ff.; Heb 1:1ff.). Without
saying anything about the manner of Jesus' conception, they acknowledged
in his coming the incarnation of One who was previously 'with God' and
now was 'made flesh'. Thus the event of the virginal conception provided a
further link for that progressive recognition of Jesus Christ's identity and
destiny which began at the end with his risen 'post-existence' and finished at
the beginning with his eternal pre-existence.

We can also spot other lesser patterns of significance to which the event of
the virginal conception contributed. Matthew's Gospel names the child
Jesus 'Emmanuel, which means God with us' (1:23). Right from his
conception and birth Jesus fulfilled and expressed the presence of Yahweh
with his people. Then at the end of Matthew the risen and exalted Christ
met his disciples as the One to whom 'all authority in heaven and on earth
has been given', and who promised: 'I am with you always, to the close of
the age' (28:18, 20). What Jesus became through his resurrection he had
already been from the start: the fulfilled expression of Yahweh's presence
with his people.

(9)   To name Christ's divinity is to speak of his relationship to the Father
in the Spirit. Hence the event of the virginal conception can naturally be
expected to yield meaning not only about Christ's divine filiation but also
about his relationship with the Holy Spirit.

Christians experienced the Spirit in the aftermath of Jesus' resurrection.
They came to recognize that the Spirit sent to them by the risen Christ or in
his name (Luke 24:49; John 14:26 etc.) had been actively present in the
whole of his life – not only at the start of his ministry (Luke 3:22; 4:1, 14,
18) but even right back to his conception. In other words, the risen Jesus
actively blessed his followers with the Spirit. But in his entire earthly
existence he himself had been blessed by the Spirit – right from his very

conception when he came into this world through the Spirit's creative power.

Thus the event of the virginal conception helps to reveal and clarify that ultimate truth: from the beginning to the end there is a Trinitarian face to the story of Jesus Christ. His total history discloses to us the God who is Father, Son and Holy Spirit.

NOTES

1 D. Hume, 'Of Miracles', *An Enquiry Concerning Human Understanding*, section X, pt. 2.

2 W. Pannenberg calls God 'the all-determining reality (*Theology and the Philosophy of Science* [ET: London, 1976], pp. 333–345). On God see H. Küng, *Does God Exist?* (London and New York, 1980) and R. Swinburne, *The Existence of God* (Oxford, 1980).

3 *Acta Apostolicae Sedis* 55 (1963), pp. 259, 262.

4 'Anima vero et corpus trahuntur ad personalitatem divinae personae, ut sic persona Filii Dei sit etiam persona filii hominis et hypostasis et suppositum . . . . Sic igitur secundum similitudinem quandam persona, hypostasis et suppositum Filii Dei est persona, hypostasis et suppositum humanae naturae in Christo' (Thomas Aquinas, *Compendium Theologiae*, ch. 211).

5 In *Mystici Corporis*, a 1943 encyclical on the Church as Christ's Mystical Body, Pius XII declared: 'By means of the beatific vision, which He [Christ] enjoyed from the time He was received into the womb of the Mother of God, He has forever and continuously had present to Him all the members of His mystical Body, and embraced them with His saving love' (n. 75). This statement, however, did not belong among the main points which the Pope aimed to teach in that encyclical. We should also remember the full context, as Raymond Brown does in 'The Importance of How Doctrine is Understood': 'Past church statements affirm that Christ had the beatific vision during his ministry, but it is irresponsible to bring them into the modern discussion of Jesus' knowledge without alerting people to two facts:

   '(a) The theory of Jesus' beatific vision was advanced in the Middle Ages as an answer to a problem: Although one could not suppose that the divine (non-conceptual) knowledge of the Second Person of the Trinity was functional in the human mind of Jesus (which operated with concepts), the Gospels portrayed him as having extraordinary knowledge about God, the future etc. – might he not have had the beatific vision which gave him such knowledge? However, now the church (Pontifical Biblical Commission, 1964) has officially explained that the Gospels do not [simply] give us literal accounts of the ministry of Jesus, but narratives into which the post-resurrectional theological insights of the Christian preachers have [also] been read back . . . . In fidelity to this church statement a Catholic may maintain that a true post-resurrectional insight into Jesus' extraordinary identity as Son of God has been given expression in the Gospels in terms of extraordinary knowledge during the ministry. This theory obviates the need for positing Jesus' beatific vision.

   '(b) Accordingly, many of the most respected Catholic theologians today, including Rahner, Ratzinger and Lonergan, have reinterpreted the theory of Jesus' beatific vision without producing any indication of ecclesiastical disapproval' (*Origins* 10, n. 47 [7 May 1981], p. 743; reprinted in *The Critical Meaning of the Bible* [New York, 1981; London, 1982], p. 87, fn. 8).

6 On the virginal conception see R. Brown, *The Virginal Conception and Bodily Resurrection of Jesus* (London and New York, 1973), pp. 21–68, and *The Birth of the Messiah* (London and New York, 1977), pp. 517–533.

7 On the charge of illegitimacy see Brown, *Birth of the Messiah*, pp. 28f., 142f., 150, 534–542. Brown is incorrectly reported by J. F. O'Grady: 'Brown has argued convincingly that the origin of this tradition [the virginal conception of Jesus] *comes from* the accusation by Jews that Jesus was illegitimate' (*Models of Jesus* [New York, 1981], p. 57; italics mine). In fact Brown clearly holds that *the historical evidence* does *not* as such allow us to conclude which was first – the charge of illegitimacy or the tradition of the virginal conception: 'There is no way to know with certainty whether the post-NT Jewish charge of illegitimacy is an authentic recollection of Jewish charges that were circulating *before* Matthew composed his narrative' (*Birth of the Messiah*, p. 537; italics mine).

QUESTIONS FOR DISCUSSION

(1) What ways of thinking and speaking about God do you find in your country and culture? How could you apply these notions of divinity to the reality of Jesus Christ?

(2) The so-called 'ages of faith' took God's existence and attributes for granted. What effect do modern doubts and difficulties have on the faith which Christians have in Jesus Christ as 'truly divine'?

(3) Was it appropriate that the Word (rather than the Holy Spirit) became flesh? Would you even argue that *only* the Word could have become incarnate?

(4) Do you agree that the Son of God could have become flesh only once? Why would you rule out more than one incarnation?

(5) Some have associated Jesus' presence in Mary's *womb* (through the virginal conception) with the absence of his corpse from the *tomb* (through the resurrection). Are you helped by this parallel between what happened at the beginning and what happened at the end?

ADDITIONAL READING

Besides the items already mentioned in this chapter the following bibliography could be useful:

J. Ashton, 'The Consciousness of Christ', *The Way* 10 (1970), pp. 59–71, 147–157, 250–259.

D. M. Baillie, *God Was in Christ* (London, 1948), pp. 106–156 (on incarnation).

K. Barth, *CD* I/2, pp. 122–202 (on incarnation and virginal conception); III/2, pp. 325–344 (on Jesus' full humanity).

R. E. Brown, *Jesus God and Man* (London and New York, 1967); this book reprints two articles: 'Does the New Testament Call Jesus God?' and 'How Much Did Jesus Know?'.

J. D. G. Dunn, 'Jesus' Experience of God – Sonship', *Jesus and the Spirit*, pp. 11–40.

Faith and Order Louvain 1971: Study Reports and Documents (Geneva, 1971), pp. 23–34 (on the Council of Chalcedon).

J. A. Fitzmyer, 'The Virginal Conception of Jesus in the New Testament', *Theological*

Studies 34 (1973), pp. 541–575; revised and reprinted in *To Advance the Gospel: New Testament Studies* (New York, 1981), pp. 41–78.

L. W. Geddes and others, 'Person', *NCE* 11, pp. 166–172.

A. E. Harvey (ed.), *God Incarnate: Story and Belief* (London, 1981).

A. Heron, 'Doing without the Incarnation?', *Scottish Journal of Theology* 31 (1978), pp. 51–71.

'Incarnation, the', *ODCC*, pp. 696f.

W. Kasper, *Jesus the Christ* (ET: London and New York, 1976), pp. 163–274 (on 'The Mystery of Jesus Christ').

J. P. Kenny, 'Was Mary in Fact a Virgin?', *Australasian Catholic Record* 56 (1979), pp. 282–300.

J. Knox, *The Humanity and Divinity of Christ* (Cambridge, 1967).

D. Lane, 'The Incarnation of God in Jesus', *Irish Theological Quarterly* 46 (1979), pp. 158–169.

J. Macquarrie, 'Kenoticism Reconsidered', *Theology* 77 (1974), pp. 115–124.

J. McIntyre, *The Shape of Christology* (London and Philadelphia, 1966).

H. Meynell, 'On Believing in the Incarnation', *Clergy Review* 64 (1979), pp. 210–216.

M. Müller and others, 'Person', *SM* 4, pp. 404–419 (= *EncTh*, pp. 1206–1225).

M. Müller and K. Rahner, 'Freedom', *SM* 2, pp. 349–362 (= *EncTh*, pp. 533–545).

J. Pannenberg, *JGM*, pp. 283–364 (on 'The Divinity of Christ and the Man Jesus').

K. Rahner, *Foundations*, pp. 176–305 (on 'Christology within an Evolutionary View of the World' etc.).

K. Rahner, 'Current Problems in Christology', *ThInv* 1, pp. 149–200.

K. Rahner, 'On the Theology of the Incarnation', *ibid.* 4, pp. 105–120.

K. Rahner, 'Christology within an Evolutionary View of the World', *ibid.* 5, pp. 157–192.

K. Rahner, 'Dogmatic Reflections on the Knowledge and Selfconsciousness of Christ', *ibid.* 5, pp. 193–215.

K. Rahner, 'Christology in the Setting of Modern Man's Understanding of Himself and his World', *ibid.* 11, pp. 215–229.

K. Rahner, 'The Quest for Approaches Leading to an Understanding of the Mystery of the God-man Jesus', *ibid.* 13, pp. 195–200.

K. Rahner, 'The Two Basic Types of Christology', *ibid.* 13, pp. 213–223.

J. F. Rigney, 'Communication of Idioms', *NCE* 4, pp. 35–37.

J. Sobrino, *Christology*, pp. 311–345 (on 'The Christological Dogmas').

J. D. Zizioulas, 'Human Capacity and Human Incapacity: A Theological Exploration of Personhood', *Scottish Journal of Theology* 28 (1975), pp. 402–447.

7
Christ beyond Christianity

I saw ... a pile of burned bodies in a water tank by the entrance to
the broadcasting station. Then I was suddenly frightened by a
terrible sight on the street ... There was a charred body of a
woman standing frozen in a running posture with one leg lifted
and her baby tightly clutched in her arms.

YASUKO YAMAGATA
(survivor of Hiroshima)

The teaching of Jesus should not be confused with what passes for
modern civilization. It is no part of the missionary call to tear the
life of the people of the East [up] by its roots!

MAHATMA GANDHI

'There is one God, and there is one mediator between God and men, the
man Christ Jesus, who gave himself as a ransom for all' (1 Tim 2:5f.). That
tiny group of people who constituted the Church of the first century were
utterly convinced that Jesus Christ was universally and absolutely significant
for the redemption of all human beings: 'There is salvation in no one else,
for there is no other name under heaven given among men by which we
must be saved' (Acts 4:12). In *Lumen Gentium* the Second Vatican Council
was doing nothing else but summarize this New Testament conviction
when it called Christ 'the source of salvation for the whole world' (n. 17).

Back in Chapter 2 I noted the *universal* way Jesus proclaimed God's
kingdom. This is not simply an historical comment about the past.
Experience today shows how well stories like that of the prodigal son (Luke
15:11–32) continue to communicate in China and other countries that differ
so much from the first-century Palestinian culture into which Jesus injected
his message. After the crucifixion, resurrection and coming of the Holy Spirit
his followers knew their obligation to reach and teach 'all nations' (Matt
28:19). The same sense of world-wide mission reverberates in the General
Intercessions on Good Friday when the Church prays for all classes of
people. In the words of absolution from the sacrament of reconciliation,

'God, the Father of mercies, through the death and resurrection of his Son, has reconciled the world to himself'.

But what of those beyond the reach of Christianity and the influence of the Church? Does the plain fact of millions of non-Christians discredit any claim about Christ's comprehensive relevance for salvation? In what sense can and does he touch their existence to deliver them from evil and share with them the life of the Trinity? Ultimately, of course, all members of the human community are called to be with Christ forever in glory. But what of the here and now? Is he already mediating life, meaning and love to all men and women – even to those who have never even heard his name? This book would be shamefully incomplete if it failed to suggest some response, albeit a brief one, to those questions.

THE UNIVERSAL CHRIST

(1) *Creation, incarnation and resurrection.* The doctrines of creation, incarnation and resurrection indicate ways of elucidating Christ's saving contact with those who have lived or now live in pre- or non-Christian societies and cultures.

First of all, the New Testament acknowledges Christ's role in *creation*: 'All things were created *through* him and for him. He is before all things, and in him all things hold together' (Col 1:16f.; see John 1:1–4; Heb 1:3; 1 Cor 1:24; 8:6). Despite their different nuances, these texts agree that through Christ all things came into being. They acknowledge him as the universal and exclusive agent of creation who preserves everything in existence, and as the model and goal of everyone and everything. This doctrine of the New Testament supports the conclusion. Whenever the created world and its history bring people salvation in some form or another, this is happening through Christ. Seen in these terms, Christ's role as mediator of salvation is as broad and as old as creation itself.

In *Redemptor Hominis* (n. 11), Pope John Paul II recalled the way St Justin, Clement of Alexandria and others saw in the non-Christian religions and cultures various '*semina Verbi*' (seeds of the Word), reflections of Christ's mysterious presence among those 'others'. Even if he was never consciously known, he was (and is) actively present to bring all people to the fullness of life. Those early Greek Fathers of the Church saw how the salvation which was offered to those living before Christ came through the Word of God who was to be made flesh in the fullness of time. As agent of creation and salvation, the Word was and is always present at least as a seed (*spermatikōs*) in every human being. Thus those who either lived before the incarnation or else lived after the coming of Christ but knew nothing of it could still be nourished by him and set on the way of salvation.

Through the *incarnation* Christ moved into new historical solidarity with all human beings, as well as with the created world. He entered history to become the focus of the human and material universe. Hereafter to be led to God through other human beings would be to be touched by the incarnate Christ. In the words of *Gaudium et Spes*, by his incarnation 'the Son of God has in a certain way united himself with each man' (n. 22). Hence to receive salvation through other men and women is to receive salvation through the incarnate Christ.

The *resurrection* transformed Christ's humanity and set it beyond the normal limits of space and time. In his glorified humanity he has become present to people of all times and places. Hence in this risen state Christ can 'show the way to' and 'strengthen' every person through his Holy Spirit, offering 'to all the possibility of being made partners, in a way known to God, in the paschal mystery' (*Gaudium et Spes*, nn. 10, 22). The omnipresent activity of the risen Christ universally mediates the divine life. To deny a universal role here is to belittle what happened to him in and through the resurrection.

(2) *Christian arrogance?* Undoubtedly some readers will be uneasy about appealing to the doctrines of creation, incarnation and resurrection so as to bolster beliefs that Christ is 'invisibly active' (*Gaudium et Spes*, n. 22) in all human experience of salvation. Does this claim express once more some traditional arrogance of Western Christians who have sought to 'take over' other religions and their cultures?

It is very much the opposite, I believe. This approach, so far from denigrating other religions, should encourage Christians to reverence Christ already present in those religions. Missionaries do not simply bring to others a Christ who has never previously been with them. He has already been there before the first missionaries arrive. The other religions and their cultures have provided the matrix in which Christ has been at work. All this should inculcate respect rather than arrogant triumphalism in Christians who encounter other religions. Such an approach could well encourage Christians to question certain settled standards and values when they see how Christ's saving influence has worked itself out in their non-Christian brothers and sisters. All those strands of European culture, through which Western Christianity has interpreted and expressed for itself Christ's role as Saviour and Son of God, can never enjoy the absolute value which attaches only to Christ himself.

In short, theological affirmations about the 'seeds of the Word' present in other religions and peoples involve a serious commitment. They pledge those who make such statements to listen attentively to what the Word might be saying *to* Christians through the religious and human experiences of non-Christians. This is much more than simply a matter of pastoral courtesy. The sincere belief that the incarnated and risen Christ is mysteriously but actively mediating life, meaning and love to and through *all* men and women among other things implies the question: What could the Christ of non-Christians be saying to the Churches?

Let me pull in a few examples to illustrate the seriousness of this challenge. (a) A famous prayer from the Indian Upanishads can remind Christians that the world's Saviour works to deliver people from that unreal situation of deadly darkness in which *all* are caught.

> From the unreal lead me to the
> real;
> from darkness lead me to light;
> from death lead me to
> immortality.

(b) Buddhists keenly appreciate the fundamental transitoriness of all created things, including human existence – that 'essential inadequacy of this changing world' which the Second Vatican Council noted as a pervasive message of Buddhism (*Nostra Aetate*, n. 2). Should Christians acknowledge in this Buddhist doctrine a call back to the one fixed point in our lives, Jesus Christ who 'is the same yesterday and today and forever' (Heb 13:8)?

(c) The first assembly of the World Conference on Religion and Peace met in Kyoto, Japan in 1970. Besides some Christians, there were representatives from most of the major religions in the world: Buddhists, Confucianists, Hindus, Jains, Jews, Muslims, Shintoists, Sikhs, Zoroastrians and others. One hardly has to read between the lines to hear the voice of the Prince of Peace calling on those who profess faith in him to repent truly and practise the good news:

> As we sat down together facing the overriding issues of peace we discovered that the things which united us are more important than the things which divide us. We found that we share:
> - A conviction of the fundamental equality of the human family, and the equality and dignity of all human beings;
> - A sense of the sacredness of the individual person and his conscience;
> - A sense of the value of human community;
> - A realization that might is not right; that human power is not self-sufficient and absolute;
> - A belief that love, compassion, selflessness, and the force of inner truthfulness and of the spirit have ultimately greater power than hate, enmity, and self-interest;
> - A sense of obligation to stand on the side of the poor and the oppressed as against the rich and the oppressors;
> - and a profound hope that good will finally prevail.
>
> Because of these convictions that we hold in common, we believe that a special charge has been given to all men and women of religion to be concerned with all their hearts and minds with peace and peace-making, *to be servants of peace*. As men and women of religion we confess in humility and penitence that we have very often

betrayed our religious ideals and our commitment to peace. It is not religion that has
failed the cause of peace, but religious people. This betrayal of religion can and must
be corrected [italics mine].

It takes very little to translate this message in terms of the omnipresent
Christ whose salvation will always wear the face of justice and peace. Is it
naïve to detect something of his influence in the fact that – even though
religious differences are often involved in conflicts and wars – *every living
religion proclaims peace*?

I have been picking examples almost at random to illustrate ways in which
the anonymous Christ of non-Christian religions could in fact be speaking to
those who believe in him as Son of God and Saviour of the world.
Furthermore, could Christians learn something about Jesus from what
Hindus, Jews, Muslims, Marxists and others have *explicitly* said and written
about him? I think here of such non-Christians as Schalom Ben-Chorim,
Martin Buber, Mahatma Gandhi and Milan Machoveč. Certainly a believer's
commitment is essential for any adequate understanding of Jesus' person and
work. Nevertheless, all access to him is not closed for non-Christians. In
fact, over some points 'outsiders' could perhaps have a valuable perception
of who the earthly Jesus was and what he stood for.

All of this is slight and impressionistic. But it cannot be otherwise. The
long answer to the issues I am raising would fill a small library. But one
further item must be added. Christ's contact with those beyond Christianity
cannot be seen simply in terms of creation, incarnation and resurrection.

(3) *Solidarity in suffering.*   The story of Jesus' passion includes the precious
detail that he did not die alone. At the place called Golgotha two others were
crucified with him (Mark 15:27 parr.). Like all men and women –
Christians and non-Christians alike – those criminals had two things in
common with Jesus: *their bodies and their sufferings*. We can differ from Jesus
in sex, age, language, culture and our period of history. But everyone has a
body and sufferings, and that creates a radical solidarity between Jesus and all
human beings (Matt 25:31–46).

The history of the world is a grim history of human suffering: from the
thousands of slaves crucified after the collapse of Spartacus' revolt (71 B.C.)
to the thirty million children who died of starvation or malnutrition in
1978, from the lepers who cried out for help (Luke 17:11–19) to those who
rot in unsanitary slums on the edge of wealthy cities, from the inhabitants of
countless occupied countries to those who use drugs to escape from a fearful
world. When Jesus 'suffered outside the gate' (Heb 13:12), his passion made
him part of that total story of ordinary and extraordinary suffering endured
by men and women in the course of their daily lives.

The two criminals crucified with Jesus stood for that whole history of
suffering which stretches from the beginning till the end, when God

will wipe away every tear from their eyes, and death shall be no more, neither shall there be mourning nor crying nor pain any more, for the former things have passed away (Rev 21:4).

Thus we can find the anonymous Christ beyond official Christianity not only in the 'seeds of the Word' but also in the face of all crucified human beings. Whether recognized or not, the saving passion of Christ goes on in every human life. Wherever we look, we meet the crucified face of God.

JESUS AND THE CHURCH

Inevitably any discussion of Christ's link with non-Christians will bring us back to the great sign and symbol of his presence in the world: the Church (*Lumen Gentium*, n. 1). It is this community which bears the primary responsibility of showing who he is as Son of God and Saviour of the world. The credibility of that message will not depend simply on carefully argued conclusions about the history of Jesus, sound interpretations of his death, or a good case for his resurrection. A Church that embodies the redemption by the witness of free, reconciled and loving lives shows that such faith in Christ is truly worth holding and practising. It is not so much right theory about him as loving discipleship which establishes that 'Jesus is Lord' (1 Cor 12:3).

In brief, there never has been such a thing as a purely theoretical Christology. All beliefs about Christ come from the practice of a genuinely Christian life and in turn should nourish such a life. To improve Christology we need *both* better scholarship *and* better discipleship. But ultimately the discipleship will prove more significant than the scholarship. We have to pay the price for Christology. It is only when we suffer, act and pray with Christ that we will truly know who he is as Son of God and Saviour of the world.

The influence of Michael Polanyi and others has made it a commonplace to observe that knowledge is participatory. More than any other branch of human research and study, Christology establishes that principle. True knowledge of Jesus Christ comes about only through being converted and following him.

In his *Foundations of Christian Faith* Rahner remarks:

> The truth of the faith can be preserved only by doing a theology of Jesus Christ, and by redoing it over and over again. For it is true here too that only he possesses the past who has recaptured it as his own present (p. 213).

It might be well to add that this truth will be preserved through *being possessed* by the past proclamation of Jesus Christ and through being *recaptured by him* in one's own present.

ADDITIONAL READING

M. Dhavamony (ed.), *Revelation in Christianity and other Religions, Studia Missionalia* 20 (1971).

M. Dhavamony, *Salvation in Christianity and other Religions, ibid.* 29 (1980).

M. Dhavamony, *Ways of Salvation in Christianity and other Religions, ibid.* 30 (1981).

X. Irudayaraj, 'An Attempt at an Indian Christology', *Indian Ecclesiastical Studies* 9 (1970), pp. 3–20.

L. Newbigin, 'Christ and the Cultures', *Scottish Journal of Theology* 31 (1978), pp. 1–22.

G. O'Collins, 'Christ and Non-Christians', *Fundamental*, pp. 114–129.

C. B. Okolo, 'Christ, "Emmanuel": An African Enquiry', *Afer* 20 (1978), pp. 130–139.

R. Panikkar, *The Unknown Christ of Hinduism* (rev. ed.: Maryknoll, 1980).

K. Rahner, *Foundations*, pp. 138–175 (on 'The History of Salvation and Revelation') and pp. 311–321 (on 'Jesus Christ in Non-Christian Religions').

K. Rahner, 'History of the World and Salvation-History', *ThInv* 5, pp. 97–114.

K. Rahner, 'Christianity and the Non-Christian Religions', *ibid.*, pp. 115–134.

K. Rahner, 'Anonymous Christians', *ThInv* 6, pp. 390–398.

K. Rahner, 'One Mediator and Many Mediations', *ThInv* 9, pp. 169–184.

K. Rahner, 'Church, Churches and Religions', *ThInv* 10, pp. 30–49.

K. Rahner, 'Anonymous Christianity and the Missionary Task of the Church', *ThInv* 12, pp. 161–178.

K. Rahner, 'Observations on the Problem of the "Anonymous Christian" ', *ThInv* 14, pp. 280–294.

L. Richard, *What Are They Saying About Christ and World Religions?* (Ramsey, 1981).

For much of Christology four further items could be added:

M. L. Cook, *The Jesus of Faith* (New York, 1981).

D. Lane, *The Reality of Jesus* (New York and Dublin, 1977).

R. P. McBrien, *Catholicism* (Minneapolis, 1980), I, pp. 367–563.

D. Tracy, *The Analogical Imagination* (New York, 1981), pp. 233–338.

Index